SECRET SERVANT

My Life with the KGB
and the Soviet Élite

ILYA DZHIRKVELOV

A TOUCHSTONE BOOK
Published by Simon & Schuster Inc.
NEW YORK · LONDON · TORONTO · SYDNEY · TOKYO

Touchstone
Simon & Schuster Building
Rockefeller Center
1230 Avenue of the Americas
New York, New York 10020

First Touchstone Edition, 1989
Published by arrangement with Harper & Row, Publishers, Inc.
First published in Great Britain by William Collins Sons & Co. Ltd.
TOUCHSTONE and colophon are registered trademarks
of Simon & Schuster Inc.
Manufactured in the United States of America

1   3   5   7   9   10   8   6   4   2   Pbk.

Library of Congress Cataloging in Publication Data

Dzhirkvelov, Ilya.
Secret servant: my life with the KGB and the Soviet élite/Ilya Dzhirkvelov.
—1st Touchstone ed.

p.   cm.—(A Touchstone book)
Translated from the Russian.
Reprint with new introd. Originally published: New York: Harper & Row,
1988, c1987.
Includes index.
1. Dzhirkvelov, Ilya.   2. Soviet Union. Komitet gosudarstvennoi
bezopasnosti—Officials and employees—Biography.   3. Intelligence service
—Soviet Union—Biography.   4. Spies—Soviet Union—
Biography.   5. Defectors—Soviet Union—Biography.   I. Title.
JN6529.I6D95   1989
327.1′2′0924—dc19
[B]   89-31204
CIP
ISBN 0-671-68299-7 Pbk.

CONTENTS

*To my wife and friend Nina
and to my children*

PREFACE

Unlike most people from the Soviet Union who find themselves in the West and feel the urge to tell the story of their life, I am neither a dissident nor, strictly speaking, a defector. I am not a dissident because I have never been an opponent of the Soviet regime. On the contrary, I have all my life been a loyal and relatively successful member of Soviet society and for many years an active propagandist for my country and the policies of the Kremlin.

I am of the generation born under Stalin which occupies a special place in the history and life of the Soviet Union. As boys at the end of the 1930s we were taught to catch spies and to expose 'enemies of the people' and as young men, at the beginning of the 1940s, to fight Fascism; when we came to manhood we still believed in Stalin; in the 1950s we took part in the 'active construction of socialism' and the 'liquidation of the consequences of the cult of personality' and, echoing Khrushchev, at meetings we proclaimed that our generation of Soviet people would live under Communism, although we no longer believed even in socialism; in the 1960s, under the 'wise leadership' of Brezhnev we became completely disillusioned in everything, but continued, out of inertia and the desire to survive, to serve faithfully a socialist system which was slowly but surely decaying from the top. One can describe my generation in such simplified terms, but it would be a gross exaggeration to assert that in the 1940s or early 1950s we could foresee what would be happening in my country today.

That does not mean, of course, that I was never critical of the Soviet regime and its rulers, but, like most Soviet citizens, I kept my criticisms to myself and to my closest friends. I knew how far I could go and how to keep out of trouble. The fact remains that, had it not been for a series of accidents, I would today be a fairly well-off member of Soviet society and would be living with my family in relative comfort in Moscow.

Nor am I, in the true sense of the word, a defector, which generally means someone who has been at odds with the regime and has been planning for some time to escape from its grip. Since it is extremely difficult to leave the Soviet Union permanently without official permission, defectors are forced to break the law. Some try to cross the heavily guarded frontier illegally, risking the mine-fields and frontier guards that constitute the Iron Curtain. Very few are successful. Some try the sea route – across the Baltic or the Black Sea, or even under water. Even fewer succeed that way.

An easier way out is to break free of controls when you are already legally outside the country – as a sailor or merchant seaman, a tourist, a journalist or a diplomat. But to achieve that takes many years of careful preparation. Recent 'successes' in this category are Arkadi Shevchenko, a high-ranking Soviet diplomat in New York, and Oleg Gordievsky, the man in charge of the KGB station in the Soviet embassy in London.

I certainly did not plan to escape. I decided almost on the spur of the moment to get away. It was as much a surprise for me as it must have been for my friends and superiors in Moscow and Geneva. I was moved by purely personal feelings – above all by sense of the cruel injustice of a regime that could treat a loyal servant with such contempt and inhumanity. I chose to defect rather than suffer any further indignities at the hands of the Soviet bureaucracy. I was in Moscow when I made my decision. How I got away I recount in my book. I was lucky. Had I failed the penalty would have been very severe. As it is, I am listed as a 'traitor'.

So here I am, a reluctant defector, so to speak, living quietly in Britain with my wife and daughter. We know we are most unlikely ever to see our native land (in my case Georgia, in the Caucasus) again.

I have no sense of guilt about quitting the Soviet Union and seeking refuge in the West. I served the Kremlin loyally for more than thirty-seven years, from the end of the Second World War to the day I slipped out of Moscow for the last time. For the whole of that time I was connected with the secret police, the famous KGB, first as a full-time officer and latterly while working in other positions as a journalist. I carried out all my duties – often very unpleasant ones – conscientiously and have a drawer full of medals to prove it. I know a good deal about intelligence and counter-intelligence work both in Moscow and abroad.

I started writing this book in 1984, before Mikhail Gorbachev initiated the process of reforming the Soviet Union. I was not out to expose the Soviet regime, although I do have criticisms to make of it, but rather to explain it. I wanted to give readers in the West an opportunity to learn what the regime looks like from the inside. Many people have written about their experiences at the hands of the KGB; I provide a glimpse of life from the point of view of the guardians of the Soviet system.

I do not claim that the events I describe were historically decisive. But I do claim that my story is true, down to the last detail. If there are things that I have had to leave out, that is because of concern for the fate of my friends in Russia and because of the need for discretion in a profession like mine. I hope the reader will find what I have to say interesting.

ILYA DZHIRKVELOV
London, 1987

Escape

IT WAS EARLY on a very cold morning in March 1980. I was speeding through the broad avenues of central Moscow in a state-owned Volga taxi, the driver of which I had paid a generous 25 roubles. People were hurrying to work along the sidewalks or standing in queues at bus-stops and taxi stations. As we swept past them the windows of the houses reflected the bright morning sun. I was on my way to Moscow's Sheremetyevo airport to catch a plane that would take me out of the Soviet Union, as I had done many times in the past.

But this was no routine journey. I was making it, I hoped, for the last time. This time I was on my own : nobody, none of my friends and certainly none of my superiors in the secret police,* knew I was leaving. I had been refused permission to do so, and it was partly because of that refusal that I had come to the conclusion that I could no longer live in the Soviet Union. I had decided to flee.

I just couldn't stand it any longer. I had served the Soviet regime faithfully for thirty-odd years, only to be spurned by it in the end. So I had decided to pit my wits against the

---

* The term 'secret police' will be used interchangeably throughout the book with 'intelligence', 'security service' and 'KGB'. Immediately after the Russian Revolution, Lenin signed a decree on 20 December 1917 providing for the creation of an Extraordinary Commission for combating counter-revolution and sabotage, which came to be known by its initial letters as the Cheka. Those who worked for the Cheka were known as Chekists, which is how people working for the KGB are still known today. The Cheka itself later came to be known by other sets of initials – VChK, OGPU, NKVD, NKGB, MGB and in 1954 KGB, the Committee for State Security.

system and leave Russia under the very noses of the authorities.

At Sheremetyevo there was the usual confusion which seems to be worse than at most other airports. My first concern was to get through the passport control as quickly as possible, and in my haste I made a mistake that might have proved fatal. The emigration officer checked my passport carefully, and then after glancing down to see whether my name featured in his black-list of people not allowed out of the Soviet Union, studied me with equal care. Then he asked me for my boarding pass. At first I did not understand his question, and this might well have aroused his suspicions, but my nonchalant manner and, most important, my diplomatic passport reassured him. He repeated his question. I pointed to my briefcase, saying with a smile that it was all the luggage I had and that that was why they had not given me a boarding pass. Smiling back, the officer accepted my explanation, and I rushed back to get the pass.

I was safely through the passport control, but there was another equally dangerous situation ahead. As I entered the departure lounge and glanced up at the board displaying the departure times I stopped in my tracks: people were still queuing up to join the Moscow–Geneva flight on which Aleksandr Kiselev, counsellor at the Soviet mission in Geneva, was due to depart, confident that I had been left behind for ever in Moscow.

Kiselev was no friend of mine. On the contrary, he had done his best to destroy me. It was he who had accompanied me back from Geneva to Moscow, and he who had made sure that I could get no hearing in Moscow. If he were to catch sight of me in the departure lounge of all places, my game would be up. I had to hide.

I slipped quickly into the restaurant and scrutinized the other customers. There was no one I knew, and probably for the first time in my life I was genuinely glad to be leaving without anyone to see me off. Despite the early hour I drank a brandy with my coffee in the hope of restoring myself after five sleepless nights. Then I made myself comfortable in a chair in a dimly lit corner so that I would not be noticed but could keep my eye on everybody and on the departure board. My flight to Vienna was due to leave in forty minutes.

Soon the light announcing the Geneva flight went out, indicating that all the passengers, including Kiselev, were aboard the plane. He would never imagine that in a matter of minutes I too would be flying westwards.

Then the Vienna flight was called. I let the other passengers through first, to make sure that there was nobody I knew on it. To meet one of my acquaintances would not have been so risky now, but it would be preferable not to. If I did run into somebody I would say that I was going to Vienna on official business, without going into details. I would never be questioned, because Soviet people have a love of secrecy instilled into them from childhood, and the more enigmatic a person's expression and the heavier his hints about the impossibility of revealing what he is up to, the more likely he is to be believed, even if he is lying. So I didn't worry much on that score.

Something else was bothering me, however. It was by now ten o'clock in the morning, and someone might call my home and discover I was not there. If my superiors were to suspect that something was wrong, they might still have time to phone the airport and stop the plane leaving. Even when airborne they could make it turn back or have it land in another Communist country.

There were other dangers too. It is not without good reason that people say that the Soviet regime has long arms. What worried me most was that it would take me at least two days to get to Geneva, where I had left my wife and five-year-old daughter: ample time for the police in Moscow to discover that I was missing and to inform the Soviet mission in Geneva. That would be the end of my attempt to get away. KGB officers would go immediately to my Geneva apartment and transfer my wife and daugher to the diplomatic mission. A few days later they would be put on a plane back to Moscow. Meanwhile the KGB would simply wait for me to turn up at my apartment. I could, of course, phone the apartment from the airport in Vienna, and I would know at once if something was wrong. But could I carry through my plan without my family? Could I abandon them? The answer was: No, I couldn't. Of that I was quite sure.

I brushed my gloomy thoughts aside. I pinned my faith on the psychological factor: the people in Moscow would never suspect that I would decide to defect, because they knew of my long and devoted service. They had forgotten that a man has his honour and his pride and, most important, that, sometimes at least, he can arrive at his own conclusions and judgements.

Fortunately, my calculations proved to be correct. But I was still a long way from being quite sure as I went out to board the plane for Vienna. Boarding a plane at Sheremetyévo is always a tedious business. On this occasion it seemed to take an eternity. I was the last person to pass through the screening device that was supposed to protect us from armed hijackers. I had no problems, perhaps because I was still holding my diplomatic passport in my hand and it had a magical effect upon the airport officials. Respect, even reverence, for documents and pieces of paper is a distinguishing feature of Soviet life. Ever since the inception of the Soviet regime forms and certificates have ruled people's lives, which is why they say: without a document you are just an insect, but with one you are a person. It was surprising that I had not attracted more attention, since I was travelling with no luggage apart from my briefcase. No Soviet official ever travels abroad without taking a number of suitcases with him, so that he can bring back all the consumer goods he intends to buy in the West. But I did not attract attention: I had the most impressive document of all, which had the effect I had hoped for. When she saw my diplomatic passport, the girl in charge politely invited me to walk round the screening device and directed me on along the corridor to the coach that would take us to the plane. Young soldiers of the frontier troops in their green caps were on guard at the exits to make sure we did not go astray.

Once aboard the plane I settled down in a window seat and gazed for the last time at the grey inhospitable buildings of Sheremetyevo airport. We stayed on the runway for a long time, or perhaps it only seemed a long time to me. I tried to turn my thoughts to other things so as to speed the passage of time. But how can a man think of something else when he is walking on a knife-edge? One false step and it would be all over.

At last the doors were slammed shut. We were off, it seemed. We were about to taxi out to the main runway. But suddenly the door at the forward end of the plane opened again and an officer of the frontier troops and another man in civilian clothes squeezed into the plane. For a sickening moment I thought they must be looking for me. Could they really have had time? Could my calculations have been wrong? But after a whispered conversation with the stewardess and a glance at the passengers the officer left without a word of farewell and the civilian went into the forward part of the plane. I let out a sigh of relief. But I knew I wasn't safe yet. For about another three hours I would be flying over the territory of the socialist commonwealth, and that was no less dangerous than standing on a shaky chair with a noose round my neck.

The monotonous hum of the engines began to lull me to sleep, so that I did not hear the stewardess offering me a glass of Georgian wine. When she saw my surprise she repeated the offer in English, apparently taking me for a foreigner because I was wearing a suit – unlike the other passengers, employees of some Leningrad enterprise who were flying to Vienna as tourists. I refused the wine, fearing that it might knock me out as I had not slept for five nights and I still did not dare to sleep. The stewardess extolled the exceptional qualities of Georgian wine. My paranoia returned. Why was she being so insistent? Who was the civilian who had joined the plane? Had somebody slipped something into the wine? There were lots of glasses and I chose one from the middle, but I didn't drink it until lunch was served, by which time all the other passengers had drunk their wine and nothing had happened to anybody. I began to see the funny side of the situation.

As I drank the Georgian wine I took my leave, probably for ever, of my native Georgia, of warm, beautiful and hospitable Tbilisi, where I had passed my childhood and youth in its green sunlit streets and where as children we first learned about good and evil, honour and dishonour.

PART ONE

Training

CHAPTER ONE

Teenage Training

I WAS BORN IN FEBRUARY 1927 in Sevastopol, the son of a naval officer who had taken part in the Russian Revolution of 1917 and was then a political commissar in the Black Sea Fleet. His name was Grigori Ilich Dzhirkvelov. I have only a vague memory of him as a tall man in a white naval uniform. I cannot recall his face. When I was six or seven I came across my mother, Yelena Yakovlevna Iremadze, a veteran member of the Bolshevik Party and an employee of the NKVD (as the secret police was then called), destroying some photographs. Amongst them was one of a man in a white uniform. When I asked who he was she told me he was my father, and that he had been killed in 1930 while on manoeuvres. The admiral's barge on which he had been serving had entered Turkish waters somewhere near Batum in a fog, struck a mine and sank. I naturally accepted my mother's account and was proud that my father had met such an heroic end. Many years later, however, I learned that this story had been invented by my mother who, anxious to protect me from unpleasantness, concealed the fact that she had divorced my father and lost trace of him. It was not until 1950 that I learned the truth about my father and why my mother had destroyed her photographs of him. And it was only in 1961 that his son by a second marriage showed me another copy of that photograph.

I spent my childhood in Tbilisi in a quiet tree-lined street close to the River Kura and the old ferry that crossed it.

Before the Revolution the house we lived in had belonged to a rich Persian. Now twelve families occupied it, each having one room, with a single communal kitchen and only one outside lavatory. In 1974, when I was last in Tbilisi, I went to look at my childhood home. It still provided accommodation for twelve families, and though the building was now equipped with central heating, and the kitchen had a gas cooker, the occupants still lived in considerable discomfort.

For us the spring of 1941 was a time of anxiety. The possibility of war loomed large and we still lived under the shadow of the mass arrests of 'enemies of the people' and the persecution of entire families. My mother complained ever more frequently of being tired, became increasingly irritable and talked about wanting to quit the secret police. She did not explain why, but I suspect that she had been deeply shocked by the recent arrest of six of our close neighbours. Nevertheless, she remained to the end of her days utterly loyal to the Soviet regime, and I cannot recall her ever having been beset by doubts about the correctness and the legality of the things that the Party leaders did.

At school our teachers frequently praised the example of Pavlik Morozov. He was the boy who had informed the secret police about his parents' conversation expressing hostility to the Soviet regime. As a result his parents were arrested, while Pavlik Morozov himself was said to have been murdered by enemies of the Soviet system. We were of course impressed by the stories of such deeds and keen to fight the enemies of our country, but we could not imagine saying anything bad about our parents, let alone denouncing them. Incidentally, Pavlik Morozov's repulsive treachery is still quoted today in Soviet schools as an exceptional example of patriotism.

On 22 June 1941, Hitler launched an attack on the Soviet Union. It was the beginning of what is known in Russia as the Great Fatherland War, in which some twenty million Soviet lives were lost. The country suffered enormous physical destruction but emerged victorious not least because, despite the horrors of the 1930s, the majority of the population believed in and supported the Soviet leaders. As one who fought in the war I can confirm that Soviet troops did indeed go into the attack shouting 'For our country, for Stalin' without being compelled to do so, as some Russian emigré writers have said. According to them it was only the security troops armed with machine-guns bringing up the rear that kept the Soviet troops advancing. To write such things is to defile the memory of the men who died in battle, to whom millions alive today, including the authors of such rubbish, owe their lives.

By the second year of the war, the front was moving ever closer to the frontiers of Georgia, and the autumn of 1942 was a frightening time. The German armies had already reached the foothills of the Caucasus mountains and it seemed certain that they would invade Georgia itself. Schools, offices and sports clubs were turned into hospitals, indeed Tbilisi itself had become one big hospital. The huge number of people evacuated from the occupied territories changed the whole appearance of the city, and the atmosphere of tension increased with each day that passed. When we came to discuss what I was to do my mother declared that there was only one correct course: to fight. The peacetime heroes – Party and Government officials in Georgia – took rather a different view. They also came to the conclusion that there was only one correct course, and that was, in case of real danger, to flee across the frontier to Iran. As a precautionary measure they would move their families closer to the Iranian border. Many of them were men perfectly fit to serve in the armed forces, but they preferred not to do so. Some of them turned out to be too ill for military service and did not recover their health until the war was over. They then completed their education and rushed to occupy safe jobs in the Communist Party and the Government as specialists with good academic qualifications.

In September 1942 a military officer visited my school and asked if I was a member of the Komsomol – the Communist Youth League – and what I intended to do to help defeat the Germans. I was a member, having joined it in the previous March out of a spirit of patriotism and in the hope that it would help me get to the front. I had visited the military Commissariat on several occasions and had tried to prove to them that I could handle weapons and was physically fit. I was an excellent marksman and had no difficulty in lifting the 100-kilogram sacks of sand with which we were barricading our houses. I later became a Master of Sport at weightlifting. Nevertheless they refused to take me into the army on account of my age.

Few children applied to join the Komsomol at that time, because their parents dissuaded them on the grounds that Tbilisi might be taken by the Germans, whose first move was to hang or shoot members of the Communist Party and the Komsomol. So when the visiting officer realized that I was burning with desire to get to the front and that my mother, far from being opposed to the idea, had herself applied on several occasions to be sent to the front, he patted me on the back and pointed out that before you could fight you had to study the military arts, and that there would be plenty of opportunity for me to get involved in the fighting, since the war would probably last a long time.

We lived opposite the school, and that evening the officer had a long talk with my mother, after which he half jokingly congratulated me on joining the ranks of the valiant Red Army. I then found he was not joking: I was not taken into the army but with my friend Boris Kelbalikhanov was enlisted into the reconnaissance group attached to a cavalry division stationed on the outskirts of Tbilisi. The officer persuaded our headmaster to transfer us to the third session, which began at seven o'clock in the evening. The schools had to work in three shifts because so many of them had been turned into hospitals.

I found the work in the reconnaissance group fascinating. We were taught a great variety of subjects: topography, orientation, the handling of fire-arms and knives, the identification of German tanks and their armament and the estimation on sight of the size of German units. But the most interesting was the horseback riding. After a couple of months' training we had a fair grasp of the elements of reconnaissance work in the field and then, dressed as Georgian village boys, we were sent for practical training into the mountains to spy for the Soviet units there. One operation Boris and I carried out was described by our leader as amazing, for we had discovered practically all there was to know about one German unit – its equipment, the number of men, and even the number of horses and donkeys that were carrying arms and ammunition. I was still impatient to get involved in the real fighting; the chance seemed imminent, since the Germans had already taken the nearby village of Klukhori, high up in the mountains, and had hanged all the top people there, including the head of the secret police. I did not come face to face with the Germans then because the Red Army drove them out of the Caucasus, but our services were not forgotten, and after the Germans had been driven out I was awarded my first military medal: For the Defence of the Caucasus. I believe this early experience did a great deal to determine my future career.

I left school in 1943 and, with help from my mother's friends, I started to work as a volunteer for the state security service in Georgia. Because I was still not seventeen I could not be taken on to the permanent staff. I had no idea what sort of work I would be doing but expected something very secret. In practice the work turned out to be more prosaic and simpler than I had expected, as is the case with most intelligence and counter-intelligence work, which rarely involves the sort of adventures seen in the James Bond films or the ones produced in the Soviet Union. Zhora Oganov, who lived in our building and who turned out also to be working for the secret police, explained to me that our job would be to follow people suspected of working for the enemy, to find out who they were meeting and talking to and what they handed over to each other. I was to act as Zhora's assistant in the business of following people about. Surveillance is difficult work, requiring considerable physical and nervous effort, because one must not let the target know that he or she is being followed and at the same time one must not allow the target to escape observation. It involves being on one's feet for many hours at a stretch. We had no motor cars, so that when a target hopped onto a trolleybus or a tram I had to run after it to take over the tailing from Zhora. At that time it was customary for only two people to follow one target, because of the shortage of manpower. Today the service responsible for surveillance has at its disposal not only cars but also sophisticated radio equipment which makes it possible to follow the target without being able to see him or her. If need be, one target today may be followed by as many as eight or ten people, all capable of changing their appearance in a matter of seconds, of using several cars, and of handing the target over to someone else by radio. But, in spite of these technical improvements, surveillance is still difficult and often thankless work.

In February 1944 I reached the age of seventeen and my work as a volunteer came to an end. I was summoned to the personnel department of the Georgian state security service and directed to work in the cryptographic section, which dealt with the monitoring of radio transmissions and the deciphering of foreign cable messages and of diplomatic codes. My older comrades tried to convince me of the importance of this work but I did not like it. It was not how I had imagined the battle against enemies of my country and foreign spies to be fought. After I had constantly nagged the deputy head of the department, Colonel Fisenko, to help me to join the operational department or be allowed to go to the front, he eventually sent me to the personnel department as being 'of no further use'. Despite this unfortunate classification, the move suited me because I was then sent on a short course of training for junior lieutenants in Navtlugi on the outskirts of Tbilisi. I finished the course in the middle of April 1944 and a few days later I was sent with a group of officers of the Georgian security service to the Crimea to take part in a special operation. Our task was to destroy the remainder of the German Waffen SS units and Death's Head divisions there as well as the military formations made up of collaborating Soviet citizens and soldiers. We had to clean up the territory liberated by the Red Army.

When our special commando unit arrived in the Crimea, we found that the fighting was not yet over. The Germans had turned the Sapun mountain into a huge and apparently impregnable fortress. The commander of the Soviet attack on the mountain decided to throw our units into the battle. The fighting was fierce and bloody, and when it was over the whole plain from the Sapun mountain to Balaklava was littered with so many bodies, both German and Soviet, that the burial units could not get round to burying them. Our special shock troops also suffered heavy losses.

The attack was halted at the end of April. The Soviet high command had apparently realized that it was useless to mount a frontal attack on the mountain without some preliminary softening-up by artillery. It was rumoured among the officers and men that Marshal Voroshilov himself had visited the Crimea and had given orders for rocket artillery, known to us as *Katyusas*, to be brought up and for the Sapun mountain to be showered with incendiary bombs. At the beginning of May the *Katyusas* did their job and on 9 May Sevastopol was liberated. The German troops were driven back to the Black Sea and hastily clambered into boats and barges. We did not pursue them out to sea but left them to the attention of our bombers.

Now we could turn to our main task of cleaning up the liberated areas of the Crimea. It was difficult and painful work, but then war is mainly work and not adventure. The remnants of the units of the German army, particularly those composed of Soviet non-Russians and Crimean Tartars, had taken to the hills, where they put up a desperate resistance, often preferring to die rather than be taken prisoner. Their struggle was hopeless and by the middle of May it was all over.

It seemed as though peace and tranquillity had returned to a land so amply watered with the blood of Soviet and German soldiers. The war was already moving towards the western frontiers of the Soviet Union, and we were ordered to remain in the Crimea until we received further instructions. Then we learnt that units of KGB special troops and some detachments from the Orenburg division had arrived in the Crimea. I was then a junior lieutenant and was put in charge of a platoon from the Orenburg division and instructed to billet them in Tartar homes in the village of Komari, near Balaklava. Practically every family had a soldier billeted on it. I found accommodation for myself in a flat belonging to a young woman with three children, whose husband was at the front. She told me that he had been a Party official in the Crimea, and we were soon on excellent terms.

Under wartime regulations we were not allowed to put questions to our superiors, so that we had no idea of the real reason for our presence in the Crimea until the day before the operation was to take place. Late one evening in the middle of May I was summoned to headquarters in Balaklava together with many other officers. The tension in the air was soon dispelled by the appearance of Colonel Shavgulidze of the Georgian KGB.

He warned us that what we were about to hear was top secret and he then read out a decree announcing the deportation of all Crimean Tartars as a punishment for their collaboration with the enemy and for planning to hand over the Crimea to Turkey as an autonomous province. The deportation was to begin at six o'clock next morning; we were to tell the Tartars to leave their houses with only the bare essentials that they could carry. They were not to be told where they were going, but were to be formed up in columns and marched to the nearest railway stations, where *teplushki* (goods wagons used in wartime for transporting troops) would be waiting for them.

After the decree had been read out there was complete silence. We were not allowed to ask questions. Orders are orders and they have to be carried out; only then can questions be asked. That is the rule in the Soviet army in both war and peace. But I could tell that, despite the bitterness we felt, most of those present were not enthusiastic about the task before us, since we would be dealing not with an armed opponent but with the peaceful inhabitants of the region, and mainly women, children and old people. We left the meeting in silence.

I do not record my distaste for such an action in order to exculpate myself; the truth is that I did not feel any sense of guilt: I was an officer carrying out an order. I had unfeelingly shot down armed Crimean Tartars who had been fighting on the side of the Germans, but I could not see that the woman in whose house I was living was blame-worthy. She had three children and a husband who was a Communist, fighting against the Germans and devoted to the Soviet regime. I could not understand why innocent Tartars who were active members of the Communist Party and who had fought the German invaders should be punished so cruelly for betrayal by a few of their fellows.

On my return that evening my landlady greeted me cheerfully and provided me with an excellent cup of tea and sandwiches made from the American canned meat which we received in our rations. She seemed not to notice how depressed I was. How was I going to tell her in the morning to gather up whatever she could carry and leave her home for ever with her three children?

It is true that I knew about the deportation of the peoples of the northern Caucasus – the Chechens, Ingushi and Karachai – because of their collaboration with the Germans, but now the enormity of what we had been ordered to do really came home to me.

I could not sleep, and lay on my bed cursing myself for sentimentality and pity when I was supposed to feel hatred. I went through in my mind all the houses in the villages and their inhabitants, and it occurred to me that they were all pretty prosperous. The houses were quite well furnished; there were usually several carpets on the floor and walls; many of them had a piano and other expensive objects. What, I wondered, would happen to all those things after the deportation? At the meeting we had all been given a stern warning against the acquisition of other people's property, which would be treated as looting. I do not believe that we younger officers had the slightest intention of taking anything from the evacuated houses, because we had been brought up to disapprove of private property. But in the case of the senior officers that might not be so, which was doubtless why we had been warned.

At half past seven in the morning my platoon blocked all exits from the village of Komari. The soldiers took up positions about a hundred metres from each other, so that nobody could leave unnoticed. We had gained our experience of such procedures when we were surrounding groups of enemy troops in the mountains and villages of the Crimea, and it presented no problem in a peaceful village. I started calling at each house, with the platoon sergeant, telling the occupants to pack their things in preparation for a long journey. This, as I expected it would, produced panic, many of the women having hysterics and fainting.

They all wanted an explanation, but I was under orders to tell them nothing. People behaved as if their houses were on fire, grabbing anything that came to hand without considering whether they would need it or not. I cannot convey what

I had to watch that day. I shall never forget my landlady's eyes, staring and lifeless, her arms hanging helplessly by her side, and her half-open, speechless mouth. I felt I had to do something to help the poor woman, although it was contrary to my orders. In one of the houses I found three tough young men, who were somehow still in the village, and two young women, and told my sergeant to bring one of them to me. He was a powerful fellow of seventeen and I asked him to take two bundles of possessions to help my landlady. He refused, saying that there was something wrong with his legs which was why he had been left at home during the war. He certainly had a limp and he may well have been an invalid, but hatred rose in me and I told him that if he did not obey my order I would shoot him. He read my expression correctly; he threw two bundles over his shoulder and we set off in the direction of the Simferopol–Sevastopol highway.

According to our instructions, the Tartars had to be drawn up along the roadside to wait for another group of deportees from the village of Alsu on the other side of the main road. That was where my responsibilities ended. From there they were to be accompanied by special KGB troops who had been sent to the Crimea for that purpose. We were to remain behind to check all the houses and the surrounding countryside for any Tartars who might still be hiding.

The group of deportees from Alsu arrived and the column moved off in the direction of Balaklava under armed guard. I did not know their ultimate destination. Perhaps the hot uninhabited steppes of Kazakhstan, or maybe the vast wastes of Siberia with their sub-zero temperatures and howling blizzards. But I was sure that they were unlikely ever again to see the Crimea, its mountains, beaches and Black Sea, where thousands of people, including foreign tourists, now go on holiday and admire the beauties of the Crimea knowing nothing of the tragedy that took place there in 1944.

The dust had hardly had time to settle before men arrived from headquarters to carry out a complete inventory of all the property left behind by the Tartars. It took them a couple of days to complete the list and then they departed. We remained in the village awaiting further orders. Next day a group of special troops arrived in the charge of five or six officers, each armed with a permit to take away the remaining property. They were all senior to me in rank, and I had no cause to prevent them from doing so; moreover I assumed the articles were going into a government store. I was, however, surprised at the care with which they selected them. They were mainly interested in carpets, silver, pianos, antiques and similar objects, while they disregarded the less valuable objects and left them lying around in the houses. 'Operation requisition' was over in a day and the heavily loaded trucks departed. When I asked one of the officers whether the remaining things would be collected later he snapped, 'Who needs that junk?' and sped off.

I learned later that all the goods that had been taken away were handed over, not to the state, but to the colonels and generals in charge of the deportation and to some of their friends. In the view of the headquarters' staff this was not looting but a way of acquiring property in short supply permitted for services performed on the battlefield. This activity reached such epidemic proportions throughout the areas occupied by Soviet troops that the Supreme Command had to intervene, and some twenty generals were reduced in rank, including the KGB Major-General Malinin. I took part in a court martial at which he was charged with having committed an abuse of his official position when on duty in Germany after the end of the war – in other words, looting. Malinin was deprived of the rank of general but, like many others who suffered similarly, he was really only a scapegoat. I realized this some years after the war, when Marshal Zhukov's daughter, who was then working on Moscow Radio, told some friends that her father still had packing cases and suitcases which had been transported to his home during and after the war and had never been opened. She said Zhukov did not even know what was in them.

Many years were to pass before the Soviet people learned about the tragedy of the Crimean Tartars. Nikita Khrushchev expressed his anger at such events when he came to expose the crimes of Stalin and of Lavrenti Beria, then head of the KGB, to whom is often attributed the decision to deport the Crimean Tartars. Khrushchev conveniently forgot that such decisions were always taken by the whole Politburo and not by Beria alone. Furthermore, elementary logic would seem to suggest that, having exposed Stalin's violation of socialist legality, Khrushchev ought to have restored that legality – that is, the right of the Crimean Tartars to return to their homeland. But that did not happen, and could not happen, because it was none other than Khrushchev himself who took steps to separate the Crimea from the Russian Federation and hand it over in 1954 to the Ukraine, where for many years he had been First Secretary of the Communist Party. That is why, to this day, the Crimean Tartars are still living in exile.

After completing the deportation of the Tartars we were given the job of guarding the main roads across the Crimean peninsula. Early in 1945 it became apparent that a major event was in the offing there and with the arrival of British and American troops in Sevastopol we guessed that it might be a meeting of the Big Three – Stalin, Roosevelt and Churchill. In the first days of February we were summoned to headquarters, where we were told to report to the main headquarters in Yalta.

There we learned to our satisfaction that we were going to be part of the security guard at the palace in which the conference was to take place. There was also a large group of KGB officers from other parts of the Crimea. I do not know why such extreme precautions were taken, for it would have been difficult for even a fly to pass unnoticed into the palace. We all wanted, of course, to set eyes on the three great men, and, as luck would have it, I did manage to catch sight of them during one of the breaks in the conference. I saw Stalin himself pushing Roosevelt's wheel-chair; it struck me as a deliberate gesture on Stalin's part to demonstrate his great respect for the American president.

A telephone cable had been laid along the highway from Yalta to Sevastopol to enable our allies to communicate with each other and it was our duty to protect it. In a number of places on my section special equipment was attached to the cable so that KGB specialists from Moscow could listen in to any conversation.

Those of us guarding the Yalta conference knew nothing, of course, about what was decided there and it was only in 1948 that I learnt what had gone on at the conference table.

At a meeting of operatives, Andrei Vyshinsky, who had been one of Molotov's deputies at Yalta, asked if any of us had taken part in guarding the conference. A few of us raised our hands. 'Do you realize what a tremendous significance the conference had for the future foreign policy of the Soviet Union and its security?' Vyshinsky asked, and he went on to say that the results of the conference reflected the experience and maturity of Soviet diplomacy and that future generations of Soviet officials handling relations with the capitalist world should learn from the example of Yalta.

After discussing in general terms the purpose of the Yalta conference, Vyshinsky described the way in which the final document of the conference was arrived at. 'We realized,' he said, 'that the most important thing would be the final document, but the Soviet Union was in a minority because, however good our relations were with America, the views of the American delegation would certainly be closer to the British point of view. So we did not want to be the ones to produce the draft of the final document. Stalin therefore proposed that the American and British delegations should produce it, because, as he said, they were in the majority.'

According to Vyshinsky, Stalin's proposal was accepted, though not without some opposition from the allies.

'We knew,' Vyshinsky continued, 'that Churchill and Roosevelt would try to draw up a document that would be unacceptable to us and then, if we refused to accept it, they would hand the job over to the Soviet delegation. Our supposition proved correct, as we realized from a first quick glance through the draft. So the Soviet delegation asked for time to study it in detail till the next day. During our study of the draft we came to the conclusion that the preliminary talks we had had with the other delegations had not achieved what we wanted, although we appeared to have arrived at common solutions to the problems confronting us. These were basically the post-war frontiers in Europe and the future of the German nation, on whose division Winston Churchill seems to have insisted in order to prevent future military conflicts in Europe; the fate of Soviet prisoners of war and that of non-Germans who had fought against the Soviet army and were then in European countries. To have rejected the document would have meant assuming responsibility for drawing up another draft which might not be acceptable to the British and American delegations, and that might not leave us any chance of achieving our aims. There were many suggestions as to what our next step should be. Stalin listened to them all with attention and then said that we should tell our allies that on the whole the Soviet side accepted the draft of the final document but would like at the same time to introduce a number of amendments. He went on to say that since we had accepted the draft, they could not refuse to let us make some amendments. "We will make the document," Stalin continued, "what we would like it to be in general terms and we won't bother about the details even if they do not quite suit our book." '

'Our allies were greatly surprised,' Vyshinsky said. 'They

could not refuse us, and in that way, by introducing amendments, we obtained practically everything we had aimed for. That was one of the most important successes of Soviet diplomacy,' he concluded. He did not, of course, go on to say that that success cost many Russians and non-Russians their lives: I am not thinking of those who fought against us, but of their families, who were repatriated along with them from Britain and other countries and sent to prison camps in the wastes of Siberia and Central Asia.

As the Germans retreated westwards they left behind in the liberated territories collaborators who were not only terrorizing the local population but were organizing terrorist acts against Soviet officials and officers. Most had belonged to fighting units formed by the Germans from among the Ukrainian, Latvian and other non-Russian nationalities as well as from Soviet deserters and captives. The Germans used these units mainly to carry out punitive expeditions against the Soviet population and Soviet partisan detachments; they were never used in battles against the Red Army. We took this to mean that the Germans did not really trust them but we had no illusions about their hostility to the Soviet regime. They were mostly genuine opponents of the Soviet system.

There were daily reports of attacks on Soviet officials who had been sent to restore normal life to the liberated areas. The whereabouts of German reconnaissance groups left in the rear to supply the German command with information about Soviet troop movements was known from constant monitoring. To deal with both these threats, the Soviet leaders set the KGB and the military counter-intelligence service, known as Smersh, the task of destroying the insurgent groups and restoring life to normal in the liberated territories as quickly as possible. It was to be achieved by using specially formed commando units, special service troops of the KGB and where necessary Red Army units which happened to be in the locality.

It was a difficult and complicated task, because the groups of nationalists and their German accomplices were operating over a vast territory from the Crimea in the south to Estonia on the Baltic. Although in Russia proper the insurgents had practically no support from the local population, the situation was entirely different in the Ukraine and especially in Latvia. So it was decided to start the cleaning-up operation in the Western Ukraine and Latvia.

I had already taken part, not only in fighting against the Germans, but also in the business of destroying German sabotage groups dropped to our rear and local people aiding the Germans in the liberated territories, but those actions had been on a relatively small scale by comparison with what now lay ahead of us. Moreover, the people we had to wipe out had made thorough preparations for defence by digging underground bunkers in pathless forests where it was impossible to employ heavy weapons. We could not have found the insurgents had we not had KGB and Smersh agents among the nationalists and had there not been elements of the local population willing to help us.

The scale of each operation depended on how numerous and how well armed the nationalist group was. For example, in order to destroy a large detachment of Ukrainian nationalists in the Lvov area, two whole divisions of KGB troops took part. The area in which the nationalists were concentrated was encircled by three rings of soldiers advancing in sight of each other. The circles were gradually reduced until we came face to face with the enemy and opened fire. The battle that ensued was bitter; no one surrendered and no prisoners were taken. The Ukrainians went on fighting to their last bullet, when further resistance was obviously useless, and they often ended by shooting themselves or blowing themselves up with a grenade. It was the same with the Latvians. Their desperate resistance was not because they hated the

Soviet officers and men but because they knew they would have been sentenced to death for collaboration.

Even after the war was over, the units I was attached to carried on with the work of cleaning up one area after another. In central Russia, Belorussia and even in the Ukraine we found it relatively easy to discover the nationalists' hide-outs. But in the Baltic states, and especially on one occasion in Latvia, we met unexpected problems. Our command had received reports that a detachment of Latvian nationalists was hiding in a forest. We encircled the area and gradually drew the ring tighter until we came face to face, not with the Latvians, but with our own men. The enemy seemed to have vanished into the ground, which, as it turned out, is just what had happened. A careful search of the area revealed nothing suspicious. Then our attention was drawn to a tumbledown barn nearby. To our surprise, beneath the piles of hay we discovered a carefully camouflaged entrance to an underground bunker. What followed defies imagination: the fighting that took place was the most horrifying of any that I had to take part in.

The officer in command of my unit, a Latvian speaker, ordered the occupants to leave the bunker and lay down their arms. Had they done so and had there been no armed resistance we would have had to take the Latvians prisoner and hand them over to the Smersh counter-intelligence service. But there was no response from the bunker. He then warned them that they would be smoked out with flame-throwers and grenades and that the air vents would be sealed. In fact we had no flame-throwers and we had no idea where their air vents were and had had no time to look for them. After a short while we received a reply to the effect that our terms would be accepted only if we withdrew to not less than two hundred metres away, that our threat to use flame-throwers and grenades did not frighten them, and that because there were civilians with them they were ready to capitulate. We agreed and withdrew, confident no one could escape through the triple ring of soldiers.

We were well aware of how exceptionally brave Latvians are and how strong their feelings of nationalism, but we underestimated both qualities on this occasion and failed to take the necessary precautions. For that we paid dearly. We waited half an hour and no one appeared. Then, as our officer approached to ask them when they intended to give themselves up, there was a sudden blaze of gunfire from the barn. Our men were cut down like ninepins by the Latvians' fire. We were taken by surprise, but we quickly recovered our wits, took cover and returned the fire. Suddenly the firing from the Latvian side stopped and to our horror we saw a column of women and children emerging from the barn. Our colonel gave the order to cease fire and allow the women and children to pass. It is difficult to describe the tension and feeling of numbness as we watched the Latvian nationalist menfolk following the women. There were not less than thirty or forty women and children and about eighty men. They had sworn not to surrender to Russians.

We realized what they planned to do, so we opened fire on the men, but the women and children dashed back into the barn with their men. Our Latvian-speaking officer had been killed, but we managed to continue negotiating in Russian. The Latvians' reply was unequivocal : either they should be allowed to leave with their families or we could shoot the lot of them. None of us had faced such a situation before, and the idea of shooting them all on the spot in the hope that such a deed would be overlooked because it was wartime was too much for even our stern commanders to stomach.

Crawling on our bellies we reduced the size of the ring to about thirty-five metres so that they could not escape under cover of darkness. We had no effective means of illuminating the scene and we had to rely on the naked eye to see what the Latvians were up to. Suddenly they opened fire again, this

time in a less organized way. One of our men could not resist
returning the fire and then all the rest of us opened up as
well.

The sound of the gunfire was unbelievable and the
branches and trunks of the trees crackled as the bullets cut
into them. Then there was a sudden explosion and in a
moment the whole barn was in flames, a huge torch which lit
up everything around, including our pallid faces. Nothing
could be heard from within, although people were being
burnt alive in there. We looked on in silence: even if they
were enemies they were a tough and courageous people.
Suddenly a figure staggered out of the fire blinded by the
smoke and badly burnt. He fell straight into the hands of our
men. We needed him alive, not only to describe what had
happened in the barn but also to make sure that our commanding officers should not be accused of setting fire to it
nor held responsible for the deaths of women and children.
Consequently he was not executed. Like all the Latvian
nationalists he hated us and did not conceal the fact, but he
had been afraid to die along with the others.

The nationalists and collaborators who realized the futil-
ity of armed resistance simply disappeared in the hope of
concealing their past. But the Soviet regime never forgives
those who oppose it and fight against it. A special department was set up in the KGB to track down and punish
former collaborators. It continues to seek them out even
today because under Soviet law collaboration with the
Germans is not extenuated by the passing of time. Many of
those who escaped us in those early post-war days met their
end later at the hands of the KGB's internal troops.

It may be asked whether I had any doubts about the
rectitude of the brutal work I was involved in. The answer
is: neither then nor now. Do I believe today, after the
passing of so many years and the change in my attitude to
socialism, that those people collaborated with the Nazis
in order to liberate their people from the Communist yoke?

No, I do not believe it, because I saw them at close quarters and I saw what they had been doing. None of the documents published today or the reminiscences of people describing their liberating mission can change my view. They are intended for the simple and ignorant reader.

I managed to survive my service with the security forces and to return to Tbilisi to rest and begin my life in my home town in peacetime. I was only eighteen, with all my life ahead of me. But it turned out not to be peaceful: fate decided otherwise.

CHAPTER TWO

•···•——◆——•···•

School for Spying and Assassination

THE LONG-AWAITED PEACE seemed to have arrived at last. But then the Soviet government began moving troops from the western fronts to the Far East, and we realized that we were still faced with a fierce battle with the Japanese in Manchuria. At the beginning of August 1945 Russia declared war on Japan and an attack was launched on the Japanese troops concentrated in Kwantung. Then the Americans dropped their atomic bombs on Hiroshima and Nagasaki. It struck us like a bolt from the blue, but Stalin seemed to regard America's possession of such an awe-inspiring weapon with extraordinary calmness. He knew perfectly well that the bomb could not be used at that time against the Soviet army, which had borne the main burden of the war against German Fascism and which was regarded by both Europeans and by Americans as an army of liberation. Moreover, work on the development of a Soviet atomic bomb was already in full swing, with the participation of such outstanding scientists as Igor Kurchatov, Mikhail Kapitsa, Andrei Sakharov and others. And the efforts of the Soviet intelligence services to obtain information on the American bomb were not unsuccessful, so that the Soviet leaders, and especially Stalin, were confident that the Soviet Union would soon catch up with America in this new field of warfare. They were right of course; and the acquisition by the Soviet Union of first an atomic and then a hydrogen bomb went a long way to compensate for the decline in prestige of the Soviet army and was the best guarantee against any form of pressure on the Soviet Union from Western governments.

The loss of life caused by the war was enormous, though no official figures were ever published. There was a serious shortage of trained manpower in Russia in general, and the sensitive field of intelligence and counter-intelligence work was no exception. For this reason we young officers were encouraged to undertake further training. Of course we already knew all there was to know and were entitled to a rest so that, when I was sent for by Colonel Avalov, the head of our department, and told that he intended to put me forward as a candidate for training at the KGB training school, I was unpleasantly surprised. Why should I have to go somewhere to study when at the age of eighteen I was already working as an operational agent and in ten years' time I would be head of a section? What's more I had no wish to leave Tbilisi and my family and friends to go and live in Moscow with its heavy snowfalls and bitter frosts, of which at that time I knew only by hearsay.

Avalov awaited my reply. I asked for time to think it over, and was told I could have until tomorrow. It was by now one o'clock in the morning, and tomorrow meant 10.30 the same day.

I arrived home at two o'clock in the morning. My mother was, as usual, waiting for me to return. For some reason she was always afraid that I would be attacked on my way back from work, although she knew perfectly well that I always carried a gun. They didn't get me in the war and they won't get me now, I told her, although I understood her concern. Muggings, robberies and murders were then a daily occurrence. When she saw the worried look on my face she asked what had happened, and I told her. In her heart of hearts my mother was certainly against the idea. She did not want to be

separated from me, but her head told her something different: she thought about her son's future and realized that to
have studied in Moscow might offer greatly improved prospects for the future, far better than just working in the KGB
in Georgia. 'I think,' she said slowly, 'that you had better
agree to go to Moscow, though I don't know what your views
are.' I told her that I had no desire to go to Moscow but
thought nevertheless that I had better accept the proposal. 'I
think so too,' my mother continued. 'Georgia is a small
country with mountains all around it, while from Moscow
you can see further.' I don't know how she managed to hit
upon such a vivid way of putting it, but I have never
forgotten her words; she was right – you could see further
from Moscow.

Eight Georgians were selected for training at the KGB
school in Moscow and we were given a grand formal send-
off. The Georgian Minister of State Security, General
Rapava, urged us in his farewell speech not to disgrace our
own KGB, to pass out with flying colours, and to return to
Georgia. He decorated three of us who had fought in the
war: For victory over Germany in the Great Fatherland
War.

It was by now the end of September, the loveliest time of
year in Georgia, when the late fruits ripen, the grapes are
bursting with golden juice and their harvest is about to
begin, when the farmers start selling the young wine known
as *machari*, sparkling, light and intoxicating, like the first kiss
of a young woman in love – yes, really in love, because wine
was ever the pride and love of Georgia. But I was leaving that
enchanting corner of the earth, not knowing that I was never
to live there again.

The journey from Tbilisi to Moscow in those days took
four whole days by train. The carriages were overcrowded
and, as a rule, had no glass in the windows, exposing the
passengers to some danger because bands of criminals along
the route could throw their *koshki* (cats) – metal devices with

four sharp hooks on them – through the windows and pull out anything they could reach. Sometimes it was a suitcase, sometimes a bag of food, but quite often the sharp claws of the 'cat' hooked into a person, who would also be dragged out through the window. The train moved slowly. There were frequent inspections to check whether people had the relevant documents for entering Russia proper. During stops at stations we often heard shooting; more often than not it was a military patrol pursuing army deserters and the like who had taken to robbery and gang warfare.

At last the train arrived at the Kursk station in Moscow early one cold morning. The pushing and shoving there was unbelievable as everyone tried to get through the document control as quickly as possible. Then we had to undergo the worst ordeal of all, at the delousing centre, which looked like something between a bath-house and a gas chamber. Every passenger had to strip naked and hand over all his clothing for fumigation. Only when we had received a certificate of cleanliness had we the right to go into Moscow. Such a process seems now strange and disagreeable, but it was necessary in those days because of the danger of epidemics.

When I emerged I took the Metro, an experience I did not relish despite its efficiency, to the Vysshaya Shkola. The KGB school was situated at that time in Bolshoi Kiselny Street in a red-brick building protected on one side by a high wall. Some three hundred metres away was the main KGB building in Dzerzhinsky Square. This is the building known in the West as the Lubyanka.

It took me about fifteen minutes to get from the Metro station to the KGB school. As I walked along I looked around in wonder; I felt as if I was in a narrow gorge with towering escarpments. In those days there were no buildings in Tbilisi more than two or three storeys high, and now stood all around what seemed to me huge structures of eight and ten storeys. I was struck by the absence of trees, which made the streets seem empty after Tbilisi, in spite of the crowds of pedestrians. But the rattle of the trams which still ran into the centre of Moscow had a reassuring effect, reminding me of home.

I presented my papers at the entrance to the KGB school and went through into the building where for the next two years I would be learning the mysteries of the knights of the cloak and dagger, the science of defeating the enemy of the invisible front and much more. First of all, however, I had to go through a medical inspection, strip naked again and hand my clothes over for treatment and then submit to a series of physical tests. The doctors declared me completely fit, although in the course of one battle I had suffered concussion when a shell exploded near me, which had left me with a twitching eyelid and eye and an inability to sit still for more than a few seconds at a time. The doctor told me that the trouble would pass off in less than a year, as proved to be the case.

I was issued with a clean and – to my surprise – neatly pressed uniform and was then handed over to the commandant of the school building. He took me to a large room on the fourth floor with sixteen beds in it. This is where I was to live with my fellow students, whom I had still not seen; I would be allowed to leave the building only on Sundays, because we were not ordinary students but undergraduates at the school belonging to the most awe-inspiring and powerful organization in the country – the KGB. Classes began at 9 a.m. and ended at 10 p.m., with short breaks for lunch and supper. The period from five to seven in the evening was set aside for us to work on our own on subjects set us by our teachers. The normal five-year course had to be completed in less than two years on instructions from above. It meant total concentration of nervous, intellectual and physical faculties. Only Sunday was set aside for rest and amusement. Anyone who was unable to cope with the course and dropped behind would be taken off the course and sent back to his place of work with a character reference which would do him little good in the future.

In such terms, briefly and to the point, we were introduced to the course by the officer in charge of the school, General Bashtakov, an unusually short man for whom a special chair had been made with legs longer than normal so that when he was sitting at a table his small stature was less noticeable. General Bashtakov always delivered his lectures sitting down and when he congratulated us on being accepted for the course he shook our hands without moving from behind the table. Because of his lack of inches he refused to go into the courtyard to greet Marshal Tito of Yugoslavia on his visit to the school in 1946. At the time some members of the Yugoslav state security service were studying there, including the twenty-six-year-old General Koča Vočić, with whom I struck up a close friendship. I later leant to my sorrow that, during Tito's purge of people who favoured good relations with the Soviet Union Vočić disappeared without trace, as did many others.

'In offering you the possibility of studying here the Party and the government have placed great confidence in you. Not everybody is given the same chance. You are being entrusted with a great responsibility – to be loyal defenders of the achievements of the October Revolution and of the Soviet people, because after you have graduated you will be on the front line of the invisible front where there is always a bitter battle taking place with a strong, intelligent and crafty enemy. The French, British and other Western intelligence services are out to undermine the foundations of socialism with the aid of every available legal and illegal means. You must always keep firmly in your minds that our main enemy is now and always will be capitalism, and in order to fight an enemy successfully you must know all there is to know about him. Your success will depend on how well you study and master the methods used by an intelligence agent, how well you study the fundamentals of Marxism–Leninism and the history and languages of Western countries, and also how well you learn to handle weapons and to use those special physical tricks which might prove indispensable in a desperate situation.'

That was how our first lecture began. The classes were really interesting, because we were introduced to a world previously closed to us in which cunning and baseness, honesty and courage, loyalty and treachery were all interwoven, in which the most ruthless and despicable methods, including abduction and murder, were used to gain victory or superiority over an adversary. It was a world that brought out the most contemptible qualities in the human character, and at the same time one in which people displayed courage approaching madness, risking their lives not for huge sums of money but because they genuinely believed in the necessity of fighting the enemies of socialism.

The secret police had no doubts at all concerning the correctness of what they were doing: they were utterly devoted to the cause. And even now, after the passage of so many years and so many changes in my view of the essence of socialism, I pay sincere tribute to their personal bravery. I shall never agree with efforts that are made to besmirch their memory or cease to be appalled that most of them were executed or expelled from their jobs during the Khrushchev 'thaw' and the fight against the 'cult of personality'. They had not understood that in the socialist society in which they were living a man's life is in the hands of the state like the rest of his property. That is the true law of socialism, despite fine talk about human life being socialism's most precious resource, and is as valid today as it was in 1945, when we were taught counter-intelligence work.

Despite the fact that most of the students at the school were officers, many of whom had taken part in the war with Germany, and it was not easy to scare us, what we learned about the Soviet counter-intelligence service, about the scale of its operations and the ruthlessness of its methods, was overpowering.

Some students on the course, especially in the faculty of foreign languages, which trained interpreters for the KGB's special services, were so shocked and frightened that they fell into a state of depression. Two of them even committed suicide. One, a young man, hanged himself in the stairway, leaving a note saying that, after what he had learned about the counter-intelligence service, life had become too frightful for him.

Of course, a suicide, and especially one at the KGB's training school, was an event of importance, and it was discussed in detail at special meetings of the Party groups on the course, not in order to elucidate its cause but to condemn it as an act unworthy of a member of the KGB. Every KGB man was supposed to be a fervent believer in the cause, to keep a cool head and lead a clean life. That was the spirit in which they trained us, convincing us of the need for asceticism, because our first concern had to be the ideas for which we were fighting and devotion to our duty and our state. Our lives were restricted and – in terms of material possessions – very simple. We had few contacts outside the KGB, because we might by chance meet people already under observation by the security service.

Although they preached the need for an ascetic manner of life, our superiors did not themselves adhere to that rule, indulging in every kind of pleasure, permissible or otherwise, and doing everything in their power to improve their material lot. The Secretary of the Party committee at the school, Colonel Peter Sharov, saw nothing shameful in using his position to force girls from the language courses to move in with him, with the promise of good jobs and promotion when they graduated. Moreover he frequently held drinking parties in his office at which it became apparent that he was a common or garden drunkard. His love of liquor and of debauchery was no secret, but as one of the bosses he was *ipso facto* faultless. There would be no point in dwelling on the behaviour of this man if similar conduct were not typical in a socialist society, where highly placed people urge ordinary people to live according to elevated moral and material criteria but consider themselves above such criteria.

The former Soviet Minister of Culture, G. F. Alexandrov, affords another example. He used to organize drunken orgies with young girl students from the Soviet Institute of Cinematography and from the ballet schools in Moscow and Leningrad carefully chosen for him by his subordinates. When this became public knowledge Alexandrov was dismissed as minister but he was not arrested for seducing minors, as required by the law. He was sent to work somewhere beyond the Urals as the Secretary of a regional committee of the Party, that is, again as an ideological preacher. Had he not belonged to the ruling caste he would have been branded as a Rasputin and might well have spent a certain number of years in a labour camp.

Many years later, when I was working in the Second Chief Directorate of the KGB in Moscow, I witnessed many a drunken orgy organized by well-known Soviet composers, poets and writers, like Aleksei Fatyanov, Vasili Soloviev-Sedoi and Valentin Katayev, who are still held up as examples for Soviet people to follow, as men who had devoted their whole lives to the noble cause of communism and had been awarded all sorts of titles and decorations. These 'pure' representatives of the ruling caste gave prostitutes champagne baths in rooms at the Moscow Hotel and indulged in group sex and all kinds of perversions, paying the prostitutes from 300 to 500 roubles a session and the waitresses 150 roubles to keep their mouths shut.

I once had an agent working for me, a beautiful and depraved young woman known as Sincerity, who took part in such orgies, but despite her cynical view of life she told me that she found these orgies revolting, and suggested that the KGB should be able to punish such people. She did not understand that members of the ruling caste cannot be dealt with even by the KGB so long as they do not overstep the limits beyond which the security of the Soviet state is affected. That was the situation then, and it remains unchanged today.

The winters in Moscow were very severe, with the temperature dropping to 20 and even 25 degrees below freezing. It was my first encounter with the Russian winter and I have to say that my initial revulsion has remained with me all my life. Although I had to live for many years in Moscow I never got used to the extreme cold and never derived any pleasure from being out of doors in the winter. I still shudder when I remember being woken at 7 a.m. and chased out into the courtyard in vest and pants to do physical jerks in the sub-zero temperature.

To those of us from the Caucasus it was a painful ordeal and we decided to protest. The attitude of the authorities towards national minorities was more considerate then than it is now; we did not feel that the Russians were dominant and we were even able to exploit their attitude to the national minorities in our own interests. Colonel Nikolai Ivanov, the head of our course, was a well-meaning and considerate man and an experienced intelligence officer who during the war had been dropped more than once behind the German lines, where he had been in charge of special sabotage groups. We knew about his past and were fond of him, especially since his experiences had not made him hard-hearted. He was married to a Georgian woman and had made several visits to Georgia, so that when we asked him to let us off exercising in the early morning frost he agreed, although it was contrary to the rules.

Although the demands made on the students were very severe, the quality of the teaching was high. The most interesting lectures were those given by such experienced and highly placed members of the KGB as Pavel Sudoplatov, who was then head of the Sabotage and Terrorism

Department. At his lectures we learned about practically every method of organizing sabotage, underground operations and the liquidation, i.e. the murder, of our enemies. He told us that a special Scientific and Technical Department of the KGB, with a staff of nameless but exceptionally able doctors, chemists and technologists, was developing and producing new types of weapons and poisons and devices for carrying out 'Liter L', which was the code name for liquidation. I should like at this point to emphasize that operations code-named 'Liter I', meaning kidnapping, and 'Liter L', can be carried out only with the approval of the Secretaries and Politburo members of the Soviet Communist Party. No one in charge of the KGB, and certainly no KGB officer in a *rezidentura* abroad, has the right to carry out such operations, and I was told that any breach of this rule was severely punished. It is a saying among officers of the KGB that 'all independent initiative is punishable'.

Operations involving kidnapping or assassination, as well as those aimed at the recruitment or discreditation of foreign statesmen and politicians or of foreign ambassadors accredited to the Soviet Union, can be carried out only with the approval of the General Secretary or certain members of the Politburo who have some connection with the KGB. The only exception to this was when Beria was in charge of Soviet intelligence and counter-intelligence : he had the right to approve such operations and to inform Stalin about them orally.

The initiative for such operations may come from above, i.e. from the men in charge of the KGB, or from below – from the *rezidentury* and departments of the KGB. In the majority of cases proposals for assassinating or kidnapping are made by the *rezidentury* of the KGB abroad or by its departments and directorates in Moscow. Permission for them to be carried out is obtained by submitting a detailed report containing well-founded evidence and arguments demonstrating the necessity and even the inevitability of executing the operation in the interests of the security of the Soviet Union. The report, marked 'top secret', is sent to the Politburo over the signature of the Chairman of the KGB. He will already have received a similar report from the head of the Chief Directorate of the KGB concerned and the head of the department responsible for putting the plan into practice. Once it has been approved by the Secretariat or Politburo the report goes back to the KGB department for implementation.

Both in the files in the KGB archives and in current files I was later to come across many such reports with Beria's approval written on them : 'I approve', but signed only with his initials L.B. and never with his full name. Once such documents have the approval of the Secretariat or Politburo they are never kept in current files but in the KGB Chairman's special file, because of their importance and the great secrecy attached to them. But the officer in charge and the one who has to carry out Operation I or L also have to see the papers. The KGB agents, however, act simply on the instructions of the officer they are reporting to.

Both at the KGB school and when I was being prepared for leading a group of militants in Iran I was taught how to employ special physical tricks and poisons to dispose of an opponent as well as, of course, how to use more familiar weapons, such as the hand-gun and knife. Even in those years the Technical Department of the KGB already had at its disposal fountain pens, cigarette cases and even fake cigarettes which could fire a fatal dose of poison. The poisons used left no traces in the body of the victim and produced the effect of a heart attack, a stroke or suffocation following an asthma attack. In addition, for kidnapping operations they had developed long-acting tranquillizers.

Did I have any doubts about the propriety of employing such methods against our opponents? I do not think so, because operations involving the kidnapping or assassination of an opponent are not organized only by the KGB : every intelligence and counter-intelligence service does the same.

Moreover, memories of the war and of battles with nationalists and other collaborators with the Fascists were fresh, and my knowledge of what foreign agents did banished any doubts I might have had.

One of the first Liter L operations was carried out in connection with the former OGPU *rezident* in Teheran, Georgi Agabekov, whose real name was Arutyunov and who defected in 1929. We were told about him at our lectures and I later looked into his case when I was working in the archives department of the First Chief Directorate. Agabekov was the first station chief ever to defect to the West. Other pre-war defectors included Aleksandr Orlov, the NKVD *rezident* in Spain, and two NKVD officers, Walter Krivitsky and Ignati Reiss. Their files showed that they had been dealt with under the heading of Liter L, with the exception of Orlov, who managed to escape that fate. There is a lot that is not clear about the Orlov story.

I was unable to find any indication of why Agabekov chose to defect. He occupied an important position and had every possibility of advancing in the secret police. His principal shortcoming appeared to be that he was too interested in the opposite sex, but this did not seem to affect his political views. Why he chose to defect remains a mystery. In his book about Soviet defectors Gordon Brook-Shepherd says Agabekov fled to the West because he fell in love with an English girl, Isabel Streeter, in Istanbul. If so, he might well be called, as the author suggests, a truly Shakespearean hero. But the fact is that Agabekov did not defect in Istanbul but from the OGPU *rezidentura* in 1929, taking with him a substantial sum of money from the safe. It said in his file that Agabekov had announced that he was going urgently to Moscow on business. All trace of him was lost, and it appears from the record that the Soviet intelligence service did not know that he spent nearly two years in Istanbul; they continued looking for him in Western Europe, where he turned up in 1931.

Agabekov had had a safe in the Teheran *rezidentura* with a combination lock which no one knew how to open. Every new arrival in the embassy was invited to have a go at opening it, but it was not until 1946 that the new deputy *rezident*, Vladimir Vertiporokh, succeeded. It contained no papers – only a revolver with two clips of bullets and a suit-length in wool.

Among our instructors on intelligence work in the field we met many experienced Soviet intelligence officers who recounted some of the operations they had been involved in abroad. Among them was Vladimir Sanakoyev (as he called himself then), who had been decorated for his work in liquidating Agabekov. He told us that Agabekov had been sentenced to death by shooting, but that in view of his absence this was changed to summary execution, which meant assassination by any means wherever he was found. Sanakoyev was ordered to carry out this mission.

Eventually Agabekov turned up in a European country and started collaborating with foreign intelligence services. But for some reason he divulged little about our spy network in the Near and Middle East, apparently because he was holding out for large sums of money. Nevertheless our whole network of agents was put into cold storage and most of them went underground. The operation to kidnap him, which cost a great deal of money, ended in failure, for which severe punishment was handed out by the Party leaders. They then ordered resolute steps to be taken to punish the traitor Agabekov who, having proved unsuccessful in France and some other countries, had by now sold himself to the Rumanian secret police who had provided him with a bodyguard and a house near Bucharest. We learned from an NKVD agent inside the Rumanian counter-intelligence service that all Agabekov's visitors were searched by his bodyguard and any potential weapons were removed.

Sanakoyev had known Agabekov for a long time and was on friendly terms with him, but he could not count on

Agabekov agreeing to a meeting with him. So Sanakoyev
was to make his way, illegally and under a different name
and nationality, through one of the countries of Europe and
arrive in Bucharest. He would phone Agabekov and tell him
that he had been sent to kill him but that he had no intention
of doing so and that he would like to meet him to discuss how
they could create the impression that he had carried out his
task. Sanakoyev pointed out that if he, Sanakoyev, did not
do the job, someone else would be found to do it. Sanakoyev
warned Agabekov that he was not to tell anyone about their
conversation or of Sanakoyev's arrival, because if he did the
NKVD would be informed immediately and the whole plan
would be wrecked. Agabekov would find himself in an even
more dangerous situation.

It appeared both from his dossier and from what
Sanakoyev said about him that Agabekov was intelligent and
shrewd enough not to be lured into a trap. Hence the head-
on approach.

Sanakoyev was heavily built, physically strong and well
trained in all the arts of killing with his bare hands people
much tougher than the rather fragile Agabekov. Sanakoyev
arrived in Bucharest in the summer of 1939 and made contact with Agabekov, who, to Sanakoyev's surprise, not only
showed no signs of fear but appeared to welcome a meeting
to find out what had been happening at the Centre, as the
KGB headquarters is known, since he and others had
defected.

Agabekov's house, Sanakoyev said, was a small fortress
surrounded by a tall fence topped with barbed wire, with
heavy wooden gates and an armed guard. After being
searched, and having all his belongings, including his
cigarettes, removed, he was admitted by one of the guards to
an office where he was joyfully welcomed by Agabekov.
The guard placed himself on a chair at the door. After a few
pleasantries in Russian Sanakoyev switched to Armenian
and told Agabekov that he wanted to talk to him without

witnesses because he could not be sure if the guard understood Russian and might report what passed between them. He was not sufficiently fluent in Armenian to explain himself properly. Agabekov agreed and signalled the guard to leave them alone.

How long they talked and what they talked about Sanakoyev did not say. How exactly he killed Agabekov also remains a secret. Sanakoyev told us only that, having carried out his task, he told the guard as he left that Agabekov had asked not to be disturbed for the time being because he was reading what Sanakoyev had brought him. He had settled Agabekov in an armchair and made it look as though he was reading, in case the guard should want to check what Sanakoyev had told him. Sanakoyev needed a few minutes to reach his waiting car.

Sanakoyev's account was borne out by the material in Agabekov's file in the archives, which points to considerable discrepancies with Brook-Shepherd's account of the incident.

In the course of his lectures Sudoplatov told us of some of his own activities. One of his most famous assignments was the assassination of the Ukrainian nationalist leader, Ivan Konovalenko, whose anti-Soviet activities conducted from Holland had been causing the KGB a lot of trouble. According to Sudoplatov, Konovalenko was connected with Western intelligence services who were supplying him with weapons and ammunition for terrorist acts inside the Soviet Ukraine.

The liquidation of Konovalenko demanded careful preparation. It was difficult to get close to him, because he was cautious, experienced and cunning, and accompanied everywhere by armed and well-trained bodyguards. Furthermore, according to our agents who had infiltrated his organization, Konovalenko never had dealings with anybody without having first made sure that the person belonged to an anti-Soviet organization and was a genuine enemy of the Soviet regime. He was kept well informed about events in the Soviet Union by sympathizers who lived there and kept in touch with him through illegal channels. The KGB, who in fact already had the Ukrainian nationalists under observation, could have destroyed them, but would then have denied themselves access to the leaders who were directing operations from abroad.

One of Konovalenko's former friends was, however, unbeknown to Konovalenko, collaborating with the KGB. It was known that Konovalenko trusted him and valued his efforts to liberate the Ukraine. Their friendship had lasted many years and had been tested by both men more than once.

This friend in fact had been offered the choice of being shot or becoming an agent of the KGB. Having 'chosen' the latter course, he directed the underground organization no longer fearful of being discovered or arrested, and provided Konovalenko with encouraging information about the work of the Ukranian nationalist movement.

In the autumn of 1936 an emissary from Konovalenko arrived in Kiev. He delivered a letter from Konovalenko requesting information about the work of the organization with especial reference to the international situation and the possible outbreak of war, which might facilitate the liberation of the Ukraine. The letter also included a request for the emissary to meet the other leaders of the organization.

Konovalenko's friend (whom I will call Peter, since his children and grandchildren are still living in the Soviet Union and I would not like to put them in an awkward situation) was at a loss to know what to do after meeting the emissary. His first thought was that the emissary was working for the KGB and that they were trying to check up on him. Then it occurred to him that, if the emissary really had arrived from 'over there', then Konovalenko had more resources than he had imagined and that, if he got to know about Peter's collaboration with the KGB, he would have little difficulty in despatching Peter to the next world for his treachery. He was frightened of contacting the KGB because there might be others of Konovalenko's men watching him. The whole affair was further complicated by the fact that the KGB had not envisaged the possibility that one of Konovalenko's people might approach Peter directly. It was a serious slip-up.

Sudoplatov explained that an oversight of such magnitude may have been due to the complacency of the KGB after the success of their operations in which hundreds of thousands of 'enemies of the people' and members of the anti-Soviet underground had been arrested. This was all the more likely because the groups like the one that Peter was running had all been infiltrated by the KGB itself, and the information being sent abroad was in fact carefully prepared *dis*information.

The Soviet leadership took the view that liquidation of the Ukrainian nationalist leaders would tend to frighten off those who remained alive. Moreover, the removal of the leaders would render the organization less effective in the event of a worsening of the international situation or the outbreak of war. It was not so long since the KGB had scored a major success with an operation known as the Trust, when a very experienced terrorist and member of the underground, Savinkov, had been lured into Soviet territory and arrested as a result of a plot organized by the KGB, which led in effect to the complete elimination of the Savinkov movement.

The conversation between Peter and the emissary lasted a long time. Peter explained to his wife that the emissary was an old school friend who had spent many years in the Far East and who had sought him out on returning to Kiev. They had a lot to talk about.

When Peter asked him how long he intended to stay in Kiev the emissary was vague but insisted on meeting the leaders of the group. Peter did not argue about this, but warned the emissary that he could not guarantee his safety. They agreed finally that the man would be put up in Peter's flat while Peter tried to collect the leaders. The emissary warned Peter that, if he were to play dirty, he would not spare his wife and two children. This upset Peter but he said nothing. Next morning, after checking carefully that he was not being followed, Peter phoned his controlling KGB officer and told him what was going on.

A couple of days later a meeting took place in Peter's flat attended by eight leaders of the underground nationalist organization of the Ukraine. All, except Peter, were KGB officers. Having been given an account of the organization's work, the emissary expressed his satisfaction and passed on Konovalenko's message, which was to urge them to strengthen their ranks by recruiting new members and to be ready for action, especially in view of the possibility of war between Germany and the Soviet Union. Armed with a letter from Peter to Konovalenko, the emissary was, with the connivance of the KGB, allowed to cross into Poland without difficulty. The main outcome of this visit was a decision to proceed at once with the liquidation of Konovalenko. The operation was entrusted to Pavel Sudoplatov, then only a member of the Special Duties Department.

Peter continued, through agreed channels, to keep Konovalenko supplied with information; he also hinted at the necessity of more direct contacts and discussion than was possible in an exchange of letters, and pressed for a meeting outside the Soviet Union between Konovalenko and a representative of his organization. In one of his letters Peter told Konovalenko that one of his more active members would be going abroad on business; he would be carrying top secret information about the Soviet armed forces and the Soviet government's plans to seize certain Western territories allegedly to ensure the security of its western and northern frontiers. He would contact Konovalenko. Peter begged him not to make the information public because suspicion might then fall on its source: an important Soviet official who held strongly nationalist views and hated everything Russian. Although Peter received no reply from Konovalenko, the KGB decided to proceed with the operation. Konovalenko might publish what Peter had told him, which would have had undesirable results for Soviet policy, even though the allegations could easily be refuted.

Sudoplatov prepared for his journey abroad, and the KGB's Technical Department proceeded to make a present for Konovalenko. Even then the department had developed some clever death-dealing weapons and poisons which left no trace.

Sudoplatov was to meet Konovalenko in Rotterdam and hand him a small package looking like a box of chocolates. The box, Sudoplatov would explain to Konovalenko, had a false bottom under which he would find messages from Peter. The box did indeed have a false bottom but it contained not the messages from Peter, but an explosive device which would be activated when the lid of the box was fully open.

Under an assumed name and with documents prepared by the KGB, Sudoplatov made his way to Rotterdam. How he made contact with Konovalenko he did not tell us; apparently Konovalenko refused for a long time to meet him but Sudoplatov finally persuaded him to do so. The meeting, in a little café in a quiet side-street, took place at about midday. Konovalenko arrived with two companions, apparently bodyguards. After giving a detailed report on the work of the organization, Sudoplatov complained that not enough help was forthcoming. They needed money and weapons for acts of terrorism against Soviet officials.

Konovalenko did not give Sudoplatov his full attention but kept eyeing the package suspiciously. Finally, looking Sudoplatov straight in the eyes, he asked whether he might now open the package, apparently on the assumption that if it was a bomb Sudoplatov would try to dissuade him or at least show signs of nervousness.

Sudoplatov agreed, and Konovalenko unwrapped the box and began slowly to open the lid, watching Sudoplatov all the time. He didn't open the lid the whole way, uncertain whether the box would explode, but the look of unconcern on Sudoplatov's face reassured him. The café began to fill with people, and Sudoplatov told Konovalenko that he didn't want too many people to see him in Konovalenko's company, and moreover he had business to get on with. He suggested that they should meet again a couple of days later, after Konovalenko had read Peter's letter. Konovalenko agreed. Sudoplatov left the café and slipped round the corner of the next street, where he waited. After a short time he saw Konovalenko leave the café with his companions. Konovalenko was blown to pieces. His mission was achieved.

Why were such stories, to which we listened with such rapt admiration, related to us at the KGB school? I suppose it was, first, to show us that there really are people who have carried out dangerous and challenging tasks, and, second, to give us an object-lesson to show what happens to those who betray the KGB and the Soviet regime. But all General Sudoplatov's skill and cunning and his long years of service to his country did not prevent a new Soviet leader, Khrushchev, having him arrested.

In the course of our lectures the idea was drummed into our heads that we had to treat everyone we came into contact with, whether a Soviet citizen or a foreigner, as a potential traitor or enemy. There was nothing extraordinary in this. A general atmosphere of suspicion was actively encouraged by the Soviet authorities, who were continually warning the Soviet population of the need for political vigilance, as they still do today. The most unpleasant and even frightening aspect of the Soviet system is that everyone is regarded by the security services as a potential criminal or lawbreaker. It is sufficient to let slip some critical comment about the Party or the government to find oneself without a job and to be classified as 'unreliable' or 'anti-Soviet' or to be deprived for ever of promotion or to be forbidden to travel abroad, even to another Communist country.

Although something deep inside me revolted against regarding everyone as a possible enemy, the examples quoted in the lectures of 'enemies of the people', foreign agents, saboteurs and terrorists served to dispel my doubts.

I had learnt a great deal by the time my course at the KGB school was over. The teaching of history, foreign languages and other special subjects was conducted very professionally and at such speed that by the end of each week I was absolutely exhausted, both physically and psychologically. But I had some results to show for it. I could already speak Turkish reasonably well and I could decipher the less complicated codes. I could also discuss the history of countries in the West, and the Near and Middle East, and knew about the work of Western intelligence services.

In the lectures about Western intelligence services the most important place was occupied by British Intelligence, which was held up to us almost as a model of how an intelligence service should work. Now, many years later, I can understand why the KGB was so well informed about the structure and policy of British Intelligence! At the time we were of course told nothing about people like Kim Philby and the other KGB agents working in British Intelligence. Our surprise at the extent of the information in the possession of the KGB increased our faith in the power and capabilities of the organization in which we were going to work. Both then and later, in the course of my work in Soviet Intelligence, I and my colleagues always had the greatest professional respect for our British colleagues, whom we regarded as worthy opponents.

In addition to theoretical training in intelligence and counter-intelligence work, some of the students, including myself, were taught how to use weapons of all kinds, special ways of dealing with an armed opponent and how to kill a man with one's bare hands. The training required a great deal of physical and nervous effort. Every sportsman knows that, unless you summon up all your will-power and nervous strength, you cannot lift a great weight or hurl an opponent to the floor. The same concentrated effort is required to strike an opponent with your hand with such force that he will be put out of action, or to fire a gun in complete darkness in the direction of a sound or a momentary spark of light and hit a target. Tastes differ, but I enjoyed the training because I concluded that, whether an agent works under cover or not, he must always be able to extricate himself from extreme situations by physical prowess and special skills.

This belief may raise a smile among present-day under-cover agents who never have to lift anything heavier than a ball-point pen. Perhaps they would be right; times have changed. Our training was different and was to stand me in good stead.

I passed all my examinations and was commissioned as a lieutenant. I even managed to marry one of the language students. She spoke better Turkish than I did, and it looked as though as a pair we had good prospects of working illegally abroad.

In May 1947 General Zarubin, the officer in charge of *nelegaly* (illegals), asked me whether I intended to return to Georgia. I told him I was not thinking of going back, because I knew that my wife would not go with me. 'In that case,' Zarubin said, 'I will think over what to offer you.' I was expecting him to invite me and my wife to agree to do illegal work abroad but to my surprise the personnel department proposed that we should go to Rumania to work under the direction of the KGB *rezidentura* there on the staff of the southern group of Soviet forces.

We were given very little time to prepare, and a few days

later we arrived in Constanza, the principal port of Rumania. The country was still ruled by King Michael, who had been awarded the Order of Victory by the Soviet Government. In exchange Joseph Stalin was to receive the whole of Rumania, and King Michael would leave his country for ever in a Soviet-made light aircraft – also a gift.

Our reception in Rumania was unfriendly and at times hostile. When darkness fell, it was not uncommon for shots to be fired at Soviet officers; it happened to me when my wife and I were returning home from the officers' club one night. Rumanian officers made a point of not making way for us in the street and refused to salute us, despite the treaty of friendship that had been signed by our two governments. The Rumanians disliked Russians then and continue to show their dislike now. It is no accident therefore that there are still substantial differences between the Rumanian and Soviet leaders or that Rumania is the only country in Eastern Europe where there are no Soviet troops: they were withdrawn from Rumania at the demand of the Rumanian leaders.

The six weeks we spent in Rumania were very hard going, because we had to work literally round the clock. Our job was to find and arrest the German agents or collaborators known to the KGB. Such a task could only be carried out with the help of the Rumanians themselves, which, in the circumstances, made our task very difficult. We arrested some of the collaborators, but our success was limited.

Rumania was my first posting to a foreign country, but in spite of much that was unusual and unfamiliar we did not really feel ourselves to be abroad, because all the shop windows and public places displayed three portraits: of Stalin, King Michael and his mother. Not counting the last two, which were in any case soon to disappear, everything was exactly what we were used to.

At the end of June 1947, to our surprise, a telegram arrived ordering us to return to Moscow and report to the main personnel department. My first foreign assignment was over. So was my basic training, in school and in the field.

CHAPTER THREE

Working in Intelligence

THE DEPUTY HEAD of the KGB's personnel department, General Vrady, interviewed me in a very friendly manner, only glancing occasionally at my file. Finally, with a sigh of satisfaction, he told me that I was being sent to work in the First Chief Directorate of the KGB, that is to work in intelligence, and told me to report next day to headquarters. It was then that I met for the first time the head of the First Chief Directorate, Lieutenant-General Pyotr Fedotov, who had been in charge of Soviet intelligence throughout the war.

Pyotr Fedotov occupies a special place in the history of one of the world's most powerful intelligence services. The qualities which distinguished this man were his intellectual distinction, his intelligence, his charming manners, and his concern for people. In the years that followed, until Fedotov was expelled from the KGB, I had frequent meetings with him on official business and I must say that each time I met him I was impressed by his powers of logical thinking and his unerring ability to take the correct decision. What really distinguished him from other highly placed KGB officials was that he did not disregard another person's opinion. If someone didn't agree with him he would not give orders but try to persuade him.

Despite his qualities and all the services he performed for the Soviet government, his ultimate fate did not differ in any way from that of others like him who had devoted their whole lives to serving the socialist regime. For reasons I am not aware of, Fedotov was driven out of the KGB at the end of 1956, not without some assistance from that faithful stooge of Khrushchev, General Ivan Serov. Fedotov spent his last years in the TASS news agency, working as an editor. It was a tremendous come-down for such a man. Neither his heart nor his nervous system could survive such humiliation and it killed him – an inglorious end to a glorious career. They say that every malicious act is ultimately avenged. So it was with Serov, the head of the KGB, whose hands were red with the blood of Soviet people. A specialist in the business of mass deportations, a man without honour or conscience, sadistic and unprincipled, he was himself thrown out of the GRU (military intelligence service) following the exposure of Colonel Oleg Penkovsky, a British agent with whom Serov had been on friendly terms. Shortly afterwards, after a heavy drinking bout, he shot himself and was found dead in the doorway of a greengrocer's shop on the Arbat.

But all that was still in the future. After my talk with General Fedotov I was assigned to the head of the Middle and Near East Department, Mikhail Natsvlishvili, a man similar in character to Fedotov. That was the beginning of my work in the Soviet intelligence service. I was assigned to espionage against Iran. Why not Turkey, I wondered, since I spoke Turkish? Because Turkey was handled by Lieutenant-Colonel Kornilov. Kornilov had been arrested in Ankara in the early 1940s, along with an employee of the Soviet embassy by the name of Pavlov, and charged with attempting to assassinate the German ambassador, von Papen. When a bomb exploded near the car from which von Papen was alighting, Kornilov and Pavlov were standing close by, which gave the Turkish counter-intelligence an excuse for arresting them. Although I was on good terms with Kornilov and it was he who recommended me for membership of the Communist Party, I never succeeded in establishing whether he and Pavlov had actually been

involved in the attempt on von Papen's life. Kornilov always
denied the charge and I was inclined to believe him because,
according to the laws of espionage, anyone who carries out
an assassination must have a wholly credible alibi. Neither
Pavlov nor Kornilov had one, which is why they spent more
than a year in a Turkish prison, not, it is true, experiencing
any great discomfort, because their food was sent in from the
Soviet embassy and they were in constant communication
by telephone with Soviet officials. The trial of Pavlov and
Kornilov was widely reported in the Soviet and world press,
but the Turks were unable to produce incriminating evidence and in the end, at the insistence of the Soviet government, they were released and deported to the Soviet Union.
So, having done his prison service, it was Kornilov who
looked after espionage against Turkey, while it fell to me and
a few of my comrades to deal with Iran.

General Natsvlishvili advised me to learn Persian at once.
Friedrich Engels is said to have taught himself Farsi in
twenty days, but I turned out to be less talented, and it took
me about a year before I could speak it reasonably well,
though with an accent. But that didn't matter, because I
could pass off as an Armenian from Iran, since I spoke
Armenian fluently – an attribute that was to play an important role later.

I started work in the Iranian section of the Middle and
Near East Department at a time when the political situation
in Iran was particularly unstable and not improving as far as
the Soviet Union was concerned. The Iranian government
had just defeated an uprising in Iranian Azerbaidjan which
had been provoked by the Soviet authorities with the aim of
detaching Azerbaidjan from Iran and annexing it to the
Soviet Union. Participants in the uprising were still being
arrested and executed, and the leaders of the Tudeh (Communist) Party who had gone underground were still being
hunted. The uprising had been led by a former Secretary of
one of the district committees of the Soviet Communist

Party in the town of Baku who had joined the leadership of the Tudeh Party when Soviet troops were stationed in Iran. After the collapse of the uprising he was taken back to Baku, where he died shortly afterwards in a car accident arranged by the Azerbaidjan KGB. He had become an undesirable eye-witness and had shown himself to be incapable of carrying out the task that the Party had given him. That could not go unpunished. The Tudeh Party leaders who had gone underground were in danger and it seemed likely that they would soon be discovered by Iranian counter-intelligence. We knew exactly where they were.

In the spring of 1948 the head of our department, Colonel Berdnikov, and I were summoned by the head of the Third Directorate, A. Otroshchenko. The presence of no less a figure than Vyshinsky, the public prosecutor in Stalin's purge trials and then a deputy foreign minister, in his office meant that the matter was of exceptional importance.

Vyshinsky gave us a brief summary of the situation in Iran and its strategic importance for the Soviet Union as a neighbouring country which we could not possibly permit to fall into the hands of the Americans. Then, to our surprise, he announced that Stalin himself had proposed that we should immediately prepare a plan for rescuing the Tudeh Party leaders still in Iran.

There could be no question of not carrying out Stalin's instructions: indeed it was a tremendous honour. With redoubled energy we set about working out plans for rescuing the Tudeh leaders. We came to the conclusion that the most practical plan would be to get them out in a plane which could land on the flat plateau some 350 kilometres from Teheran. The KGB *rezidentura* in Iran would have no difficulty in assembling the leaders at the landing place, as it had at its service an experienced group of young Iranian revolutionaries who had more than once taken part in operations involving the kidnapping of undesirable persons and even their liquidation. If the operation were to misfire the

Soviet embassy could declare that the whole affair had been an act of provocation by the Iranian authorities in an effort to upset relations with the Soviet Union. It would be difficult to prove that the KGB or the embassy had been involved because we planned to use a plane of American or German manufacture piloted by Iranian airmen who had fled to the Soviet Union. It was an excellent scheme, but, according to Vyshinsky, Stalin rejected it. I was reminded of it many years later when a number of American helicopters, sent by President Carter to rescue the American hostages seized by the Khomeini regime, were destroyed on that very same plateau.

In the end it was decided to smuggle the Tudeh leaders one at a time across the frontier. Whether this method was really better than the one we had proposed was doubtful, but there was no question of discussing orders issued by so high an authority. We had to work round the clock. There was an endless stream of telegrams from the Teheran *rezidentura* replying to our enquiries as to what and when and where. But before actually carrying out the operation we tried to exert some influence on the young Shah, Mohammed Reza Pahlevi. There was then a Soviet hospital in Iran with a very high reputation among leading Iranian officials. The head of the hospital at that time was Ovanes (Onik) Baroyan, a member of the Soviet intelligence service but a doctor by profession, Assistant General Secretary of the WHO in the 1960s, and now a member of the Soviet Academy of Medicine. He was on good terms with the Shah, because he treated not only the Shah but all his brothers as well. Ministers in the Shah's court also took advantage of the hospital's service. Treatment there was confidential and no Iranians hostile to the hospital's distinguished patients could obtain any information about their illnesses. Baroyan was so close to the Shah that we used to say that, although the Shah's ministers had to wait for an audience, Onik could see him at any time of the day even without telephoning. There was an element of truth in this.

The KGB *rezident* in Teheran, Herman Akzhigitov, was instructed to bring his group of revolutionaries to a state of complete readiness, and Dr Baroyan was told to try to persuade the Shah to allow the Tudeh leaders to go to the Soviet Union. Baroyan was noted for his sharp wit and his persuasiveness, but even he did not succeed in obtaining the Shah's agreement, though there had been a moment when it seemed as though a deal might be struck. In response to Baroyan's request the Shah replied that he might agree to let the Tudeh people go on the condition that the Soviet Union gave him its moral and practical help in obtaining the return of the remains of his father Reza Pahlevi, who had died and been buried in exile. He also demanded that the Soviet embassy (i.e. the KGB *rezidentura*) should warn him of any threats to his regime. These demands were not acceptable and Baroyan's plea had no result, except that it considerably increased Iranian surveillance of the Soviet embassy.

It was time to put our plan into practice. I had begun to prepare for the day when I would be sent to Teheran to take over the leadership of the group of young revolutionaries. That meant intensive study of Farsi and another course of training similar to the one I had been through at the KGB school, but this time more thorough, because I had to have complete command of every kind of weapon and all forms of unarmed combat, not to mention surveillance techniques.

My departure for Iran was planned for 1949, though I knew events might force me to go earlier. The Soviet authorities were in a hurry to rescue the Tudeh leaders, but we could take no chances and weighed every move carefully. Two members of the staff of the *rezidentura* in Teheran arrived from Iran: Fedor Bykovsky (father of the Soviet astronaut Vladimir Bykovsky) and Vladimir Vitkovsky, an enormous fellow of great physical strength who had worked as a cipher clerk but had at the same time been carrying out special missions about which he told us later over a bottle of vodka. One of his stories sticks in my mind because it concerned the operational group that I was about to take charge of. It appeared that a certain Orlov, a Soviet diplomat who had worked in Iran some time before, had secretly established contact with the Americans and, it later came to light, intended to ask them for political asylum. So he was put under observation and was eventually seized by the operational group as he was quitting his flat with his suitcase and setting off in the direction of the American embassy. He was led off to a street close to the Soviet embassy where some members of the *rezidentura*, including Vitkovsky, were waiting. Once inside the embassy building, when accused straight out of betraying his country, Orlov put up a desperate fight. Eventually Vitkovsky grabbed the leg of a grand piano and brought it down with such tremendous force on Orlov's head that the poor man died on the spot. Vitkovsky said he had had no alternative but he omitted to point out that the order to liquidate Orlov had already been signed and approved in Moscow. They were only waiting for Orlov to confirm by his actions the reports they had received.

There was in fact nothing particularly unusual about this episode. What is more, nothing has really changed: even today an official who defects to the West is signing his own death sentence; and it is only a question of when he will be discovered and when the possibility will arise of carrying out the sentence. Exactly how it is done is of no significance – whether it is with an axe, a gun, a dose of poison, a poisoned umbrella or a car accident.

Then Vladimir Vertiporokh arrived from Teheran. He gave us a detailed account of the situation in Iran and helped us with the plans for rescuing the Tudeh Party leaders whom he knew personally. He was tall, with fair curly hair and strong masculine features, and he was not only greatly respected by all of us but also enjoyed much success with the ladies. I worked with him closely on the planning of the operation.

There was no difficulty about crossing the Iranian frontier. The problem was to pass unnoticed through the village near the frontier in which Iranian military and police units were stationed. We had to make sure that when the Tudeh leaders were passing through the frontier districts there were no soldiers or police about. Our final solution was approved by Stalin. We then told the *rezidentura* in Teheran exactly what to do and when to do it and the operation began. The Tudeh leaders were brought closer to the frontier by our young activists, some on horseback, some on donkeys and some in carts, all disguised as peasants.

And so, one day in the summer of 1948 there appeared on the frontier between Iran and Azerbaidjan, to the great surprise of the Iranian observation posts, a dense smoke-screen, and at the same time there was a roar of engines, the screech of tank tracks on the roadway and the sound of heavy gunfire and bursts of machine-gun fire. The noise was terrifying. The Iranian officers decided that it was the beginning of a Soviet invasion and they were so confused that they lost all control of the units under their command. There was complete panic. The soldiers dropped their weapons and scattered in every direction, trying to get as far away as possible from the Soviet frontier. Soviet monitors listened in to all the exchanges taking place among the Iranian commanders and overheard an Iranian general, no less scared than his men, enquiring of his superiors in Teheran whether to put up some resistance or to retreat. In fact, as we learned later, he did not wait for a reply but took off in a hurry by car in the direction of Teheran. It was like a musical comedy. In the confusion the five members of the Central Committee of the Tudeh Party crossed the frontier unchallenged, together with the group of young revolutionaries led by our agent, who was known as Boxer because he had recently been an Iranian boxing champion. The Tudeh leaders were sent off to Moscow, while the young activists went back to Teheran.

A few days later the Iranian government summoned Sadchikov, the Soviet ambassador to Iran, and delivered a strong protest about the Soviet army's operations on the frontier, which had provoked a panic on the Iranian side. In reply, the Soviet government said that their troops had been conducting manoeuvres on Soviet territory, as was their right, and that, as far as the panic in Iran was concerned, that did not fall within the competence of the Soviet authorities.

One leader of the Tudeh Party, however, was still in Iran. His name was Kombakhsh, and it fell to my lot to organize his escape. Along with Boxer and the other young fighters I made my way to Teheran, where I telephoned the *rezidentura* and, having given an agreed code-word, announced my arrival.

Kombakhsh was in effect the General Secretary of the Tudeh Party and was considered to be the most intelligent of its leaders and the best trained in political affairs, because he had been through special courses at the Higher Party School of the CPSU and was utterly devoted to the Soviet regime. The defeat of the recent uprising had had such a powerful psychological effect on Kombakhsh, who was then in hiding near Teheran, that he refused categorically to attempt any crossing of the frontier independently or with the help of Iranian friends of the Soviet embassy, despite the fact that the other leaders had succeeded in getting away. Nevertheless, Stalin's command that all the surviving Tudeh leaders were to be rescued had to be carried out. That is why the Soviet intelligence service decided on a course that would have been quite out of the question in normal times: to send a trained intelligence officer to rescue a foreign Communist leader.

The man who briefed me for the operation, Colonel Viktor Sosnin, pointed out that, in the first place, it would be excellent training for me and a good way of testing in practice what I had learnt at the school, and in the second place I would be carrying out a task set personally by Comrade Stalin, and that was not entrusted to everyone.

'If – perish the thought – you get caught,' said Sosnin, 'you realize of course that you admit to no connection whatsoever with us. You are an Armenian living in Iran; you have no family and no parents as far as you know, and the person you are accompanying had asked you to show him the way to Meshed and had paid you well for it. You have no idea who he is : why should you bother when he pays you more money than you've ever seen? You know, of course,' Sosnin continued in a more friendly tone, 'that we are never forgiven for betraying our country – and to confess is to betray.'

I understood exactly what he meant, of course, and was ready for anything. We have more courage in our youth than in our later years.

The *rezidentura* in Teheran sent me Kombakhsh's address through a secret letter drop and I went there with Boxer. We talked for a long time before he was convinced that I really had come from the Soviet Union and that Stalin himself had given me the task of taking him to Moscow. But, once convinced, he relaxed and agreed to come with me. Boxer got hold of a woman's dress, in which we dressed Kombakhsh with the veil lowered over his face, then we set off on the road for Meshed. Waiting for us was the KGB *rezident* Manapov, who had prepared a 'window' by which we could cross the border into Turkmenia. For a whole week we trudged along, trying to avoid places where we might meet the police. We ate whatever we could find.

Manapov had found somewhere where we could rest and recover from the journey. Next day he got us a donkey, which Kombakhsh rode, disguised as my deaf and dumb mother. I was taking her to Turkmenistan, where we had relatives who would enable her to have the treatment we were too poor to obtain in Iran. This was the story made up for the benefit of the two Turkmen whom Manapov had paid to take us across the frontier. They were smugglers who knew all the crossings well, since they made regular trips in each direction, trading in hashish and *teriyak*. Manapov provided me with a German Walther revolver and several clips of bullets, just in case our guides were to try any tricks on us. In the event Kombakhsh and I and the donkey crossed the frontier without incident and waved our guides good-bye.

We had arrived in Turkmenia. Members of the Turk-menian KGB were waiting for us, and our people in Moscow were soon reporting to Stalin that his instructions had been carried out to the letter. Then Kombakhsh and I, with officers of the Turkmenian KGB, were flown by special plane to Moscow.

I was given a week off to rest, then I started to prepare myself for work inside Iran, where my chief job would be to take charge of the group of young militants and to carry out what were known as hush-hush operations. These ranged from kidnapping Iranian and foreign spies and other opponents of the Soviet regime to penetrating foreign embassies to photograph confidential documents. Another of my jobs would be to check up on Iranian citizens who were in contact with us or were candidates for recruitment or collaboration with us.

I redoubled efforts to learn Farsi and studied photography, microphotography and methods of conducting surveillance and of evading observation by the enemy. I practised armed and unarmed combat, and was introduced to those weapons specially manufactured for use in secret operations.

As I was due to take charge of a group of militants connected with the *rezidentura* in Teheran, Colonel Viktor Sosnin, a Russian brought up in the Caucasus, where he appeared to have absorbed a great deal of Eastern cunning and duplicity, suggested that I study the Djafar case carefully and submit a proposal. It was sufficient for me to read the later documents in the file to know what proposal I had to make.

In the middle of 1935 it had been reported that a young Turk had arrived in Tbilisi to study at the State Medical

Institute. He said he had decided to become a doctor and a cardiologist after his father died of a heart attack. His father, he claimed, had been a colleague of Ataturk, who had concluded a treaty with the Soviet Union in 1917 by which Turkey acquired territories belonging to Georgia and Armenia in the Kars-Erzerum-Ardahan region. There was nothing to support the young man's claim, but the fact that the Turkish government had pressed the Soviet authorities to allow him to study at the Tbilisi Institute suggested that he came from a prosperous family with contacts among the top people in Turkey. As with every foreigner the young man was put under surveillance by Georgian counter-intelligence, not so much to stop him spying as to prepare him for recruitment.

The Turk was given the code-name 'Djafar' and that is the name I will use for him. Djafar worked hard learning Russian and Georgian with the help of a teacher who was in fact an NKVD officer pretending to be a fellow student. The NKVD officer made great efforts to persuade Djafar of the virtues of the Soviet regime and of the need for Turkey to have good relations with the Soviet Union, especially in view of our common frontier and the possibility of a military conflict between the USSR and Britain. Because Turkey was known to be drawn towards Nazi Germany, Djafar was told that the Soviet leaders regarded Fascism as being just as hostile as capitalism and that, in the event of a military conflict, Turkey would not be considered neutral and that the Red Army might strike a warning blow. This was, of course, all calculated to frighten the young Turk and feed him with information which he would report to the Turkish authorities when he took his holidays in Turkey. It was intended to act as a warning to the Turks.

The NKVD *rezidentura* in Turkey reported, following one of Djafar's visits home, that he had been called in by the Turkish counter-intelligence service and that he had been interrogated at length about his contacts in Georgia, asked to

write a full report and in future to maintain contact with the
Turkish consulate in Batumi.

The *rezidentura* reported that Djafar had also had meetings
with politicians to whom he had passed on the warning. It
was assumed that Djafar was inclined to collaborate with the
Turkish intelligence service and that he would act as an
informer for the Turks. This did not represent, it is true, any
danger for the Soviet Union because Djafar was not a professional intelligence officer, but the fact that he had been called
in by Turkish counter-intelligence and had been in touch
with the Turkish consulate in Batumi could be made use of
in our efforts to recruit him : we could threaten to prosecute
him for espionage. Djafar had also witnessed the mass
arrests of 'enemies of the people' and members of Hitler's
Fifth Column in Georgia and, although he was regarded as a
Soviet sympathizer, the NKVD, with the authority of Beria
(who was then Secretary of the Central Committee of the
Georgian Communist Party), arrested Djafar in 1937 on
suspicion of espionage and held him for two months in the
NKVD prison in Georgia.

After lengthy interrogation which produced no results at
all, the Georgian NKVD decided to use its trump card – the
fact that Djafar had been called in by the Turkish counter-
intelligence and had written an account of his stay in Georgia. He could not deny this. After he had written a detailed
account of his dealings with the Turkish counter-
intelligence, he was told that if it fell into the hands of the
Turkish authorities he would be punished as a traitor on his
return to Turkey. At the same time, as a Turkish spy, he was
liable to a sentence of death.

He was then told that this could be circumvented and he
would even be allowed to complete his medical training if he
admitted his guilt and agreed to work with the NKVD.
Djafar had no choice.

He was set free and provided with a certificate for his
institute which said that he had been undergoing treatment

at the spa town of Mineralnye Vody because of some stomach trouble, and he returned to his studies at the institute under surveillance by the NKVD. He also fed the Turkish consulate in Batumi with information, but now under the direction of the NKVD.

Soon after his release Djafar was invited to dinner in a house on the outskirts of Tbilisi, where he met Beria. Beria wanted to get to know at first hand the foreigner who had been recruited and to assess his potential for Soviet intelligence, since it was then exceptional for a foreigner to be recruited by the NKVD in Georgia.

When Djafar went on holiday to Turkey he was given detailed instructions by both the Georgian NKVD and the First Chief Directorate in Moscow. Djafar was to provide detailed portraits of politicians and other people who had come to the attention of the Soviet secret police, and his work in this field produced excellent results.

Djafar finished his medical training before the outbreak of war and then went either to Turkey or to Germany. He provided information about both countries. Just before the end of the war Djafar turned up in Moscow and Beria gave instructions that he was to have a two-roomed flat in Stoleshnikov Street in the centre of Moscow. Beria, accompanied by Merkulov, the Minister of State Security, had frequent meetings with him and questioned him at length about the situation in Turkey and the intentions of the Turkish government.

As I came to the last document in Djafar's file, a letter from our *rezidentura* in Turkey made it clear, from information supplied by a recently recruited Turkish agent, that Djafar had been for a long time a double agent working both for Turkey and for Western intelligence agencies. The most damning evidence of Djafar's double game was a report that his meetings with Beria were known to the Turkish intelligence service.

Beria had been furious when he learnt of Djafar's double

game, and had written the letter L in inverted commas and his own initials, L.B., on the letter from the *rezidentura*. It would have been dangerous to arrest Djafar, who was still a Turkish citizen, and try him because he might have revealed something about his meetings with Beria and other matters embarrassing to the Soviet authorities. But it would also have been difficult to stage a closed trial, because there would have been no certainty that the Turkish authorities would not make enquiries about him.

After studying the file I went to Sosnin and asked him what I had to write on it when Beria's decision made it perfectly clear what had to be done. Sosnin's reply was simple: 'Don't argue – just write a memo proposing that Liter L should be carried out.' Letters of this kind were then sent to the Central Committee without being addressed to any one individual. The letter was signed by the head of a Directorate of the KGB and the Chairman of the Committee of Information. It came back to us marked 'I approve – L.B.'

A separate report to the head of the Directorate said that to effect Djafar's liquidation it was proposed to use a woman agent of the Second Chief Directorate of the KGB who was on intimate terms with him, and that tablets which would produce a fatal heart attack would arouse the least suspicion, since his father had died from a stroke.

In the course of a regular visit to Djafar the agent was to wait for a telephone call which would necessitate Djafar's going into another room to answer it, giving her time to put the dissolving tablet into his tea, coffee or wine. The woman agent was told that the tablet would simply upset Djafar's stomach, which would enable us to transfer him to a hospital for treatment and to discuss with him a number of questions that interested us. She did not know that Djafar was our agent and thought he was just a foreigner in whom we were interested. We could not reveal to her our true intentions: she might have wrecked the whole operation by being at the last moment too scared to drop the tablet in Djafar's cup.

After our telephone call to Djafar she was to leave him within thirty minutes, by which time the tablet would have begun to take effect.

At eight o'clock in the evening one of our men rang Djafar and, after giving the password, told him that some of the senior people wanted to meet him in the next few days and asked him to put down on paper his proposals for increasing our pressure on the Turkish authorities in connection with the negotiations going on about our joint administration of the Dardanelles and the Bosporus. The conversation took ten minutes, which was quite sufficient for our purpose. Colonel Shluger, who controlled the woman agent, called me up and said everything had passed off as planned and the tablet had been dropped into the glass of wine. Djafar was no more.

The time had come for me to be briefed about my forthcoming activities in the Teheran *rezidentura*.

At that time both the Soviet leaders and the heads of the KGB believed that the fewer representatives of the non-Russian peoples of the USSR there were living abroad the less opportunity there would be for foreign intelligence services to prepare agents to send into the Soviet Union. There would also be fewer of them to conduct anti-Soviet activity abroad. For this reason, at the end of the 1940s a major campaign was organized to encourage Russians and Armenians living in Iran, in other countries bordering on the Soviet Union, in the Middle East as a whole and in Manchuria to return to their homeland. A committee was set up to organize the return of the emigrés. It was, of course, under the control of the KGB.

Meanwhile the Soviet intelligence service was given the task of dispersing and getting rid of the leaders of the anti-Soviet emigré organizations abroad and kidnapping or assassinating those members of the Soviet national minorities who were collaborating most actively with foreign intelligence services. An example of this sort of operation is provided by the case of the former Soviet spy Nikolai Khokhlov, who was sent in 1954 to kill Georgi Okolovich, one of the leaders of the Russian emigré organization known as the NTS. Khokhlov failed to carry out his mission and paid dearly for his failure with his life in 1957, when he was poisoned. Bogdan Stashinsky was more successful, killing both Stefan Bandera, leader of the Ukrainian nationalist military formations during the war, and Lev Rebet, another Ukrainian nationalist, by means of a revolver which fired poison.

Colonel Berdnikov and his deputy Sosnin sent for me and we soon got to the point. 'It looks as though you will have to go and work again across the frontier,' Berdnikov said. 'The fact is, the repatriation of Armenians and Russians is going quite satisfactorily and the Party is pleased with our work, that is to say, the work of our Repatriation Committee. But we are encountering serious problems with the return of the Armenians. The Iranians, who have close links with British Intelligence, are taking advantage of the repatriation to send their agents into our country – both established agents and new ones recruited from the people being repatriated. We have this information from Kazbek, but his facts are of dubious value, because, apart from one Armenian who has only recently been recruited by the Iranians, and has had no time to do anything, the counter-intelligence in Azerbaidjan has come across no one and is getting nowhere.'

Kazbek was an agent of ours working inside the Iranian intelligence service. He was Armenian by origin, called Sarkisyan. He had been collaborating with us since 1942 and was well thought of. But what Berdnikov had to say next surprised me, because I had thought that I was going to be ordered to go through all the reports received from Kazbek over the years to see if there were any contradictions in them that would help us to determine whether he was a plant.

'Sarkisyan is a double agent,' Berdnikov said, 'but not in our interests. He has been fooling us for a long time now and doing it very skilfully, not because he is so clever himself, but because his bosses have experienced advisers. He knows a lot, especially about the repatriated Armenians and Russians.'

I took it upon myself to ask how they could be so sure that Sarkisyan was a plant. 'We've got it from the British department,' Berdnikov said sharply, 'and it's certain – so it has been decided to carry out Liter I in his case and you have been chosen for the job. You won't have actually to kill him yourself: you'll operate under the direction of the *rezidentura*, using your future team – Boxer, whom you know already, and the others.'

I was flattered at being given this task and uneasy, because I had never had to remove anybody, and certainly not on foreign territory. Noticing my hesitation, Berdnikov asked me whether I agreed to take the job on. 'Of course,' I said, but Berdnikov suggested that I should think it over till the next day and then give him my reply. We would then, he said, discuss detailed plans for the operation, which had already been agreed in principle by the Instantsia. That was the term we used to refer to the Party leadership, which has to approve all operations carried out by the Soviet intelligence services aimed at liquidating and removing people or at compromising high-ranking politicians and diplomats in the Soviet Union or abroad.

Next day I told Berdnikov that I was ready to do the job, and he proposed that we should get down to studying the plan of operation which had already been drawn up in outline and could be accepted as a basis for action at once. The plan was in fact practically complete: it had, I gathered, been prepared by the *rezidentura* and sent to the Centre for approval. It was extremely simple on paper and we reckoned that it would be equally simple to put into practice, bearing in mind that the Iranian counter-intelligence service was very weak from the technical point of view: it did not even have its own men for carrying out surveillance, but instead made use of beggars and other vagrants for keeping an eye on Soviet diplomats and employees, for which it paid them very little. Whenever people working in the *rezidentura* noticed a beggar or someone in tattered clothes following him he would stop him and give him two or three times what the man was getting from the Iranians and he would immediately leave our man in peace. We were sure we should have no difficulty in kidnapping Sarkisyan.

Berdnikov explained that Sarkisyan had denounced to us agents who were no longer of any value to Iranian intelligence with a view to increasing our confidence in him. At the same time, however, he had been recruiting a lot of Armenians who were working against both us and the Tudeh Party and who could now be on their way to the Soviet Union as repatriates. We could not get anything out of him so long as he was in Iran, but once he was in the Soviet Union we would be able to make him talk. In short, Berdnikov said, he knew a great deal that we needed to know, and that was why this very important task was being entrusted to me.

Everything was done according to the approved plan. I travelled to Teheran as a diplomatic messenger with two others. According to the plan, the other two messengers would continue their journey to Iraq, while I would remain in Teheran and return later to Azerbaidjan through Resht as a diplomatic messenger accompanying a 'special consignment' from the embassy.

Discussing the details of the operation with Major Pekelnik, who was deputizing for the *rezident*, and agreeing them finally with Ambassador Sadchikov, we came to the conclusion that the best thing would be to seize Sarkisyan on one of the dark, quiet streets near the embassy. I would lure him there by telling him that I had come specially from Moscow to talk about some serious questions. Most of the meetings with him took place in the street or in an Armenian restaurant, but on this occasion he would be told that it would be undesirable for me to show myself in a restaurant. Strange though it may seem, in practice the simpler and more straightforward a story is the less it is likely to arouse suspicion. That was the case with Sarkisyan, though he was a very cautious and cunning man. He fell into the trap.

The meeting was arranged for ten o'clock in the evening when it was already dark. The BMW car in which I had arrived was parked near me. Sarkisyan turned up on time. I exchanged passwords with him and when he asked why the car was there I told him we were going to drive around a little so as not to be seen standing on the street. He nodded in agreement. Boxer and two of his comrades were standing nearby in a dark passageway between two houses, and I had left the car so that the passenger door was opposite the passage. As soon as I opened the door for Sarkisyan and he bent down to enter the car, Boxer and one of his men grabbed him. Sarkisyan was a tall man and in good physical condition; he put up such resistance that Boxer had to knock him out. Once we had satisfied ourselves that Boxer had not killed Sarkisyan with his left hook, we used chloroform to make sure that he did not come round and start trying to fight his way out again. We had foreseen everything except the fact that it would be impossible to get the six feet of Sarkisyan into the little BMW. However much we tried, his feet still stuck out of the window. It had all happened very quickly and quietly, without attracting any attention. Now it remained for me to deliver Sarkisyan to the embassy. There were always two Iranian policemen on guard duty but we had softened them up with bribes so that they no longer paid any attention to our comings and goings. But what would they do when they saw feet sticking out of the car window? I could only think of pretending to be a drunk delivering an even drunker member of the embassy staff. The trick worked. The policemen grinned, and gave us a friendly wave. They suggested asking the embassy duty officer to help us, but he was in the know and was only waiting for us to arrive.

When he came round Sarkisyan at first was unable to understand where he was or what had happened to him. But when he saw familiar faces he apparently realized what had been done to him and burst into tears. A special packing case had been prepared for him and, next day, after he had been given an injection of a slow-acting sedative, he was put into it and labelled 'special diplomatic consignment'. In that state I transported him across the frontier in an American jeep without any difficulty whatsoever, because the Iranian frontier police were so slack. I never discovered Sarkisyan's ultimate fate, but he disappeared from view for ever. According to the laws of the spy world, nothing is ever said about people who are kidnapped, whether they survive or not.

I was thanked by my superiors and congratulated on the successful fulfilment of an important operation. Having thus tested my abilities I sat down again at my desk in the department and began to prepare for my posting to Iran, for a longer stay this time as a member of the embassy staff. I did not know at the time that my posting was never in fact to take place.

I was not a member of the privileged élite, so that when I was getting ready to go to the KGB *rezidentura* in Teheran I had to go through the screening process, even though I was employed by the intelligence service. I had joined the KGB in wartime and had therefore not been given a sufficiently careful screening.

In the summer of 1949 I was summoned to appear at the personnel department of the Information Committee on the Gogol boulevard in Moscow. I was expecting to discuss my forthcoming job. I was sent in to see a Major Mikhailov, who told me to sit down while he silently studied my personal case history. As the silence remained unbroken I began to sense that all was not well. Finally Mikhailov raised his lacklustre eyes, looked straight into mine and said, stressing every word : 'Why did you deceive the Party and the KGB?'

His words rendered me speechless, my throat went dry and my eyes clouded over. Thoughts began to race madly through my head as I asked myself when, where and how I could have deceived the Party and the KGB. Obviously I could not remember something that had never happened. It seemed like a bad dream until Mikhailov's voice brought me down to earth again.

'So what about it : are we going to tell the truth or continue with the deception?' Mikhailov asked with a note of sadism in his voice.

I had recovered from the shock sufficiently to say that I had never deceived either the Party or the KGB. 'That is the honest truth,' I asserted.

'All right, in that case perhaps you would like to tell me about your father,' Mikhailov said in the same mocking tone.

I could not understand what was going on, so I said simply that my father had been a deputy commander and commissar of the Black Sea Fleet and had lost his life in 1929 or 1930 while on manoeuvres, at least according to my mother. I knew nothing more about him, and could not even remember what he looked like, since I had been only three years old at the time.

'All right,' said Mikhailov again in a manner calculated to let me know that he didn't believe a word I said. 'So you stand by what you said and know nothing more than that about your father?' he continued.

'Yes,' I said. 'I have told you all I know.' But frightful things were going on in my head. Something unbelievable had happened. But what? After all, my father had died nineteen years ago, and I had already been working for the KGB for five years. Surely I had already proved my devotion to the Soviet regime and the KGB?

'So how about this,' Mikhailov said in a deadly calm tone. 'Your father did not perish in manoeuvres in 1930 but was arrested by the NKVD in 1934 as an enemy of the people and sentenced to ten years. However, while he was still in the prison camp he continued his anti-Soviet activity, for which he was re-sentenced and in 1937 he was executed. That is what you have concealed from the Party and the KGB.'

I remained silent as cold sweat trickled down my back and my face. This was, I decided, the end. The son of an 'enemy of the people' would have to be kicked out of the KGB and would never find a job anywhere because everybody despised such people. I could see only too clearly what the future would be like for me and my family. My wife, who also worked for the KGB, would be dismissed. We had an eighteen-month-old daughter, and my wife was pregnant. We were living in the KGB hotel on Mayakovsky Square (now the Hotel Peking), waiting for a room in one of the KGB blocks. We would be thrown out of the hotel. We had no money nor any possessions. Where were we to go, what could we do?

Somewhere in the distance I heard Mikhailov's voice telling me to report to him again in a week's time, when he would tell me what the KGB bosses had finally decided, because he was not authorized to decide the matter himself. He told me I was suspended from my job from that moment and was at the disposition of the personnel department and should hand over all the papers in my possession.

I have only the vaguest memory of leaving the building. I telephoned my wife from my office and asked her to meet me at the KGB's Dzerzhinsky club. When she saw me she realized immediately that something serious had happened. I tried to tell her about it as calmly as possible because I knew that any nervous shock might be harmful to her in her pregnancy and even lead to a catastrophe. 'When all is said and done,' I said, once she had grasped what the trouble was, 'why should both of us lose everything? If I am to be kicked out as a son of "an enemy of the people" you must say that you knew nothing about it when you married me and, now that you know, you no longer wish to live with me and want a divorce. In this case right is on your side and we shall be able to minimize the consequences of what has happened. You can go on working and so have a salary and a roof over your head. I will manage somehow, and then we shall see.'

There seemed to be no other way out. But we had to await the final decision.

I handed over all my papers, telling my comrades what had happened. They advised me to go to the Central Committee of the CPSU and prove that I had fought in the war, had recently crossed the frontier into Iran illegally, and so forth. They were genuinely anxious to help me, if only with advice, but my bosses, who had only the day before sent me to the devil, maintained a graveyard silence. At practically the same time as Colonel Otroshchenko and Colonel Sosnin and other high-ups were receiving military decorations for rescuing the secretaries of the Tudeh Party, I was being excluded from the lists of awards and would be without a job.

In spite of my low morale I found it in myself to congratulate Sosnin on his award. He understood my position perfectly well but kept his own counsel. He always remained silent when he thought that speech might harm him or give his superiors cause for doubts.

A week later I presented myself to Mikhailov as instructed. I had to wait a long time to see him, but at last I was summoned into his office. Mikhailov again repeated, very slowly, the story of my father, whom he called an enemy of the people and who, he said, had deserved to be executed. But, he went on, my father had divorced my mother when I was only two years old and he could not therefore have instilled any anti-Soviet ideas into me or have brought me up in an anti-socialist spirit. For these reasons,

Mikhailov said, the people in charge would let me continue to work in the intelligence service, not on operational work but in the archives section.

My relief was enormous. Work in the archives was not particularly attractive, but the main thing was that I had not been kicked out and would not have to go around wearing the label 'son of an enemy of the people'. After a short pause, during which Mikhailov appeared to be studying me and my reaction to his superiors' decision, he advised me to embark on a serious study of the works of Lenin and Stalin. Oh yes, Mikhailov was a skilled operator who knew just the right moment to strike a blow to humiliate a helpless opponent and so assert his own importance.

I was later advised, when filling in questionnaires, to write 'father unknown', which is what I did for many years. The distinguishing feature of the retired KGB officers who work in the personnel departments of civilian organizations is their vigilance. So when in 1974 I came to assemble documents for my last tour of duty in Switzerland an official in the personnel department of the TASS agency, Sergei Sergeyev, who had worked previously, as I had, in the First Chief Directorate but in a different department, asked me why I had said that I didn't know my father.

'Because I really never knew him,' I replied, adding that this must be the hundredth questionnaire in which I had written the same answer.

'But I can't send off such a questionnaire to the KGB for checking,' said Sergeyev. 'You know very well that the question will come up immediately as to how and why . . .'

I lost my temper and said that I had been given the right to reply in that way thirty years previously for reasons I had no intention of revealing, and that if he was that interested he should telephone the Central Committee.

That appeared to cure Sergeyev of any desire to pursue the matter. But the incident was none the less instructive. The years may pass, but if something in a questionnaire raises doubts, then, until those doubts are dispelled, the person concerned remains in a state of suspension.

Many years later I came across Mikhailov again. He was retired and working in the personnel department of the Novosti press agency. I saw him while on a visit to the director of Novosti, Boris Burkov. He was much older and much balder and had even less light in his eyes. He gave the impression that he had not recognized me, but I reminded him of our little chat with a certain degree of malice, since I had now come out on top: I was deputy to the General Secretary of the Soviet Union of Journalists, while he was just an employee in the personnel department, a dreary civil servant. When I reminded him of our past encounter he simply smiled bitterly and muttered: 'That's the way things were at the time.'

CHAPTER FOUR

In the Archives

WORK IN THE ARCHIVES of the KGB is not highly thought of by officers of the security services, many of whom have no idea of the wealth of material contained in those ageing and often faded pages of print and photographs stored on the shelves. They provide a fascinating picture of the operations of the security organs against enemies and potential enemies of the Soviet regime. What is most striking is the extraordinary scope of the surveillance exercised by the secret police over the Soviet population, especially in the mid-1940s. What is more, this surveillance was maintained not only within the frontiers of the Soviet Union but also beyond them, and not only over people travelling abroad on duty or to work in Soviet missions abroad but also over people who had left the Soviet Union for good and were living permanently abroad.

This degree of surveillance was based on the principle that the network of informers had to cover not only the country itself but foreign countries too. The more informers there were, the greater the supply of information about people who interested the security services and the greater the responsibility for checking on the informers themselves. One often came across cases in the dossiers of individuals where one informant had written a report on another. If their reports gave rise to any doubts then a third informer was brought in to find out the true situation. Not surprisingly case officers themselves often became confused.

The informers' reports went into great detail about the behaviour and opinions of the target being studied or of some individual who had happened to come to the informer's notice. For example, in the dossier on the famous Soviet author Konstantin Simonov the informant said that his name was not Konstantin but Kirill. Against this was a note by the case officer: 'Find out why he changed his name.' The appropriate instructions were given to the informant. At first sight this appears simply laughable, since many authors use pseudonyms and change not just their first names but their surnames too, as the case officer must have known. This check on Simonov was being carried out because he was due to go abroad and the KGB had to give its approval. But because of the uncertainty with regard to his first name, instead of the words 'nothing compromising' that should have appeared on his record, there was a pencilled note saying: 'Hold until matter of name is cleared up.'

In another dossier concerning the application of a 'national artist of the USSR', Mikhail Nazvanov, to travel abroad was a report from an informer which said that among his friends Nazvanov had said that he was a real Russian artist, no less talented than Stanislavsky or the Jewish Meyerhold, but that his talent had not yet been recognized. There was, of course, nothing anti-Soviet in such a statement, only evidence of ambition. But the informant had described his remarks as unhealthy and anti-Semitic. Since, in addition, Nazvanov came from a formerly well-off family he was refused permission to travel.

Any Soviet citizen travelling abroad, for the first or the tenth time, is subjected to this type of screening, irrespective of his official position and rank, unless he is a member of the Soviet élite.

With every day that I worked in the archives my knowledge of the way the security services worked grew. I would sit there reading the documents till late at night, which it was possible to do in those days because we often worked until one o'clock in the morning, so that there was nothing suspicious about my behaviour. In any case I had no unlawful aims in view: I just wanted to get to know as much as possible about the past work of the organs of the KGB.

It was there that I read up the whole story of the arrest of the British agent Sidney Reilly. Despite his experience and knowledge of Russia, Sidney Reilly did not learn from an earlier operation carried out by the Cheka/KGB in which Savinkov, an experienced and cautious enemy of the Soviet Union, was lured back to Russia and arrested. Savinkov, having admitted defeat and recognized the Soviet regime in order to save his skin, refused to collaborate with the security services and during a conversation with KGB officers on the fourth floor of the main KGB building on Dzerzhinsky Square, realizing that he would never see freedom again, threw himself out of the window of the interrogation room and fell to his death. (Thereafter all the windows of interrogation rooms were covered with metal grilles and metal nets were suspended in the stair-wells.)

Sidney Reilly had been one of the leading Western agents during the first Soviet government. Arrested by the Cheka and interrogated personally by the head of Soviet counter-intelligence, Feliks Dzerzhinsky, Reilly was released but continued to engage in anti-Soviet activities. According to the official version, in 1925 he tried to cross the Soviet frontier illegally from Finland and was killed in an exchange of fire with Soviet frontier guards.

However, I came across documents which made it clear that Reilly was *not* killed in the frontier incident but was taken alive by Soviet security police. The Soviet authorities announced that he had perished, in the hope that the news would cause confusion and defeatism among his supporters.

It emerged from Reilly's file that he hoped that the British government would take steps to free him and, despite being under arrest, he still had hopes that the Soviet regime would soon be overthrown. He told this to a KGB informer sharing

his cell. His hopes of being freed were dashed when, in the
course of being questioned about a year later, the inter-
rogator showed him a report in the Soviet press saying that
Sidney Reilly had been killed as he tried to cross the Soviet
frontier.

'You no longer exist in this world,' Artuzov, the officer in
charge of the operation, told him. 'Your hopes of being freed
will come to nothing. The British Government is hardly
likely to demand the return of the corpse of someone who
crossed a frontier illegally. You have lost, Reilly, and if you
want to remain alive you had better tell us everything you
know that might interest us.'

According to his file, Reilly ultimately provided detailed
information about the work of the British and other Western
intelligence services and of the Russian emigré organizations
hostile to the Soviet regime. But this did not serve to prolong
his life. He fell ill and in a few years he died in the Lubyanka.

It would take years to read through even a selection of the
cases preserved in the KGB archives. What struck me was
not so much the quantity as the detail and care with which
the KGB studied every person who came to its attention.
One of Stalin's closest comrades, Sergo Ordzhonikidze,
once told employees of the Soviet security services that if
they were to take the most 'pure' Bolshevik and put him
under constant observation and record everything he said it
would be possible within a year to imprison him as an
'enemy of the people'. Ordzhonikidze apparently understood the sort of tragedy that surveillance on such a scale
would result in for the Soviet people, and that was probably
why, unable to put a stop to the process, he committed
suicide when he learned that the KGB had arrested his
brother. The official version, published in the Soviet press,
was that he had died of a heart attack.

What lay before me in the archives was not simply sheets
of paper covered with writing: I was immersed in the lives of
real people, many of whom were already corpses. In the case

of everyone accused or condemned, there were so many informers' reports, often from several different sources, that the guilt of the suspect seemed to be beyond doubt, however great his past services to the Soviet regime. Whether the informers' reports and other evidence corresponded to the truth was difficult to say because to disprove the charges, which often included a confession by the person concerned, it would have been necessary to spend more time on the defence than on the prosecution. Statements made by Soviet officials, after Khrushchev had criticized Stalin's actions, that the files of many of the people arrested contained nothing other than an arrest warrant are not correct. It was not, in any case, a matter of the quantity of material in the files. The point was that the KGB agent attached to the target had already been prepared by the case officer and instructed to expose the target as an 'enemy of the people' or a foreign spy. Consequently the agent, concerned for his own well-being, anxious not to disappoint the KGB officers and so land among the 'enemies of the people' himself, would simply provoke the target to discuss anti-Soviet subjects and to criticize the Soviet system or to praise the West. All this evidence would be produced at the next meeting with the case officer as a report from an informer. Many people became victims of this provocative method of dealing with a suspect.

The majority of authors writing about those troubled years, perhaps carried away by their subject, depict the 1930s as a period of total lawlessness organized by the NKVD and Stalin personally. In fact, the whole tragedy of those years consists in the very fact that all the arrests were carried out in strict accordance with laws that are still in force today. As someone who worked in Soviet counter-intelligence and who has personal knowledge of the matter I can say that not a single member of the Soviet Communist Party could be arrested, then or now, without the approval of the Party leaders and the government prosecutor, while people who were not Party members could be arrested only with the approval of the prosecutor. A member of the Politburo, a secretary of the Central Committee of the Party, the First Secretaries of the republican Communist parties and members of the Central Committee of the Party could be arrested only with the approval of the General Secretary of the Party, at that time Stalin. Secretaries of the regional and town committees of the Party could be arrested only with the sanction of the secretaries of the republican party, and ordinary members of the Party with the approval of the district secretaries. Without the approval and the signatures of these people neither the NKVD nor the KGB was able then, and is not able today, to carry out an arrest.

I do not mention these technicalities in order to excuse the deeds committed by Stalin and the NKVD but to make it clear that it was not Stalin alone but all the Party leaders who took part in those crimes against the Soviet people that were exposed by Nikita Khrushchev at the 20th Congress of the CPSU. It should be added that Khrushchev himself, as Secretary of the Moscow committee of the Party and First Secretary of the Ukrainian Communist Party, was directly involved in the arrests and execution of thousands of leading Party and government officials in Moscow and the Ukraine.

The exposure of Stalin's cult of personality, which had in fact been created with Khrushchev's active participation (he had, on Stalin's seventieth birthday, cried out 'Long live our dear father Stalin'), was a necessary step for Khrushchev and his supporters, not to advance the democratization of the Soviet system but to strengthen his own position as leader. I was working in the Second Chief Directorate at the time of Khrushchev's advent to power, when it was fashionable in intellectual circles to speak about the thaw that was taking place. Even today that period is spoken of as if it had been an especially happy time. I was able to follow then, in 1954, how, on instructions from the Central Committee and cer-

tainly not without Khrushchev's knowledge, a Fifth
Department of the Second Chief Directorate (now the Fifth
Chief Directorate) was created for dealing with the dissident
intellectuals, writers, poets, musicians and other representatives of creative, scholarly and scientific circles. The so-
called thaw meant no more than playing at democracy : it did
not last long and its consequences are now known to many,
especially those who were obliged reluctantly to leave the
Soviet Union and those who are serving terms in Soviet
prison camps. There is nothing to be surprised at in this;
since it first came into being the Soviet system of socialism
has never allowed any opposition. According to the Constitution of the USSR the Communist Party organization is
empowered to rule and direct the Soviet Union, which
means that its decisions, whether political, ideological or
economic, have to be obeyed unquestioningly.

As I went through lists of 'enemies of the people' and spies
who had been sentenced to death or to long terms of im-
prisonment I found among them well-known journalists like
the *Pravda* correspondent M. Koltsov, scholars, writers,
doctors, workers and peasants : representatives of all sections of the population. But what amazed me most were the
cases of such prominent political and military figures as
Bukharin, Rykov, Radek, Kamenev, Zinoviev, Tukhachevsky, Blucher and others who had taken part in the
Revolution. I have to say that the cases were prepared in a
wholly professional way : there was a sufficient number of
reports and personal confessions to convince me that they
were guilty of espionage or anti-Soviet activity. I was particularly struck by the file on Marshal Tukhachevsky, which
contained agents' reports about his behaviour at the time he
was in Germany in the early 1930s, detailed information
about his conversations with highly placed German military
and political figures, during which he was alleged to have
revealed to the Germans the Red Army's lack of prepared-
ness for action, to have spoken admiringly about German

military might and even to have accepted a proposal for closer co-operation with Germany to counter British and French plans. Whether these reports were true or not would be difficult to establish today, but most important was the fact that the NKVD was watching even such an important and powerful man.

There was also material on the famous trial of the men alleged to have taken part in the Bloc of Rightists and Trotskyites which took place in Moscow in March 1938 and was attended by foreign diplomats and journalists. Surprisingly, although they knew they were facing the death sentence, all the accused admitted to being guilty of anti-Soviet activity and even of contact with foreign states. Rumours were put around in the 1950s to the effect that Stalin himself visited Bukharin, Zinoviev and Kamenev in the NKVD internal prison and urged them to confess to crimes they had not committed in exchange for being granted their lives; this is pure invention. Stalin was too vain to do anything like that and had plenty of other people to do it for him. Bukharin and the others were undoubtedly opponents of Stalin's policy and said so openly under interrogation; it would have been naive of them to deny it since their views had been made clear throughout the struggle that had taken place at the Party congresses. But they were in opposition to Stalin and not to the Soviet system and they were certainly not 'enemies of the people'. Like Lenin before him, Stalin was well aware that any genuinely democratic administration which permitted opposition groups within the Party or outside it would inevitably lead to the collapse of the socialist system based on the dictatorship of the proletariat. That in itself was a fiction, since the dictatorship was established not by the proletariat but by a small group of leaders who were anything but proletarian and who lorded it over the genuine proletariat.

Once he had destroyed his opponents, both physically and morally, Stalin and the people around him created the

Soviet model of socialism which exists today. But, while Stalin had to sweep aside only a group of people at the top who threatened his power, Party and government officials at a lower level who wanted to remove *their* enemies and opponents found this a conveniant moment to do so, which led to the mass arrest and execution of thousands of people. Of course, many of those who were guilty of killing so many innocent people were themselves arrested and executed, especially after the arrest of Beria in 1953.

Since then there have been some changes. Hundreds of thousands of case histories have been destroyed, an enormous number of people released from camps and prisons, and those who were executed have had their memories rehabilitated. Today there are fewer executions and the KGB is a different organization from the NKVD of the 1930s. But as the principles on which the Soviet system is based have not changed, people continue to be accused of conducting anti-Soviet propaganda, distributing prohibited literature and so forth, and the KGB's archives and current files are constantly replenished with more case-histories. This will go on until such time as the Soviet leadership rejects the principle that the idea must take first place and the individual only second place, in short until it permits the creation of democratic institutions.

After nearly two years of work in the archives and having completed a course of evening classes at the Higher Party School, I was regarded as having completed my political education and having rehabilitated myself, so to speak, after the revelation of my father's guilt. In August 1952 I was transferred to work in the American Department of the KGB, then headed by Colonel Raina.

The person who helped me to escape from the archives was Colonel Pavel Yakimets, with whom I was on good terms and who knew Raina well. Yakimets was an old Chekist who, although because of his lack of education he was only the head of the secretariat of the Middle and Near East

Department, enjoyed considerable authority among his superiors. In the course of conversations over a glass of vodka he would tell me stories about how, in the 1930s, he took part in the arrest of saboteurs who were trying to blow up arms factories and industrial plants. I suppose he was telling the truth since it is difficult to deny that German agents and enemies of the Soviet regime, linked up with anti-Soviet emigré organizations, had penetrated the country and aimed to overthrow the Soviet regime – to play the game of those who wanted to turn back the wheel of history and refused to face reality.

Pavel Yakimets came to a tragic end. Following the exposure of Stalin's crimes in 1956 Yakimets lost all faith in the future and, aware that he had committed crimes himself in the past, threw himself out of the window of his ninth-floor flat. He was by no means the only one to suffer such a fate: many other old Chekists preferred suicide to suffering the shame of a trial.

Colonel Raina gave me a friendly welcome, as though I was an old friend, despite the fact that – he being a colonel – I had seen him only at a distance. Distinctions of rank were strictly observed in both the military and political intelligence services, not only in the interests of maintaining discipline but also to ensure that we, the middle operational staff, regarded our superiors not just as being higher in rank and position but as separated from us by a sort of invisible chasm which we could cross only when our chiefs considered it essential. This was Stalin's method of rule, the point of which was that the further the superior officers were removed from their subordinates and the less democratic and accessible they were the greater the authority and the power that they wielded. The same situation prevails in the Soviet Union today: apart from the rare and carefully orchestrated encounters with the employees of a factory or collective farm, the leaders of the Party and the government of the people's state show themselves to the population only on public holidays and then at a great distance and behind a living wall of secret policemen. This system is observed throughout the country, including government ministers, chairmen of state committees and heads of other organizations, from top to bottom of the whole vast bureaucracy. For example, when Leonid Zamyatin, now ambassador in London, was the General Director of the TASS agency, he not only refused to shake hands with newsmen when he met them, acknowledging their greetings with a very casual nod of the head, he even arranged to have his own personal lavatory which he could lock and which he permitted only his first deputy to use, and then only in his absence.

This explains my surprise at Colonel Raina's direct and friendly attitude towards me. He asked me what I had learnt in the course of my work in the KGB archives and whether I had forgotten how to perform the duties of an agent, and then said that he had heard about my successes (meaning my operation in Iran), and that he hoped I would be just as successful in my work in the American Department. As a start he was going to entrust me with a serious affair which would also serve as a test of my ability.

Raina explained that it was becoming ever more difficult for us Russians to operate in America. The Americans had greatly improved the quality of their counter-intelligence work against us, and our embassy and other missions were literally besieged by their agents, who were provided with cars and radio telephones, so that it had become practically impossible to evade observation. In spite of the fact that, when they had to make contact with a source, our men would spend five or six hours making sure they were not being followed – they switched from one means of transport to another, dodged into shops, stopped off in restaurants and cafés, entered into conversation with strangers so as to confuse anyone following them – the results were pathetic. The planned meetings often failed to take place and sometimes were actually disastrous. One of our men, Guk, had recently been caught in the act and had been obliged to leave the United States. True, the agent himself had apparently been a double, but that did not make things any better. KGB mechanics had examined all our cars after they had been serviced in American garages and had discovered special transmitters which sent signals to the American observation centre near the embassy and to the surveillance cars, making it possible for them to track our movements even if we managed to break away from them for a while. Raina told me that there were something like ten American observation cars constantly on duty near the Soviet embassy in Washington.

My job, as an officer well acquainted with surveillance work, was to plan how we could neutralize, at least temporarily on important occasions, the American surveillance. Raina told me that I had a month to get acquainted with the whole business and to make some suggestions.

I began by reading the reports made by case officers in the Washington and New York *rezidentury* about the American agents, some of whom had been photographed by cameras hidden in jackets and briefcases. There were also photos of the cars they used, with their registration plates, which, as we well knew, the Americans could easily change.

At that time the accepted way of checking whether you were being followed was to stop in front of a shop window and use it as a mirror, or to bend down and tie up a shoe lace that had conveniently come undone. But these tricks had not produced much in the way of results: indeed they had put the American agents on their guard, making it more difficult to identify them and impossible to be sure that they had been thrown off the scent. So the technical department designed sunglasses and ordinary spectacles which had little magnifying mirrors set in the outer corners of the lenses making it possible to observe who was coming up behind without turning your head. The spectacles were heavily built and were not very popular with the staff of the *rezidentura*.

After I had spent a few days thinking over the problem Colonel Raina had set me I had what seemed to me to be a quite absurd idea. I recalled that, when I had been studying the methods used for keeping people under observation, I had been told of the way the members of the staff of certain foreign embassies in Moscow always left their missions at the same time to go to lunch and scattered in various directions. At first our agents had been at a loss to know what to do because they did not know which of the targets to follow, since there were more of them than there were agents, and it was too late to call up extra men to help out. I thought it might be a good idea for us to carry out the same manoeuvre in Washington, but on a much bigger scale. What would the Americans do if practically the whole staff of the embassy were simultaneously to leave it, some by car and others on foot and all in different directions? They would of course follow the main targets but they would not be able to follow everybody and the person who had to keep a rendezvous would not be a main target but a less important employee from the point of view of surveillance. Such a mass exodus from the embassy would of course have to be agreed with the ambassador, a suitable day would have to be chosen, and the embassy staff would have to be told what was happening, but these were minor considerations. I imagined the *rezident* would have no difficulty in persuading the ambassador, since it was not so long since all ambassadors had been the principal *rezidents* and responsible for all intelligence work. I set out my proposal in detail in a written report and then asked to see Raina, fearing that at best he would ridicule my plan and that at worst he would regret ever having taken me on to work in his department.

Raina's secretary – a sexy young woman called Valya whose intimate relations with Colonel Avakimyan almost put an end to his career – asked me to leave my 'opus' for Raina to study. I had to wait a painfully long time, almost a week, before I was called to the great man's presence. He enjoyed considerable authority with us and his opinion had great influence, so I entered his office with trepidation. This time he greeted me in the normal manner of senior officers – coldly and politely – so that I quite expected him to dismiss my proposal with scorn.

To my surprise Raina approved my idea. 'I like it on the whole,' he said. 'It has to be done on a big scale, of course, so it can hardly be used very often, but we can try it out. Incidentally, you failed to give the operation a code name. Let's call it *Tumàn* [Fog].' And that was how my idea was referred to subsequently in correspondence between the Centre and the Washington *rezidentura*, where it was put into practice for the first time towards the end of 1952. According to reports from the *rezidentura* the American agents who were keeping our embassy under observation were completely confused and lost track of three of our men, who managed to make contact with agents whom they had not contacted for a long time. It was clear that such a ruse was cumbersome but it could produce results in case of necessity. Raina advised me to make a serious effort to learn English, saying I should think of the future and the possibility of having to work abroad. I was promoted to the rank of senior case officer, apparently not only for *Tumàn* but also for my past services. My promotion gave me an opportunity to work more independently without 'advisers' looking over my shoulder and poking their noses into everything. The men in charge of the Information Committee (the combined political and military intelligence services) apparently realized that they needed to introduce new blood among the intelligence officers, so new, younger cadres began to be promoted to positions of responsibility, to the discomfiture of the old men, who were then only a little over forty.

At an operational conference in January 1953, Colonel Raina announced that the Politburo had set us the task of extending our intelligence-gathering operations, especially

within and against the United States, since America was the
leader of international imperialism and co-ordinator of
Western intelligence directed against the Soviet Union. For
that reason we must not repeat the mistakes we had made in
the past and must know in advance what the imperialists
were planning to do. Raina said the Politburo believed that
we were not making sufficient use of the possibilities that
existed in the United States for extending our intelligence
network. We should be exploiting the United Nations
Organization in New York and other international organizations in Europe. The Soviet Foreign Ministry had made a
mistake when it had missed the opportunity to have the same
number of men on the United Nations staff as the Americans
had, with the result that UNO was full of Americans, many
of whom were spies. The Foreign Ministry had therefore
been instructed to redress the situation. Without interfer-
ing with the work of the Soviet diplomatic service, we must
have in the UNO as many of the staff jobs as was necessary
for carrying out the Politburo's instructions. I can remember
this announcement by Raina very well, because it was the
first and last time I was to attend such a conference in the
American department.

Just over twenty years later, when I was working in the
WHO in Geneva, the Central Committee of the CPSU was
still demanding that steps should be taken to increase the
number of jobs occupied by Soviet officials in the WHO and
in other United Nations agencies in Europe.

I continued my employment in the American department, dealing with operation *Tumàn*, studying the files,
entering up reports from the *rezidentura*, replying to
enquiries and preparing for a trip to the United States. In
one of the dossiers I came across some indecent photographs
that almost turned my stomach. They showed two
homosexuals from the moment of their meeting on the street
until their sexual performance. One of the men was an
American sergeant working in Moscow. The photographs

had come to us from the Second Chief Directorate, which, it appeared from the papers, had recruited the American by means of blackmail. It was suggested that we should make use of the sergeant as an agent and that if he refused to collaborate we should threaten him with publication of the photographs. Raina, however, had his doubts about the reliability of the recruited sergeant and feared that we might succeed only in revealing the identity of our own man in America and, even worse, in getting involved in one of the FBI's games, with a double agent who would be feeding us disinformation. I recalled that sergeant much later when, in the late 1950s or early 1960s, a friend and neighbour of mine, Vladislav (known in America as Vladimir) Kavshuk was sent to the United States to remind a sergeant – possibly the same one – that the KGB had not forgotten him. Kavshuk was head of a section in the American department of the Second Chief Directorate and had recruited the American sergeant.

The men in charge of the Information Committee set the American department the task of completely rebuilding the agent network in the United States, because the agents we had been using during the Second World War had practically all been exposed and were mainly people who had been recruited on an ideological basis – that is, people whose political views were close to those of the Communist Party or had belonged to it in the past. Most of them, according to our information, were already known to the FBI but could not be called to account for lack of evidence. Apart from that, many of the so-called agents were so careless that they made no attempt to conceal their contacts with Soviet officials, and were therefore quite useless to us. We were instructed to rectify this unsatisfactory position as quickly as possible without recruiting anybody belonging to the Communist or other left-wing parties. This was not simply because they were known to hold left-wing views but also to avoid giving grounds for accusing those parties of being in touch with Soviet intelligence. Since that time the Soviet intelligence services have rarely recruited such people either in the United States or in other countries. Contact with Communist and other left-wing opposition parties in Western and developing countries is maintained by representatives either of the International Department of the Party or the Directorate for Foreign Cadres (the body which supervises the employment of Soviet officials abroad). They are based at the Soviet embassy, usually with the rank of First Secretary or Counsellor, and direct the activities of those parties in a friendly way. *Pravda* correspondents are sometimes also involved in this work.

One of our major problems was the 'illegals'. We needed to introduce fresh and younger blood among them and make more practical use of them in political and military intelligence work. Apart, that is, from those who had been posted abroad and intended to remain inactive for a long period (on 'prolonged settlement', as it was called). Those who had been engaged in illegal work in the pre-war years had not only aged but were also exhausted by their wartime efforts and were no longer capable of meeting new demands. For this reason the directorate in charge of the illegals, then headed by Aleksandr Korotkov, embarked on a vigorous search for younger men who could be employed on illegal work abroad.

Two of the men I had got to know when working in the archives went through the training course and had already been posted abroad. One of them, Alesker Mamedov, an Azerbaidjani with jet-black hair and eyes, was somewhere in the Middle East and would later go to Europe as a commercial traveller and businessman, and the other, Yura Savin, was a priest in the Russian Orthodox Church in Jerusalem. Mamedov was very successful at his work and was decorated for it. When I saw him in Moscow on leave, he was a completely changed person, on the surface not at all like a Soviet citizen. But Savin very soon went astray. Unable to tolerate the discipline demanded by the Church, he forgot he was a priest and had an affair with a nun, as a result of which he was thrown out of Jerusalem, out of the Church and – ultimately – out of the intelligence service, on the grounds that he had not justified the trust placed in him by the Party and the government. Savin then shaved off his beard and had his long priestly locks cut off and became an ordinary Soviet man again. With two foreign languages to his credit, he managed to get a job on Moscow Radio, where he worked as an editor preparing programmes for transmission abroad.

My own career in intelligence turned out to resemble something that the famous Soviet poet, the late Vladimir Vysotsky, once wrote: 'My fate is really great: full of ups and downs . . .' I had hardly had time to feel at home in the American department when I was summoned by Colonel Korotkov, and found he had in his office Fedor Bykovsky, with whom I had recently been involved in work connected with Iran. Bykovsky had worked for some years prior to 1948 as a cipher clerk in the KGB *rezidentura* in Teheran and was later responsible for training future illegals in the cipher business and the other mysteries of cryptography. Korotkov, every inch a sportsman, with a square jaw that suggested a strong character, gave me a powerful handshake, asked me if I knew why he had summoned me and then, without waiting for my reply, asked me straight out: 'Do you want to be an illegal?' This kind of frontal attack did not bother me, because I had heard a lot about Korotkov, his manner of addressing you without beating about the bush and his brusque and outspoken manner. In spite of this, no one complained about him because he was not malicious and was always ready to stand up for his subordinates. He himself had risen from the ranks, starting as a footballer and then becoming a courier, carrying papers from one office to another within the KGB. At the same time he was teaching himself German. Having attracted the attention of his superiors, he was finally promoted to be a case officer and spent several years doing illegal work in Germany, first in the Hitler years and later in the Western sector of occupied Germany. I replied to his unexpected question in just as unexpected a manner. I said: 'Yes, I do.' It was a perfectly reasonable reply, since in my opinion illegal work is for real men who are neither cowards nor have weak nerves.

'I have spoken to Raina and everything has been fixed,' Korotkov said. 'So, if you are interested, write me a note to the effect that you wish of your own free will to switch to illegal work, because we never force anybody to do it against their will. You have a family from whom you will probably be separated for a long time. So write the note, but think it over carefully. We can wait.' Next day, after a talk with Raina, I went to see Korotkov again and the day after that I started – for the third time – on a course of special training.

On 2 March 1953, Korotkov called the staff together for an emergency meeting at eight o'clock in the evening. Then he made a brief announcement. Stalin was seriously ill. The prognosis was uncertain. Our superiors called upon us to increase our vigilance, not to go out of Moscow, not to leave our homes for any length of time, and always to leave note of where we could be found.

Korotkov's news stunned and depressed us. It had never occurred to us that Stalin might die: he was our saviour and our idol, our leader and father-figure, not simply because we worked in the Soviet intelligence service – it was the same for the majority of Soviet people. Three days later we were informed that Stalin had died. While the women on the staff started crying, we began to wonder what the future held, how on earth we could get along without Stalin. On his authority, it seemed, rested the whole Soviet system. Who was worthy to replace him?

We knew the first contender for the position of leader was Malenkov: that had been apparent ever since the 19th Congress of the Party at which Malenkov, and not Stalin, had delivered the main report on behalf of the Politburo. I was among the guard at that Congress and well recall Stalin's brief speech in which he said that Communists must take up the banner of struggle for freedom that had been dropped by the Social Democrats. Stalin had not given the impression of being a sick man, but it was rumoured that he had decided to retire from active political work because he had been exhausted by his wartime efforts. This was apparently true, because if Stalin had not wanted to abolish the post of General Secretary of the Party and make himself simply the Secretary it would never have come about, whatever tricks Malenkov, Beria, Khrushchev or anyone else in the Politburo had got up to. Stalin's authority was too great among the Soviet population, not to mention among the state security services and the Soviet army. We who were employed in the special services knew that better than anybody. Theoretical analyses by specialists on Soviet affairs in which they argue that there was an internal struggle within the Politburo directed against Stalin are far from the truth, because the Soviet political system itself excludes that possibility even today, let alone in Stalin's time. The bloody palace revolution organized by Malenkov and Khrushchev against Beria and his supporters in 1953 and the bloodless revolution of 1964, when Khrushchev was overthrown by Brezhnev, were not typical of the Soviet system. What is more, Khrushchev and Beria possessed only a fraction of Stalin's authority and power.

On 6 March 1953, the security services and the Soviet army were all brought to a state of maximum readiness for action. When the coffin with Stalin's body was mounted for the lying-in-state in the Hall of Columns in the House of the Unions and it was announced that people would be able to pay their last respects, something happened which the heads of the KGB, who were responsible for maintaining public order in Moscow, could not have foreseen. People simply swarmed, quite out of control, through the streets of the capital in the direction of the Hall of Columns. The ranks of the KGB internal troops who were ringing the building were broken and several streams of human beings met at one of the entrances. The people at the back kept pressing forward so that those in front were being squeezed into the narrow entrance or against the walls of the building. People started to shout and panic and to make the confusion even worse. Dozens were crushed to death and hundreds were injured.

Nowadays, when a man like Brezhnev or Chernenko dies, nobody rushes of his own accord to pay respects to the late leader : there is no desire to do so. The district committees of the Party decide which organization and how many people will attend the lying-in-state. Consequently there is no confusion and nobody is crushed to death, because faith in the exclusivity and irreproachable honesty of the Party leaders and in their concern to provide their people with real freedom and well-being has also been weakened. The great majority of my generation, myself included, certainly had faith in our idol. But after he died not only we but the younger generation as well ceased to believe in any idol, in any devil or god, and certainly not in any single individual swept up on the crest of a political wave to the summit of power. Power is like a high cliff, the top of which can be reached only by eagles or by reptiles. The number of eagles is getting smaller and smaller.

Stalin's funeral took place on 9 March 1953. To avoid a repetition of the tragic events that had taken place at the Hall of Columns all streets leading to Red Square were closed off with trucks and soldiers of the internal security troops at a distance of some two kilometres from the centre. Apart from men from the directorate that provided bodyguards for the leaders, the whole operational staff of the KGB, including those of us from the Information Committee, took part in the security arrangements surrounding the funeral.

In the course of our preliminary briefings we were told that there was no danger of any counter-revolutionary actions, but that it could not be excluded that there would be some scattered outbursts by enemies of the Soviet regime who might take advantage of the difficult times we were living through. If there were such acts of provocation we were to employ the most severe measures and, in case of people resisting arrest, to use our weapons even if it meant killing a man on the spot.

I had previously taken part in protecting members of the government at the physical culture parade in the Dinamo stadium in 1947, which was attended by all the members of the Politburo, headed by Stalin, and in the security arrangements for the military parade and demonstration on Red Square in November 1952. I am consequently able to assert that the steps taken to protect the Soviet leaders are on a very high professional level that practically excludes any possibility of acts of terrorism or sabotage. For example, on the occasion of the gymnastic display in the Dinamo stadium, the whole of the stand in which the government box was situated was divided into small squares composed of plain-clothes KGB officers, all of whom were armed. The squares were then filled with trusted Soviet workers who were under our constant observation. No movement on their part could go unnoticed by us.

If, in the event of an emergency, we killed someone, we would not be held personally responsible. In the same way, the people who act as personal bodyguards to members of the Politburo, today as in the past, bear no responsibility for any steps they take to deal with a dangerous situation. I will cite just three instances to support what I say, which took place at different times.

In the late 1940s Beria was riding in his armour-plated car accompanied by a second car containing his bodyguard. As they were going down Dzerzhinsky Street Beria's car slowed down (government cars normally travel at great speed), apparently because something had caught Beria's eye. Suddenly a small car shot out of Kiselny Street and got in between Beria's car and that of his bodyguard. Dzerzhinsky Street, which leads to Dzerzhinsky Square and Varovsky

Square, where the Soviet Ministry of Foreign Affairs was situated at that time, is very short and narrow, and the driver of the little car could not obey the bodyguard's signals to turn off. So Beria's bodyguard, consisting mainly of Lezgians (a very courageous and rather wild Caucasian people), opened fire with their revolvers and killed the driver on the spot. Beria and his bodyguard simply swept on without stopping.

A similar tragedy befell the mother of a friend of my wife in the mid-1950s. As she was crossing Kutuzov Avenue on a pedestrian crossing not far from the building where Brezhnev and Andropov lived, she was knocked down and killed by an official government car speeding in the direction of Borvikha, where many members of the Politburo have their country houses and the suburban section of the Kremlin hospital is situated. Once again, neither the 'servant of the people' on his way to the country nor his bodyguard thought it necessary to stop.

Finally, a third incident, which took place in the mid-1970s. Aleksei Kosygin, then Prime Minister of the USSR, was returning with his bodyguard from Zavidovo. Leonid Brezhnev had his country estate there, complete with well-organized shoots and specially constructed roads on which he drove Rolls-Royces and Mercedes which had been presented to him or bought with government funds. A middle-aged couple who had just bought themselves a small Moskvich car were driving slowly along the Leningrad highway in the direction of Moscow. In some places the highway is very narrow and drivers normally slow down there. But not members of the Politburo or other top officials. When Kosygin's bodyguard saw an obstacle – the little car with the middle-aged couple – in their way they switched on their siren. The little car did not give way but continued slowly along the road. So the bodyguard overtook Kosygin's car and drove straight into the little Moskvich, which shot off the road, turned over and landed in the ditch. The couple, who were killed, probably never knew what was happening to them. The official cars continued their journey to Moscow as though nothing had happened.

In none of these tragic affairs did anyone suffer any penalty, because nobody has the right to slow down or stop official cars. The traffic police stationed on such streets as the Kutuzov Avenue, the New Arbat or the Leningrad highway, which are all known as government routes, are actually officers of the Ninth Chief Directorate of the KGB, though they are dressed in policemen's uniform to conceal the fact. Consequently it is not unusual on these routes, especially when members of the Politburo, not to mention the General Secretary himself, are expected to come through, to have majors and lieutenant-colonels standing in the middle of the road directing the traffic.

This particular precaution originated in a strange way. In the late 1930s Stalin was on holiday at his estate in Georgia on the shores of the mountain lake of Ritsa. Beria, who was a crafty courtier and extremely ambitious for power, was then Secretary of the Communist Party of Georgia. One fine day he suggested to Stalin that he should make a trip on the lake in a motor launch accompanied by other Georgian Party officials. When the launch reached the middle of the lake, there was a sudden burst of machine-gun fire. Beria was the first to rush to where Stalin was relaxing in an armchair, threw him down on to the deck and covered him with his own rather overweight body. The others followed his example and in their enthusiasm they nearly suffocated Stalin. Where the firing came from and what it was all about was never made known. The criminals simply vanished. True, no traces of bullets were found on the launch, but it was accepted that there had been an attempt on the life of the leader. The incident was quoted as an example of an act of terrorism in lectures when I was studying at the KGB school and I heard more about the affair when I worked with the Georgian KGB. After Stalin's death, but before Beria's arrest in 1953, there were persistent rumours going around among KGB officers to the effect that Beria himself had organized the incident to show Stalin how devoted he was and to convince him that he had enemies in his inner circle. Whatever the truth, after that incident the heads of the KGB gave top priority to Stalin's protection. And not only during his life; at his funeral the security measures taken were just as thorough.

Everybody involved in the security arrangements on the day of Stalin's funeral – and that included myself – was issued with a special pass permitting him to get into Red Square, where we had to appear at seven o'clock in the morning. It was an unusually cold and windy day, with a blizzard sweeping across the square. Nobody apart from officers of the KGB and detachments of the internal troops was allowed on to the square. At about 7.30 the units of internal troops were drawn up in squares. We took up position in front of them – two rows of 'civilians'. I found myself in the front rank immediately opposite the entrance to Lenin's tomb, where a platform had been put up to display Stalin's coffin. But it would not arrive until after midday. There was nothing, no tea or even hot water, to warm us up. When we asked one of the officers in charge whether we could get some hot water because we were freezing, he replied sharply that we were not having a day out but attending a funeral, and he told us not to move about so much and to talk less. I am amazed that we didn't get frostbite. The time passed painfully slowly, and the only thing to distract us from the tedious business of waiting for the funeral to be over was the tireless activity of the film cameramen, who kept begging us to put on expressions of grief and suffering so that they could record our faces for posterity. Finally the workers, or rather representatives of the workers, began to arrive in the square. They were admitted through narrow gaps into the squares made by the soldiers. I am quite sure that not one of them could see

Stalin's coffin without jumping up, which was something not to be recommended. Then the sounds of the funeral march were heard and shortly afterwards the funeral procession appeared in Red Square. Stalin's coffin, in which the dead dictator's face could be seen beneath a plastic dome, was placed on the platform. Malenkov, Beria, Molotov and the others made their speeches, and then it was all over and the coffin was carried into the tomb.

There were no incidents during the funeral ceremony or afterwards, either in Red Square or elsewhere in Moscow.

If I am not mistaken, the ceremonies ended at about 2.30 in the afternoon. We had been standing for seven and a half hours in the freezing cold and wind and we could scarcely walk, our legs and feet were so numbed with the cold.

But that was not the end of the story as far as laying Stalin to rest was concerned. Nikita Khrushchev, who had been appointed chairman of the commission for Stalin's funeral, buried Stalin twice: first in Lenin's tomb and then beneath the Kremlin wall behind the tomb. But when it came to his turn his ashes were placed in the rather second-class cemetery at the Novodevichi Monastery on the outskirts of Moscow at the insistence of Brezhnev. What a comedy, when history can be re-shaped at the will of a single individual; but a nation gets the government it deserves.

PART TWO

Decision-making in Moscow

CHAPTER FIVE

····—◆►—····

The Seat of Power

WHEN SOVIET PEOPLE refer to the Central Committee of the Party, they do not have in mind the Central Committee elected at the Party's congress, consisting of more than 500 members and including, apart from the senior Party officials, a number of factory and farm workers and a few intellectuals and scholars. They are referring to the Party's permanent staff in the building on Old Square, Staraya Ploshchad. This – rather than the better-known Kremlin – is the holy of holies of the Soviet regime, the true seat of power, the place where the General Secretary of the Central Committee of the Party has his office, where meetings of the Politburo and Secretariat take place, and – most important – where members of the *apparat* of the Central Committee work.

The Central Committee *apparat* came into being shortly after the Revolution of 1917 as a small body of technicians to back up the Party leaders. Today it has grown into a vast institution employing several thousand Party officials which has become the nerve centre of the Soviet state. It is here, in the headquarters of the Communist Party, that policy is made and the fate of the Soviet people decided.

It stands to reason, of course, that the Central Committee, with its 300-odd full members and 150 candidate members, cannot be a policy-making body, although it is the body which from time to time approves – always unanimously – policy documents. But there is never any serious debate or exchange of views at Central Committee meetings, which are brought together to give the appearance of democratic procedure to Soviet policy-making. The overwhelming majority of the members of the Committee are high-ranking Party officials, but a few ordinary people – a fitter from a factory in the Urals or a milkmaid from a collective farm in the Ukraine – are also included as a sort of token to show that the Soviet Union is a state of workers and peasants. For some people membership of the Central Committee is almost automatic when they have reached a certain level in the Party or Soviet society: Party first secretaries of the more important provincial centres; ministers of the more important industries; some marshals and generals of the Soviet army and the security services; editors of leading newspapers, and so forth. For others membership of the Committee is an honour and a sign of confidence: distinguished scientists, academicians and writers, for example.

For all these chosen people membership of the Committee carries with it considerable moral and material advantages. They are able to enjoy certain privileges where they live and at their place of work and especially when they visit Moscow, where they have access to special shops selling goods which are in short supply elsewhere and which they can acquire at low prices. All they have to do in return for these privileges is to raise their hands to vote in favour of whatever is being proposed or occasionally to read from the platform the text of a speech that has been written for them in advance in the building of Old Square.

For seven years I maintained close contacts with the *apparat* and the Secretariat of the Central Committee, and several times a week I went round to the Old Square to visit them. What always struck me on my frequent visits to the Party headquarters was the atmosphere that prevailed in the place. It is decorated in the ascetic style laid down in Stalin's days. The offices are notable for their modest but at the same time solid furnishings. There is no way of distinguishing between the office of the head of a department and that of a lower-grade official except by its size. The tops of the desks are covered with green cloth. There is always a small side-table with a bottle of mineral water; no refrigerators or food stores; a safe; wall-to-wall carpeting. The corridors in the building are covered with the carpet called 'Kremlin runner'. Nobody rushes about or makes a noise. The walls in the corridors and offices are partly panelled in wood. Everything gives the impression of solidity.

The office of the General Secretary of the Party is on the right-hand side of the building as you enter, quite separate from the other offices, entered by metal gates which are painted black. Only the General Secretary uses this entrance, except on special occasions when other members of the Secretariat may use it. Access to the right-hand side of the building is controlled by a special KGB guard. The General Secretary's office, like the offices of the other secretaries, is provided with a retiring room and a dining room. A door leads out of his office into a conference room which has a long table, also covered in green cloth, at which meetings of the Politburo and the Secretariat take place as well as any special conferences that may be called.

Also accommodated in the right-hand part of the building is the General Secretary's personal bodyguard, his secretariat, and his group of *referents* – the aides who prepare all the papers he needs for his speeches in public and at meetings with foreign statesmen and politicians. In practice, all the departments of the Central Committee play some part in the preparation of policy papers, and when necessary special brigades are organized, consisting of journalists, Party officials, scholars and experts in various fields who can contribute something to the subject being discussed.

Such brigades do not necessarily work in the building on the Old Square. The Central Committee has at its disposal special houses on the outskirts of Moscow where the brigades can produce their official speeches and reports.

Occasionally they also write real 'works of literature' such as the volume that was produced describing Khrushchev's visit to America, *Face to Face with America*, and the works attributed to Brezhnev. Similar works will doubtless appear under the name of Mikhail Gorbachev.

The visitor to the Central Committee headquarters receives a strong impression of quiet power and self-satisfied superiority. The people who sit behind the desks in those offices have developed what I call the quiet style: that is to say that, even if you have been summoned to the building to be informed that you are being expelled from the Party and deprived of all the benefits you had been enjoying up to that point, you will be told about it in a calm and polite manner, without any emotion and even with a friendly smile.

I hated the quiet manner and the whole Central Committee *apparat*, because none of the people working in it represented the interests of the Soviet people: they were concerned primarily about their own personal well-being and the preservation of the system which had brought them so many benefits and given them the right to decide other people's fate. To be drunk from power is much worse than being drunk from alcohol, against which General Secretary Gorbachev has waged his campaign. If he were to expose the primary cause of the spread of alcoholism in the Soviet Union he would not campaign against vodka but against the present political system which, while proclaiming freedom and equality, first has created a totalitarian system in which the people are subordinated to a relatively small group of Party bureaucrats at the top.

The Central Committee *apparat* is not concerned just with matters connected with the Party and ideology. It reviews and has the power to approve or reject all economic, foreign policy, scientific, cultural and other plans drawn up by government and other public bodies and even by some individual intellectuals. No official can start to put a plan into effect without the approval of the Central Committee. Once the plan has been approved by the *apparat* the Secretariat of the CC confirms it automatically, because the members of the Secretariat have complete faith in their *apparatchiks*. In the course of many years working in the Union of Journalists I cannot recall a single case when any proposals we put forward that were approved by the *apparat* were turned down by the Secretariat. Consequently it is not the Central Committee and not the Party but the *apparat* of the CC that is the leading and guiding force in the Soviet state. If all the ministers and their subordinates both in Moscow and in the republics were to be removed and only their executive officers were to be left in place, nothing would change, because they would go on working as they did before under the direction of the *apparat* of the Central Committee.

None of the ministries or departments, not even the KGB or the GRU, can put any domestic or foreign policy plans into practice without a decision by the Central Committee. Of course, the Politburo discusses them, but all the proposals submitted are prepared by the CC *apparat*, that is to say by the CC departments in charge of the relevant ministry. No one has the right to conduct any talks, political actions or international meetings, to send Soviet delegations abroad or to receive foreign delegations in Moscow without the approval of the International Department of the CC and a decision of the CC.

Every ministry and organization has to submit all its proposals to the *apparat* of the CC. The *apparat* examines them and decides on their political or economic usefulness and what they will cost in foreign currency. Only exceptionally important matters are submitted to the Secretariat and the Politburo.

Once proposals have been approved they are sent back to the body which drew them up, marked Secret or Top Secret. Consequently if the Secretariat of the CC has approved proposals from ten ministries and departments, only the relevant ministry will be told of the decision concerning its own.

The secrecy that surrounds the work of the *apparat* and its members and its remoteness from both the members of the Party and the Soviet people are now taken for granted. No member of the Party can walk unhindered into Party headquarters and talk to members of the *apparat*, let alone the heads of its departments and secretaries. An ordinary member of the Party can enter the CC building only if he is summoned or if he has asked for an audience in advance and been granted one by the *apparat*. If he is invited to headquarters he must take his Party membership card or his identity card; he is then issued with a pass but he still can only gain access through heavily guarded entrances, manned by an officer and two armed soldiers from the KGB troops. So much for the democratic nature of the leaders and *apparat* of the Central Committee.

The people who work in the *apparat* constitute the most privileged section of Soviet society. Their salaries, housing and ability to buy consumer goods are incomparably greater than those enjoyed by employees of the ministries, the KGB, GRU, and other privileged Soviet organizations.

The head of a department of the Central Committee is the equal in status of a minister in the Soviet government and indeed is more important than some ministers. The head of a sector has the status of a deputy minister. Heads of departments, who are also secretaries of the Central Committee, constitute the top élite, more powerful than the government itself. It was therefore no accident that under Brezhnev both the Minister of Foreign Affairs and Defence and the head of the KGB were taken into the Politburo, to ensure its control over them. It is true that under Gorbachev the Minister of Defence, the elderly Marshal Sokolov, has been made only a candidate (or non-voting) member of the Politburo, but that is likely to change when a younger man closer to Gorbachev is appointed minister.

People working in the CC *apparat* are also cut off from the rank-and-file members of the Party and the Soviet population by their living conditions. They do not have to queue to obtain a state-owned apartment, referred to modestly as 'an apartment of improved type', a description not found in any official document but understood by every Soviet citizen. The *apparatchiks* do not live in new apartment blocks on the outskirts of Moscow but in the centre. An ordinary Soviet citizen is permitted to have a maximum of nine square metres per person if he is allotted a new apartment, but there is no such limit for the *apparatchiks*. Some of the people I knew working in the *apparat* had four- and five-roomed apartments although the size of their families did not warrant them. An ordinary citizen may wait years for an apartment, but even a recently appointed *apparatchik* will get one with no delay.

The people included in the *nomenklatura* of the Central Committee enjoy similar privileges. These are the senior officials of the Party, the government, the so-called trade union organizations, and other organizations who are appointed by the Secretariat of the Central Committee and cannot be dismissed without the permission of the Committee. The *nomenklatura* includes the heads of all ministries and committees and of such organizations as the Union of Journalists and the Society for Friendship with Foreign Countries, the editors of the national newspapers and periodicals, the heads of radio and television, of the news agencies, and so forth. Also included are the heads of scientific research institutes and leading academicians and scholars. There is also a *nomenklatura* system operating in the republics, regions and other districts of the Soviet Union, though its members have fewer privileges.

The *apparatchiks* and members of the *nomenklatura* are provided with special polyclinics and hospitals, known as *kremlyovki*, in which the treatment, equipment and medicines are incomparably better than in places provided for the public. These clinics and hospitals are closed to the public and guarded by the KGB.

The *apparatchiks* and members of the *nomenklatura* do not take their holidays in the homes and sanatoria belonging to the trade unions and used by factory workers and their families, but choose the special sanatoria on the Black Sea coast, in the northern Caucasus or in other such attractive resorts. Black caviare and other delicacies that most Soviet people have long forgotten about are part of the regular diet, and transport, accommodation, medical treatment and food are all free. No wonder the élite feel themselves to be superior or that they are out of touch with the lives of the ordinary people.

Marx said, 'Reality determines consciousness', and when I was a member of this élite I too came gradually to forget about the realities of Soviet life and even the bitter cold of the Moscow winter, because I never had to experience them. This division in society is unquestioned, and moreover, in the case of the élite, the process of becoming removed from Soviet society is entirely natural. Nobody ever voices any doubts concerning its legitimacy; after all, Lenin said that universal equality did not mean a levelling out of everybody. In other words, even in the Soviet state there must be rulers and ruled.

Nobody can tell how long a member of the *apparat* or of the *nomenklatura* will be able to hold his job, but while he is in it, whether in the top or middle ranks, he will try to extract from his position as much as he possibly can before he falls. Even in recent years there have been cases where members of the Politburo and even the General Secretary himself and the President of the country – men such as Malenkov, Molotov, Kaganovich, Bulganin, Khrushchev, Podgorny, Kirilenko and Mazur – have been ousted from their apparently powerful positions. More recently Grigori Romanov and Viktor Grishin have disappeared from the Soviet political scene.

This is why I am unable to accept Milovan Djilas's theory of the 'new class', because the term 'class' means something fixed, stable and unchanging with time. If I am a member of the working class or the peasantry, my origin and my position in society are unchangeable. I can be dismissed from my job or expelled from my farm, but I do not for that reason cease to be a worker or a peasant. That is what it means to be a member of a class. But what exactly is the Central Committee *apparat* and *nomenklatura* which Djilas called the 'new class'? It is not a class but a superstructure transcending all classes in society, composed of privileged and carefully selected Party and government bureaucrats. A man can be a member of that superstructure today and be thrown out of it tomorrow.

Unlike politicians and statesmen in the West, members of the Soviet superstructure, even those occupying the highest positions, have no significance for the Soviet system as personalities, on the principle that the idea comes first and the personality second.

If a Western politician or statesman loses his job or retires, he is not automatically stripped of his material possessions or his right to continue political activities or publish critical comments on the government and its leaders. With Soviet officials the position is exactly the reverse. If one of them loses his place among the Soviet élite he immediately loses everything. He will certainly not be able to return to political or government work nor permitted to make any public statements; he simply disappears from public life.

There are many examples to illustrate this, from the old revolutionary and Bolshevik Vyacheslav Molotov to Grigori Romanov, recently a colleague of Brezhnev and Andropov and a rival of Mikhail Gorbachev. A typical case was that of Dmitri Polyansky, whom Brezhnev threw out of the leadership. When he learnt that he was no longer a member of the Politburo and had been given the relatively unimportant job of ambassador to Japan, Polyansky left the headquarters of the Central Committee and stood there looking round for his bullet-proof limousine. One of his former bodyguards, now assigned as his minder, explained that he now had only an ordinary Volga car. Certain other questions, including the use of his Politburo apartment, his house in the country, and so forth, would come under scrutiny the next day. (All the members of the Politburo and their families are provided with bodyguards to protect them from terrorist acts against them on the part of the CIA, the British Intelligence service, the Sureté Générale and other Western special services, though what they fear most is their own people and getting too close to them.)

But, however unpleasant the consequences of losing one's rights as a member of the élite, those in it enjoy very considerable advantages and if they play their cards carefully can survive in a state of 'advanced socialism', moving steadily up from one job to another. A good example of this was the late Anastas Mikoyan, member of the Politburo and President of the Supreme Soviet. His ability to know where to turn in a difficult situation is exemplified by the story which recounted that, when he left the CC headquarters in the rain after a meeting of the Politburo at which Molotov and others in the 'anti-Party group' had been reduced to the ranks, Mikoyan's bodyguard offered him an umbrella. Mikoyan refused it, saying: 'Don't worry – I'll get to the car between the drops.'

People in the *apparat* and in the *nomenklatura* possess a conditioned reflex for self-preservation. I spent many years of my life in their company, so I have reason to know them. In all the years that I was a member of the Communist Party I do not recall a single case when a member of the Party who approached the CC *apparat* for help obtained it. As it was in Stalin's days, so it was under Brezhnev and Khrushchev, and so it is today, because to defend a rank-and-file member of the Party inevitably involves a conflict between an *apparatchik* and a member of the *nomenklatura*. I have always hated this indifference to other people's fate hidden behind the quiet style of the *apparatchiks*. On all my visits to the

Old Square for whatever reason, the officials would make me feel their sense of superiority. When, after many previous trips abroad, I was due, in 1974, to go to Zambia as a TASS correspondent, I was interviewed by a new head of section of the Department of Agitation and Propaganda. After some initial small talk, he turned to his subordinate and asked in a condescending way: 'What do you think – shall we let him go to Zambia?' And he immediately answered his own question: 'Oh well, let him go.'

Despite his quiet manner, he made his superiority clear with the obvious hint that, if *he* didn't wish it, I would go nowhere.

The Central Committee *apparat* consists of a number of departments, each of which is in charge of one aspect of the country's social and economic life. Thus, the Department of Agitation and Propaganda is in charge of the whole of the press, radio and television, mainly as far as domestic issues are concerned. The Department of Party Organs is responsible for the organizations within the Party. The Department of Administrative Organs supervises the appointments and functions of the KGB, the GRU and other secret agencies. The Department of Science and Culture handles all scientific and cultural matters. This does not mean, however, that bodies such as these are entirely unable to display initiative: on the contrary, they are expected to put forward plans and proposals for approval by the Central Committee.

Each Central Committee department plays a key role in its own field. The International Department handles foreign policy. It was headed for thirty years, until 1986, by the veteran *apparatchik* Boris Ponomarev. Despite the existence of the Ministry of Foreign Affairs, the KGB and other organizations concerned with international questions, it is not they but the International Department that determines foreign policy and relations with foreign Communist and other left-wing parties. When the Politburo comes to decide upon strategy it listens most closely to the views and propo-

sals of the International Department. The International
Committee was originally a small section of the Central
Committee *apparat*, responsible for maintaining contact
with the Communist parties abroad; it replaced the Comintern, dissolved by Stalin during the war. It has gradually
developed into one of the most powerful departments of the
CC and its head has the rank of a Secretary of the CC and
candidate membership of the Politburo.

The International Department is divided into sectors on a
geographical basis and staffed by experts in political and
economic conditions in the countries for which they are
responsible. They maintain close working contact with
Foreign Ministry and other Soviet organizations connected
with foreign countries. All officials going abroad must pay a
visit to the International Department, where they are advised
about the specific immediate job as well as how to spread
propaganda about Soviet foreign policy and the Soviet way
of life.

The International Department agrees with each relevant
organization its proposals about the undertakings for the
coming year. In the last quarter of the year these are sent to
the Central Committee as official proposals. They are usually approved without any changes by the Secretariat of the
CC in the following January. As I have said, when I was
responsible for the international contacts of the Union of
Journalists there was not a single instance when the provi-
sionally agreed plan was not approved.

In addition special commissions consisting of specialists in
international affairs representing various organizations and
interests are set up to vet the proposals before they are sent
for approval by the Secretariat and the Politburo. In this
way foreign policy is worked out on a collegial basis, taking
into account the latest information about the international
situation and political events in various parts of the world.
Foreign policy is planned for a year ahead, but may be
changed on an *ad hoc* basis. The Soviet leaders do not have

any five-year plans for foreign policy, though many Western observers seem to think they do. Certain long-term objectives of course do remain unchanged : spreading the idea of socialism and the superiority of the Soviet system; influencing public opinion in the countries of the West and the Third World in favour of Soviet policy and against imperialism; organizing movements for peace, against nuclear weapons and Star Wars; giving moral and material support for the national liberation movements; emphasizing the possibility of a peaceful co-existence with pluralist countries.

Bearing in mind the hostility towards the West of many African countries which had been liberated from colonialism, even under Khrushchev the Central Committee had come to the conclusion that the idea of socialism in its classical version – that is, a collectivized economy and the development of the economy without capitalist help, with armed forces to defend the country's independence – could prove very attractive to Africa. This was to some extent borne out in practice.

As for the advanced industrial countries of the West, it was decided that, however wide the spread of the ideas of Marxism–Leninism, the possibility of proletarian revolutions taking place in those countries was practically nil, in spite of economic and political crises, the growth of unemployment and the existence of Communist and left-wing parties operating freely there. Consequently, while still holding to the view that the capitalist system would be replaced by a socialist one, it was decided to talk in future about the 'evolutionary' way of changing the social system, still maintaining that capitalism must inevitably perish. So the long-term plans provide for the creation of social and political instability in the countries of the West by the means referred to above, in which not only the diplomatic and propaganda services but also the other special services will continue to take part.

The Secretariat and the Politburo attach great importance

to the activities of the Communist and pro-Communist political parties in Western Europe and the USA, although they do not have great influence on the economic or political life of their countries, with the exception of Italy and France. Even with the Communist parties of these two countries the CPSU has serious differences of opinion, but these relate to the reluctance of the European parties to accept the Soviet model of socialism and not to any differences of principle in the field of Marxist–Leninist theory and the replacement of the capitalist system by a socialist one. On this subject they are in complete agreement.

'We must not forgive capitalism for a single mistake made, however small, but exploit it in order to undermine its foundations politically and morally,' Mikhail Suslov said at a meeting in the Central Committee. 'But,' he added, 'to carry out this task you need not so much the desire to do so as the knowledge of Marxism–Leninism and its application in practice to everyday life.'

These remarks were directed not only at Soviet Communists but also at members of the foreign Communist parties. The *apparat* and Secretariat of the Central Committee usually attributed differences between the CPSU and other Communist parties to ignorance of, or the incorrect interpretation of, Marxism–Leninism by the leaders of the Western Communist parties. The fact that the parties operated in a capitalist environment, were exposed to its influence, and tried to adapt themselves to the situation led to an abandonment of many of the fundamental principles of Marxism.

In an effort to improve the situation and to avoid mistakes in the application of Marxist theory in practice the Central Committee set up a Higher Special School for members of foreign Communist parties, many of whom were staying in the Soviet Union illegally, that is, without indicating the true purpose for which they had left their own country. This Party training school is controlled by the International Department of the CC and is situated in Moscow, on

Leningrad Avenue, opposite the Airport Metro station. There is nothing on the outside of the building to indicate what goes on inside it, but it is guarded as strictly as the CC headquarters, except that the guards wear a different uniform. The Communists who come to study there are provided with everything necessary for their comfort and for mastering the teachings of Marx and Lenin. Every sort of food is available to them, and I have to admit that a friend of my wife's who worked in the school used to provide us with things in short supply.

The students at the school, who normally complete a two-year course, are members of Communist and other left-wing parties from practically all the countries of the West and also from the Third World. In this way the Soviet leaders count on increasing their influence and making the foreign Communist parties more effective and more pro-Soviet, so that along with other opposition movements they may gradually undermine the foundations of the capitalist system and may be able at a suitable moment to take power into their own hands. Present-day Marxist theoreticians believe that this process of transition from the capitalist system to socialism will be long and complex, but they believe it to be inevitable and, to speed the process, they need well-trained people.

There is also a need for well-trained people in the *apparat* of the Central Committee and to staff the Party organizations in all the republics and regions of the Soviet Union. There is another Higher Party School for training them which is controlled by the Department of Party Organs of the CC. The course there lasts two years and, although the conditions are not as good as in the school for foreigners, they are much better than in ordinary educational institutions. After completing the course the students return to their home towns but are usually promoted to better jobs. They are the ones who, so long as they behave themselves properly, have a good chance of becoming members of the ruling élite.

It is a measure of the effectiveness of the International Department that Boris Ponomarev has remained at its head for so long, though I suspect this is not so much the result of his ability as of the efforts of his staff. I met Ponomarev on many occasions at conferences in the CC and on trips abroad, and I formed the opinion that he was a narrow-minded person, one well stuffed with Marxist–Leninist formulae, stubborn, pushing, and not well disposed towards anyone who challenged his views. I saw how sharply he put down people whose statements did not please him, and I also witnessed his behaviour in Egypt shortly before President Anwar Sadat threw out several thousand Soviet advisers in 1972.

CHAPTER SIX

·····━━◆━━·····

Power Struggles

In the early years of the Soviet regime the security organs recruited to the Cheka, or security service, mostly people with a working-class background. In fact the main criteria in selecting people for such work were their proletarian origins and their devotion to the new regime, rather than their educational level or intellect. In these early years and in the mid-1930s and late 1940s the Cheka–KGB, on instructions from the Party leaders, dealt with the Soviet people with great brutality, destroying hundreds of thousands of intellectuals, working people, Party and military leaders and even its own officers. There have been many books published recalling the terror that reigned in the 1930s in the Soviet Union, the authors of which generally place all the blame for what happened on the security organs and Stalin himself. I have to say that I cannot agree entirely with this view of events. As I have explained, all the Party leaders – Molotov, Voroshilov, Kaganovich, Khrushchev, Kalinin, Bulganin, Beria, Mikoyan, Suslov and many others lower down the scale, including the bosses of Party organizations throughout the country – took part in that campaign of terror. When he came to expose Stalin's cult of personality, Khrushchev was aiming to conceal from the Soviet public and the world at large the part he himself played in those crimes when he was First Secretary of the Moscow committee of the Party and later of the Communist Party of the Ukraine. He was counting on the ignorance of the majority of the Soviet population and the world public. Moreover, he and those around him, who had also played their part in liquidating 'enemies of the people', were assured of the silence of those who survived and had witnessed the frightful events of the past, because silence and the fear of speaking one's mind had become an automatic reflex in Soviet people. By heaping the blame on the security organs and on Stalin, Khrushchev was trying to demonstrate that the large-scale repressive measures taken against Soviet people were due to the cruel character of certain individuals rather than the Soviet system itself or to the collective leadership of the Communist Party.

Stalin and the people around him used the secret police in their struggle to hold on to power and to dispose of their political opponents. There were of course plenty of people opposed to the new regime. It could hardly have been otherwise, in view of the extent and violence of the upheaval in the social, economic and political life of the country, which had swept some to the top and others to the very bottom and could not fail to give rise to bitter internal battles. In that crude struggle for power, Stalin applied Lenin's principle: an alliance even with the devil if it will serve your ends. Stalin and those who sided with him did not choose the devil in their efforts to achieve their ends; they chose the secret police – the NKVD as it was then – and the Party *apparat* which commanded all the media of propaganda and public information. The alliance brought Stalin and his supporters victory over the 'enemies of the people', chiefly thanks to the organs of state security which had arrested and executed leading Party and military figures and members of Lenin's Old Guard as well as an enormous number of less prominent Soviet citizens.

By 1947, however, despite the creation of the United Nations Organization, the international situation had worsened and the world had entered the period of the cold war. America's possession of the atomic bomb, coupled with the fading prestige of the Soviet army, created an unfavourable situation for the Soviet Union. In wartime the army plays the principal role in achieving victory, but in peacetime results can only be achieved by the intelligence service. Stalin understood this and in September 1947, on his instructions, Soviet political intelligence – the KGB – and Soviet military intelligence – the GRU – were merged. A Committee of Information attached to the Council of Ministers was also set up, headed by Molotov, whose deputies were Andrei Vyshinsky, Jakob Malik, Lieutenant-General P. Fedotov, Lieutenant-General A. Serenko, Lieutenant-General Aleksei Yepishev (until 1985 head of the Chief Political Directorate of the Soviet army) and Vice-Admiral Radionov.

The Information Committee was instructed to strengthen and extend intelligence work, both political and military, abroad and to integrate the two services. Its formation marked the beginning of a new era in the history of the Soviet intelligence service. It is today the largest intelligence service in the world and the Soviet Government provides it with all the material resources and manpower it requires. It can be said with certainty that 40 per cent of the Soviet citizens working abroad in international organizations and in diplomatic and other missions are full-time employees of the intelligence services. A similar proportion of other Soviet people sent on duty abroad are also agents.

The Information Committee was given the buildings previously occupied by the Communist International, which Stalin officially dissolved in 1943. The buildings were on the outskirts of Moscow next to the site of the Exhibition of Economic Achievements, which was not functioning at the time, and the 'Gorky' film studios. They were chosen because it was thought that they would provide a better cover for employees of the Soviet intelligence service, who would be less likely to be photographed by foreign spies, which was easy when they worked in the KGB building on

Dzerzhinsky Street in the centre. But it was only a matter of months before everybody knew where the intelligence service was housed. It was not difficult to understand why. Buildings which had previously been empty were suddenly filled with people mostly dressed in foreign clothes, which was unusual at the time, reading foreign periodicals and occasionally showing off their knowledge of foreign languages. The No. 9 trolleybus, which normally transported a few film actresses and students, was now overcrowded. On one occasion a couple of drunken workers in dirty clothes wanted to get on to the bus. But the conductress would not let them on, and that provoked noisy protests. The conductress then asked them if they realized the sort of people who were using her bus, and, when they said they didn't, she told them proudly that her passengers were either actors and actresses or secret service agents. Thereafter we were forbidden to read foreign papers or books in the trolleybus. We remained in the former Comintern building until the beginning of 1953.

After the formation of the Information Committee its head, Molotov, who was also then Soviet Foreign Minister, decided to put all Soviet ambassadors in charge of Soviet intelligence work abroad, with the title of Chief Residents. The KGB residents were subordinate to the ambassadors and had to take orders from them. This resulted in incredible confusion. The residents, the professional intelligence officers, resorted to incredible subterfuges to avoid informing their ambassadors about their work, since the diplomats had only amateurish knowledge of intelligence work and its methods and it was thought that their lust for power might be counter-productive. In the course of many years' work abroad, I came to the conclusion that the majority of Soviet ambassadors, however well educated, remain narrow-minded, over-ambitious career diplomats.

Towards the end of 1951 important changes took place in the structure and staff of the Information Committee. The

KGB and the GRU were separated again. Lieutenant-General Serenko was made head of the Committee and his new deputies were Aleksandr Panyushkin (former ambassador to the United States and, following the disbanding of the Information Committee in 1953, head of the First Chief Directorate of the KGB) and Yevgeni Pitovranov, later Chairman of the Soviet Chamber of Commerce. Molotov, Vyshinsky and other men in charge of the Soviet diplomatic service were removed from the direction of intelligence work. This development was to be explained partly by the strained relations between Stalin and Molotov at the time but also by the fact that the merging of the political and the military intelligence services had not produced the desired results: even when they were united in one organization neither the KGB nor the GRU ever revealed their cards to each other and were never particularly fond of each other. The KGB considered the GRU to be professionally inefficient, while the GRU was dissatisfied because it was, and still is, constantly under observation by the KGB's counter-intelligence – the Third Chief Directorate in the Soviet Union and the counter-intelligence officers in *rezidentury* abroad. For example, one of the future heads of the GRU, Colonel (later Colonel-General) Seskin, when he was working in the GRU *rezidentura* in Japan, was kept under close observation because he was suspected of having intimate relations with his Japanese domestic servant, who was an agent of Japanese counter-intelligence. Quite a fat dossier was put together on Seskin which for some reason came into my hands. After his return from Japan in the late 1940s I came to know Seskin personally and we were on quite good terms, though I never said anything to him about his dossier. Tall and well-built and with a very full moustache, he may well have made an impression on the ladies of Japan, of whom he apparently took advantage, allowing them to interfere with the way he carried out his official duties. It was at the same time that Yuri Rastvorov, a KGB employee and son of a highly placed official in the Central Committee, got so involved with Japanese geishas that he refused to return to the Soviet Union despite pleas from his father and the heads of the KGB.

We parted company with the GRU quietly and without any fuss since, as I pointed out, our connection had been purely mechanical and had not affected our or their intelligence work. That is why I am inclined to doubt whether Igor Guzenko, the cipher clerk who defected in Canada in 1945, could have had any real knowledge about the KGB's agents in Britain, particularly among members of the intelligence service, because the KGB *rezidentura* never used the GRU's communications system.

Shortly after Stalin's death the Information Committee was disbanded and Soviet political intelligence once again became the First Chief Directorate and moved into the Lubyanka.

The Ministry (later the Committee) of State Security and the Ministry of Internal affairs (MVD) were merged and Politburo member Lavrenti Beria became the head of the whole system. Then the *apparat* was reorganized, with cuts and expansions, dismissals, arrests and releases from prison. It was difficult for the staff to make out what was going on. But one thing was clear: in spite of some slowing down in our work and a certain confusion, the security services were moving up several leagues in importance and influence. Semyon Ignatiev, who became head of the KGB after the arrest of Viktor Abakumov, did not enjoy the slightest authority with us. It was he who concocted the notorious 'case of the Kremlin doctors' not long before Stalin's death; politically, however, he emerged unscathed, speaking at the 20th Congress of the CPSU practically as a witness for the prosecution, exposing the crimes of the cult of personality. Aleksandr Panyushkin, formerly a Party official and later a diplomat, was made head of the First Chief Directorate and General Pyotr Fedotov (who had been in charge of Soviet intelligence throughout the war) became head of the Second Chief Directorate (counter-intelligence). He replaced Lieutenant-General Raikhman, who had been sacked at the time when Jews were being ousted from the security services and was later arrested and very nearly accused of being a spy.

But the most important event, though one that is little known, was the setting up, on Beria's instructions, of a special secret group within the telephone-monitoring service. Its job was to listen in to Soviet officials in their homes, offices, country houses and even in their cars. Beria was provided with photographs of all the people working in the group, together with the basic facts about them. There were about fifteen people involved, all of them screened three times over before they could be entrusted with such a sensitive and dangerous task. It was dangerous for them because Beria could have them executed, as witnesses, once the job was done. And dangerous for him too, because if they were to tell anyone what he had ordered them to do he would lose his head very quickly. Because there were so few of them, members of the group had to work long hours with no time off. I know about the group because one of its members was a friend. I shall call her V. She told me that it was not so much the work that was tiring but the constant fear : they realized that at any moment they might get a bullet in the neck either from their chief, Beria, or from the people they were bugging.

When V. told me what she was working at I asked her who was in charge of the group and what was the point of listening in to the Party leaders' conversations. I was curious to know what explanation they had been given. She replied that their boss was Colonel Kuzmin, the head of the monitoring service. He had been in the secret police almost since the day the Cheka was formed : though not known for his intellect and without higher education, he was totally loyal to the service. Kuzmin had explained to the group that the Soviet

intelligence service had received a report from an agent
abroad that one of the top leaders of the CPSU was in contact
with a Western intelligence service and was concerned not so
much with spying as with plans to organize a counter-
revolution at a suitable moment. Stalin's death might well
have provided such a moment. The agent did not know the
name of the person concerned, because he was referred to in
the foreign intelligence reports only by a code-name. Consequently it had been decided to listen in to all the Secretaries
and members of the Politburo, except Beria himself, who
was in charge of the whole enquiry.

Such an explanation might well have been accepted
because memories of the events of the mid-1930s, when
more than one important Party and government official had
been executed for contact with foreign intelligence services,
were still fresh in everyone's mind.

There could in fact be no question of there being a foreign
agent among the Secretaries and members of the Politburo.
Beria wanted them bugged not so much as a weapon in the
struggle for power but to protect his own position and even
his life. To imagine that after the Georgian Stalin, Beria,
also from Georgia, would become head of the state was, to
say the least, absurd, not least because Malenkov, Molotov
and Khrushchev possessed obvious advantages.

For us working in the KGB, and for many other people as
well, it was no secret that Stalin's favourites were Malenkov,
Khrushchev and Bagirov, Secretary of the Communist Party
in Azerbaidjan. But Beria represented a danger to these men
because Stalin trusted him and because the security services
were in his hands. We knew that some differences of opinion
had arisen in the Politburo after Stalin's death, but we did
not know exactly what they were about and we could not
possibly have imagined what would happen later.

My friend V. told me what she had overheard in the
conversations of Malenkov, Khrushchev, Bulganin,
Kaganovich and others. My relations with V. were more

than close and there were no secrets between us. At the time we were not really interested in what the members of the Politburo said; we were much more concerned about what would happen to her if the whole enterprise were to be exposed. For what she had heard showed that the leaders of the Soviet Union were very far from being the near-saints they were presented as.

The things that V. told me upset my whole way of thinking about a socialist society and its leaders. In place of the crystal-pure Bolsheviks I was presented with figures of a completely opposite kind. V. said that Khrushchev and Bulganin drank themselves into a shocking state, used the worst possible swear words, smashed their glasses and dishes and called Stalin and Beria all sorts of vulgar names. Voroshilov drank without restraint, and once Malenkov had even had to ask him not to come to meetings quite so drunk. Malenkov was the only one who did not drink, but he was very talkative at home and was heard working out plans, not only for the country's future, but also for the composition of a government that would suit his needs. He disliked Khrushchev, whom he considered to be a primitive and not very intelligent person, greedy for power. He did not trust Beria but considered him the most useful person for his own purposes.

The most important thing to emerge from the bugging was a discussion between Khrushchev and Bulganin about how to get rid of Beria. It had occurred during one of their regular drinking bouts, judging from their voices. This conversation was immediately reported to Beria himself, who then summoned V. to his presence to question her personally and to make sure there was no mistake. Beria could have listened to the recording himself, V. told me, but he apparently considered that beneath his dignity. 'I nearly died from fright,' V. told me, 'when Kuzmin told me that Beria himself wanted to see me. But he received me politely and there was nothing affected about him. He asked me whether I had understood everything correctly, since in transcribing the recording I had indicated in some places "loud background noise" or "not very audible". When I assured him that I had, Beria thanked me and said he hoped I would appreciate the great responsibility of the task I had been given and the necessity for observing absolute secrecy.'

V. kept the secret, telling no one but me. But someone in the know – a supporter of Krushchev or Bulganin, or an eager careerist – must have taken fright when he realized that he and others were in great danger so long as the eavesdropping continued. However it came about, Khrushchev, Malenkov and Bulganin got to know that their telephones and flats were being bugged, and that decided Beria's fate.

Beria was arrested on 28 June 1953. His close supporters, Kabulov, Merkulov, Dekanozov and a few others, were arrested with him. That day we were ordered not to leave our places of work until we received further instructions. At that time I was doing practical work in the Second Chief Directorate, where I had been sent by Colonel Korotkov to study counter-intelligence work in the Fifth Department, which was responsible for the Moscow embassies of the countries of the Near and Middle East. At about ten o'clock in the evening the head of the department, Colonel Davidyan, went round all the offices and advised us to check our personal weapons and to be in a state of maximum alert. We were never told what it was all about and I still have no idea. At half past two in the morning we were permitted to leave the KGB premises and go home. In all the side streets were tanks of a guards division, covered with dust and mud, ready if necessary to surround the KGB building and prevent access to it.

Next morning we were informed that Beria had tried to carry out a *coup d'état* and had been arrested together with his accomplices. It was only then that we understood what might have happened if Beria's deputy, Bogdan Kabulov, inside the KGB building, had managed to issue an order to the staff and the internal security troops to put up resistance to the 'counter-revolutionaries' or something like that. There would have been a blood-bath in which people would have perished without knowing why. My friend Gennadi Burkov, then working as secretary to one of the deputy ministers of state security, told me how, when Kabulov, a very fat man, was arrested and army officers dragged him out of his office, he shouted hysterically : 'Comrades, Chekists, help! – they are arresting your deputy minister!' But no one came to his aid. One must give the military commanders their due for having carried out the arrest of Beria and his accomplices so successfully and quickly, thus preventing a conflict between the KGB and its troops on the one hand and the army on the other.

Beria's arrest had the effect on us of an exploding bomb, but it did not produce any unrest within the KGB. Another reorganization of the service was begun. In order to strengthen the operational staff of the KGB a large group of people from the Central Committee's *apparat* was transferred to us, including Leonid Zavgorodny, with whom I worked in the Fifth Department of the Second Chief Directorate and who, after a short stay in the KGB, became an assistant to Nikita Khrushchev until his overthrow in 1964.

Because Beria himself was from Georgia all the Georgians of the KGB staff were taken off their jobs and were either given a new one or dismissed from the service. One of those to be dismissed was Colonel Datiko Nakashidze, who revealed to us after Beria's arrest that he was a nephew of Beria. His sister, also a KGB employee, had at one time acted as governess to Stalin's daughter Svetlana.

I was the last of the Georgians to be summoned to the personnel department, because my surname does not have a typical Georgian ending and the fact that I was a Georgian was only discovered after someone had been through my personal file. My russified surname served me in good stead, and the personnel people, unable to detect anything typically Georgian in my accent, proposed that I should go on working in the Fifth Department of the Second Chief Directorate. That was how I started to work as a counter-intelligence officer in the Directorate headed by General Pyotr Fedotov with General Oleg Gribanov as his deputy. The head of the Fifth Department, Colonel Davidyan, became deputy head of the Department, to be replaced by a man transferred from the Central Committee *apparat* who had not the slightest idea of operational work with agents but was experienced in the sort of Party work essential for putting across the Party line. He turned out to be a pleasant person who did not put too much pressure on us with his Party mission, realizing full well that he was totally ignorant of our work.

The Ministry of State Security (MGB) was renamed the Committee for State Security (KGB) and attached to the Council of Ministers of the USSR, which was intended to make it clear that the KGB was no longer an independent organization but was subordinate to the government. The man appointed to be Chairman of the KGB was Army-General Ivan Serov, notorious for having carried out the deportation of whole peoples (the Ingushi and Chechens and other peoples of the North Caucasus) and other large-scale military operations. He was short in stature and limited in outlook, a cruel man with little education, with little understanding of the finer points of operational and intelligence work, which is why he did not enjoy the authority he should have had among us operatives. We knew all about his ruthless character and his fondness for bossing people about and punishing them. I was later to meet up with him on two occasions at meetings of the Collegium of the KGB after a visit of inspection to Armenia and Georgia by a KGB commission of which I was a member.

In 1955 we were sent to check up on the work of the KGB in those two republics. We naturally discovered certain shortcomings in the KGB's work there, and discussed them at the KGB Collegium under Serov's chairmanship. Without going into details and not bothering to sort out what had really been going on, he started by demoting the heads of the Armenian and Georgian KGB present. Surveying everyone with a menacing look and trying to give a steely firmness to his voice, he ordered the Deputy Chairman of the Armenian KGB, Mikhail Agayants, to be reduced to the rank of colonel, the deputy head of the First Department of the Georgian KGB, Nikolai Gvinadze, to be reduced to lieutenant-colonel, and so on with every representative of the Georgian and Armenian KGB present. But tragedy soon turned into comedy. The truth was that Agayants was not a general but a colonel, and Gvinadze was not a colonel but a lieutenant-colonel. Serov had demoted them – and the others – to the rank they already held. Serov's attitude to Armenia and Georgia could be explained by his intense Russian nationalism and his hatred of Caucasians. He made no attempt to conceal it, taking advantage of his position and knowing that Khrushchev, whose faithful servant he was, was also known not to be especially fond of Georgians and Armenians. But, despite Serov's devotion to Khrushchev, however superficial and calculated it was, and the help he gave Khrushchev (which will be described later), the Soviet leader removed him from the chairmanship of the KGB in 1958 and put him in charge of the GRU, a less important position.

After the arrest of GRU Colonel Oleg Penkovsky, who became an agent of British Intelligence and with whose family Serov was on close terms, Khrushchev turned him out of the GRU as well. Finding himself in disfavour and, indeed, at last getting a taste of his own medicine, Serov took to drink and, in a state of drunkenness, shot himself in a back alley on the Arbat near a greengrocer's shop where an old friend of his worked. Such was the inglorious end of the cruel general. He did not even merit an obituary notice apart from the announcement of his death, signed by an anonymous group of comrades.

The change of name from MGB to KGB was a pure formality, a political trick on the part of the new Soviet leadership intended to persuade the Soviet population that Beria and his accomplices had wanted to set the MGB above the Party, and to prevent anything similar happening in the future. To make it impossible for the men in charge of the state security service to 'violate socialist legality' the security ministry became a committee attached to the Council of Ministers. This did not, however, change anything in the way the security services worked: we went on as before, because the Party officials were not able to suggest or devise any new ways of working, and those who had been transferred from the Party *apparat* to the KGB, once they had learnt the secrets of the special services, themselves became ordinary operatives applying in their work the classical methods of intelligence and counter-intelligence.

In spite of the fact that I took a sceptical view of the claims that Stalin and his colleagues knew everything, were experts in matters of science, art and culture, and were always right about everything, I was still inclined to believe in their honesty and respect for principles as Party members. I also believed that their efforts were directed at building a socialist society, and that the problems were the natural result of the fact that they were creating a brand new social and political system.

But the 20th Congress of the Party in 1956 and the events that followed it completely destroyed my illusions. Under the guise of fighting against the consequences of the cult of personality Khrushchev and the people around him, who included Suslov, Malenkov, Kaganovich, Voroshilov, Bulganin, Molotov and others, physically destroyed those who had served Stalin and themselves faithfully and loyally.

The first victim was Lavrenti Beria, one of the people closest to Stalin. Arrested on a ridiculous charge, he was executed without any proper investigation or trial. The story that he was tried at a closed court does not, to say the least, correspond with the truth. When I was still working for the KGB in Moscow I took part in a five-hour meeting where the indictment concerning Beria was read out. It was immensely long, but I still remember the essentials. Beria wanted to put the KGB above the Party : as a member of the Politburo and one of the leaders of the Party himself, why should he want to do so? Beria, it was alleged, had been an agent of British Intelligence and of international imperialism. British Intelligence, unfortunately, did not know that it had such a valuable agent in the Politburo and so could make no use of him. As for being an agent of international imperialism, there was no such organization for him to belong to. A serious charge was that Beria was a lecher and not averse to using Colonel Sarkisov, the head of his personal bodyguard, to procure for him the women he selected from the window of his bullet-proof car as he drove round Moscow.

The most important point in the indictment was that, while the other leaders wept at the side of Stalin's death-bed, Beria, unable to conceal his joy at the imminent demise of the leader, proposed the formation of a new Politburo and government. Malenkov was the chief exposer of Beria's criminal and espionage activities and was thanked for his political vigilance.

Nevertheless in 1957 Khrushchev expelled Malenkov from the Politburo and his posts, alleging that Malenkov had shown no such Party vigilance and had been in league with Beria. Similarly Bulganin met his political end, although Khrushchev had recently spoken of him as his close friend.

Khrushchev, Bulganin, Malenkov, Kaganovich and the others had not been able to restrain their tears when they saw their leader and teacher Stalin dying, but three years later, on the excuse of correcting mistakes committed under Stalin's rule, they contrived to lay the entire responsibility for the crimes committed by the Party leaders on to Stalin, denying their own complicity and pleading ignorance.

This kind of nonsense made a bad impression on many of

us working in the security services, because we knew more than most people what had happened in the past: that, for example, it was none other than Khrushchev himself who, as head of the Moscow and the Ukrainian Party organizations, had sent thousands of Party officials and members to the camps and to be executed. It was no secret that tens of thousands of Soviet people had been arrested and executed in the 1930s on orders from the Central Committee and the Politburo. Those orders were carried out by the NKVD. Similar purges were known to have taken place at the end of the 1940s. So what did Khrushchev reveal that was new to Soviet people in his secret speech of February 1956? Nothing whatsoever, apart from the obvious: that he and the other 'true Leninists' had done everything they could not to lose their jobs and, like spiders in a jam-jar, had destroyed each other. The survivors were those who had been most obedient and loyal to Stalin and had conscientiously carried out his wishes.

Such revelations by the leaders of the Party were simply intended to create the impression that a new, more liberal era was approaching, and, since the period came to be described as the 'thaw', was to some extent achieved.

Those of us who worked in the KGB were concerned by this turn of events because the security services were associated with Stalin. Many KGB officers who had conscientiously carried out the task set by the Party and who were not connected with Beria in any way found themselves regarded as criminals; indeed many of them, such as General Rukhadze, General Ysereteli, General Kavtaradze and others, had been violently opposed to Beria.

While Stalin, who liked to have compromising material on his colleagues, was alive, Beria was unable to settle accounts with Rukhadze and the others. But when Stalin died in 1953 and Beria became head of all the security services he arrested his enemies but he did not have time to execute them because he himself was arrested and executed on the orders of

Khrushchev. The men in charge of the KGB and other organizations who had been appointed by Beria were also arrested. One would have thought that those whom Beria had arrested as his enemies would be released, but Khrushchev and Malenkov were too preoccupied with the power struggle in the Politburo. Consequently it was decided to try both groups together as Beria's men and as inveterate violators of the socialist legal system. The job of doing so was handed over to Rudenko, Prosecutor General of the USSR.

I attended the trial, which took place in Georgia in 1955. To add to the drama only relatives of people who had been executed or imprisoned under Beria's rule were admitted to the courtroom. The atmosphere was tense, as was to be expected when those present were told that the men on trial had killed their husbands, fathers, mothers and brothers. But the audience had no means of knowing which of the accused had done the killing.

The accused were asked how their victims had been eliminated – by a hammer, an axe or a bullet? General Tsereteli could not restrain himself and shouted: 'What does it matter what someone was killed with? What matters is that he was liquidated on the orders of the Party.' General Rukhadze, the former Minister of State Security in Georgia, asked Rudenko repeatedly to produce the files held by the Georgian KGB and let the court study the material he had collected against Beria, because he did not want to be tried as one of his supporters. Rudenko paid no attention to Rukhadze's request, and at the end of the three-day trial all of them were sentenced to death.

The accused were permitted to make a final statement. All, as in the case of the Stalinist show trials of the 1930s, admitted their guilt, expressed their regret and asked for their lives to be spared. This is normal procedure in a Soviet court. General Tsereteli, who unlike the others had not lost his human dignity and spirit, impressed me as he looked proudly at his judges and said: 'In my final speech I wish to thank the Central Committee and the Politburo of the CPSU for assessing my work so highly and for permitting me the honour of being shot and not hanged.' Rudenko could not contain himself and shouted: 'Accused Tsereteli, don't blaspheme – these aren't the old days any more!' But Tsereteli turned his back on him.

Similar trials took place throughout the country, but they were not publicized, and very few people knew about them, apart from those working in the security services.

Many people, especially among the creative intelligentsia, were favourably impressed by the reports about these trials, which confirmed them in the belief, especially following the innumerable and verbose speeches by Khrushchev and others, that an era of liberalization or even democratization of the Soviet political system was beginning. The crude propaganda poems of the young Yevtushenko and others, as well as the works of most of the other major writers, encouraged this mood of optimism and the intellectuals began to sing the praises of the new leadership of the Party. They did not know, however, that the KGB had already gathered a huge quantity of reports from informers indicating that the concept of freedom of the individual was getting out of hand.

This is why, in 1954, a new department was created to observe the Soviet intelligentsia and to counteract unhealthy and anti-Soviet tendencies. In 1958 the department was transformed, on account of its importance, into the Fifth Chief Directorate of the KGB, designed to protect Soviet society from penetration by capitalist influences and to conduct a campaign against any developments running contrary to Communist ideology.

My comrades and I understood, though, with some difficulty, that the exposure of the cult of personality, the arrest and execution of Beria and the others, the removal from the Politburo of some, like Malenkov, and the elevation of others, like Khrushchev, were measures designed to bring about radical changes, not in the political system itself –

about which there could be no question – but in the economy and in scientific development. But the expulsion from the Politburo of Molotov, Malenkov, Kaganovich and Bulganin in 1957 on the grounds of their anti-Party activity not only created a bad impression on me but also radically changed my attitude to the leadership of the Party and to socialist ideology.

I could believe that Molotov and Kaganovich were opposed to Khrushchev's secret speech which, after all, had no effect except to discredit the socialist system and cause a split in the ranks of the Communist parties abroad. I do not know whether or not Molotov and Kaganovich realized this, but the fact that Khrushchev's speech had harmed the Soviet Union, both internally and internationally, was obvious to those of us who were working in the KGB.

I was later to learn from Khrushchev's son-in-law, Aleksei Adzhubei, and from Leonid Zavgorodny, who worked as an assistant to Khrushchev, that Khrushchev's differences with Molotov, Kaganovich and Malenkov were not so much about the country's economic and political development as about his desire to establish his personal rule. In short, history was repeating itself, but whereas under Stalin the struggle for power was a tragedy, under Khrushchev it turned into a farce. To accuse Molotov, the revolutionary and Bolshevik, colleague of Lenin and one of the founders of the Communist Party and Soviet state, of anti-Party activity could only be regarded as farcical. It might have been nearer the mark to accuse them all of anti-Khrushchev activity.

Voroshilov and Mikoyan had certainly sided with the 'anti-Party group'. But when they saw that Khrushchev was winning they behaved like good Leninists and switched quickly to his camp, thus ensuring that for a time they remained among the top people. The conflict between Krushchev and the 'anti-Party group' was finally resolved at a meeting of the Central Committee in 1957.

For three days and three nights the battle of words went

on. Nobody left the General Secretary's office. A KGB guard provided them with food and accompanied them to the toilet. Khrushchev needed to gain time, because his faithful satrap, Ivan Serov, the Chairman of the KGB, had ordered all the republican KGBs to deliver all the members of the Central Committee of the CPSU to Moscow, instructing them to support Khrushchev. It was not Marshal Zhukov, as some people have written, who assembled the members of the Central Committee in Moscow and thus enabled Khrushchev to survive, but General Serov. I know this because at the time I was deputy head of the First Department of the Georgian KGB and saw Serov's orders. At the time we did not know the reason for these instructions and only understood why they had been given a few days after the Central Committee meeting ended.

Having expelled all his opponents from the Politburo, Khrushchev became the autocratic ruler of the USSR, and his arbitrary decisions did the country a lot of harm, both in foreign relations and in economic terms. Having condemned the cult of personality, with the aid of his advisers Khrushchev invented a new term, the 'authority of the leader', which led to a cult of Khrushchev as the down-to-earth, omniscient leader of the people. Shortly before he was overthrown the Central Committee decided to celebrate the 'glorious' tenth anniversary of his becoming General Secretary and of the 'great successes' achieved under his leadership in the fields of economics and politics, despite such serious failures as the Cuban missile crisis, the 'maize epic' which inflicted such harm on Soviet agriculture, and other such mistakes. It is true that, in his early days, Khrushchev had made life a little easier for the creative intelligentsia, raised the iron curtain a little, and promised some economic improvements in the near future, all measures which had aroused a certain enthusiasm. But this was soon replaced by scepticism, which frequently took the form of vulgar jokes about Khrushchev.

Although personally I was not a dissident nor held anti-Soviet views, I was becoming disillusioned. But I realized that I had to go on as before, working and living under the system as it was, because there was no alternative. Western democracy and the Western way of life did not tempt me at that time. I did not believe then, and I do not believe now, in the possibility of any radical restructuring of the Soviet system or in any democratic reforms on the Western model. This is not simply because it would be technically difficult to bring about, but because Russia has never had democratic institutions, except for a brief period before the February and October revolutions of 1917. The Russian empire, like the Soviet Union and its people, needed a strong hand at the helm. Most but not all of the intellectuals and an insignificant number of thinking people, both under Tsarism and under socialism, have fought for democratic reforms, but almost always without success, because they have never had the support of the people. The only exception was the October Revolution of 1917, when the armed masses of the people supported the Bolsheviks to gain real freedom. The majority of the Soviet people, in spite of all the shortcomings and difficulties, believes in the present system and in its superiority over capitalism.

PART THREE

The KGB at Home and Abroad

CHAPTER SEVEN

────◆────

The KGB

To BELITTLE THE SUCCESS of the security services in the twenties and thirties against potential enemies of the Soviet regime would be to distort the truth. To explain that success only by reference to the severity of the methods employed would be to fail to understand the historical process and the changes which took place at that time in the minds and disposition of many representatives of the West. The widely advertised claims made by the Soviet Union after the October Revolution about how it was creating 'a society based on absolute equality and the absence of exploitation, unemployment and other shortcomings common to capitalism', linked with the lack of any accurate information about the real state of affairs in the country, and the impossibility of visiting the Soviet Union freely or exchanging information with the Soviet population, played an important part, paradoxical though it may seem, in swinging opinion in the West in favour of the Soviet Union.

That is why the basic principle upon which the recruitment of Westerners in those years was founded was ideology – that is to say, candidates for recruitment were chosen according to the extent of their attachment to or sympathy for Soviet ideas and policy. The ideological basis was used by the Soviet intelligence service for recruiting many a Westerner, among whom was the well-known agent of the British intelligence service, Kim Philby. In the years to come, I had frequently to deal officially with agents who were foreigners recruited on such a basis, and I must say that they were genuinely sincere supporters of socialism who believed in Marxist ideas and served the KGB faithfully as the representative of socialism. Consequently the frequently repeated view that the KGB recruited mainly by compromising people, resorting to bribery and blackmail, is not entirely true. Blackmail and bribery were only employed by the KGB as the principal means of recruitment much later, when Westerners who had previously been pro-Soviet began to realize that socialist ideas which appeared so attractive in theory turned out very differently in practice; also that the socialist system in the Soviet Union itself, instead of being a system of social equality and freedom, had become a cruel totalitarian regime disposing of its opponents mercilessly by means of severe repressive measures and executions, as was the case in the years 1937 and 1938 and at the end of the 1940s.

What changes have taken place in the conduct of Soviet counter-intelligence since Stalin's day? The principles underlying the work remain the same, but different methods are used. The Soviet brand of socialism does not allow any deliberate or involuntary deviation from or criticism of the domestic or foreign policy decided upon at the top. Nor can there be any criticism of the actions of the Party leadership. It is the function of the state security organs to prevent any form of opposition and where necessary to take repressive measures against dissidents. However, today there are fewer executions, though I am not convinced that it is better to have to drag out one's life doing hard labour in a prison camp because one's thoughts and opinions do not coincide with the official views or because one would like to emigrate abroad, a right recognized by the Declaration of the Rights of Man to which the Soviet government subscribes.

To carry out satisfactorily the intelligence tasks set it by the Party leaders the KGB requires enormous material resources, to maintain both its operational staff and its network of agents. Apart from the Party leadership and the KGB bosses themselves nobody knows what sort of budget it disposes of: nothing has ever been published on the subject. However, one of the main differences between the early years of the Soviet regime and today is that the permanent staff of the KGB now consists of highly educated people, whose selection does not depend on their proletarian origin or avowed devotion to the Party ideology. They speak one or more foreign languages and are quite capable of passing themselves off as professional men.

During the Second World War, when our country was in danger, people of my generation, including myself, were attracted to work in the KGB out of a desire to fight the country's enemies and Fascism. Today the KGB is an élite corps, entry to which is virtually impossible for the average Soviet citizen, especially to the central offices in Moscow or the republican capitals. The KGB now recruits most of its staff from the universities and academic institutes on the recommendation of Party committees or highly placed and influential individuals. Many of those accepted into the KGB have already been recruited into its service as informers or agents.

In educational institutes such as the Moscow State Institute of International Relations, the Foreign Languages Institute and the Moscow State University there are KGB officials working in the personnel departments. Apart from being responsible for counter-intelligence, it is their job to study students' behaviour, abilities and interests to discover if they are suitable for employment in one of the KGB agencies. Those who are selected and have completed their higher education are usually sent on an initial one-year course. They attend the KGB school in Moscow, now on the Leningrad highway near the Belorussian station, where they continue their general education, studying foreign languages, Marxist–Leninist theory and the special disciplines connected with work in the secret police. In addition the

KGB occasionally recruits staff from among full-time Party officials, usually when the Central Committee thinks it necessary to reinforce the KGB *apparat*, as for example following the 'quiet' palace revolutions of 1953 and 1964.

The demands placed on a case officer are rigorous. The service requires absolute honesty, devotion to the Party and the work entrusted to him, unhesitating fulfilment of orders from his superiors, and strict self-discipline in his work and in private life. A case officer has to be discriminating in his choice of acquaintances among Soviet people, to avoid intimate relations with women, to exercise moderation in drinking and to observe the strictest secrecy with regard to official secrets. On joining and on leaving the service an employee has to sign an undertaking not to reveal in any circumstances anything about his work in the KGB in written form or by word of mouth. The undertaking ends by saying that, in the event of a breach of trust, the signatory will be subject to prosecution on a charge involving a prison sentence. The KGB thus not only prevents leakage of current secret information but also deters former members of the KGB from publishing their memoirs. Publication of any literary or documentary work about the KGB is possible only by prior agreement of both the KGB and the Central Committee and then under strict censorship. Of course, in spite of the high standards demanded of them, and the severe penalties for breaches of those standards, drinking too much, getting involved with women and quarrelling at home are no less prevalent among KGB employees than they are among employees of other government departments.

It is not easy to define exactly what it is that attracts young people to work in the KGB. There seem to be two main motivations. One category of person joins the KGB for patriotic reasons, believes that by working in intelligence or counter-intelligence he will serve the state, in the knowledge that it is work for real men and not for rarified intellectuals. The other category sees in the KGB an opportunity of joining a privileged and financially secure group and also of wielding power over others. Many KGB employees are motivated by both.

The salary of the average desk officer in the KGB is twice or three times that of a qualified doctor, teacher or engineer. Such high salaries are intended to ensure that KGB employees experience no material difficulties that might prevent them from devoting themselves entirely to their work, and also to make them less likely to yield to bribery. In addition to his salary every case officer has the right each year to a free rail or air ticket for himself and his wife to any place in the Soviet Union or the Communist countries of Eastern Europe, as well as two practically free vouchers to a sanatorium or rest home. The KGB has its own private polyclinics and hospitals for the treatment of its employees and their families. The doctors and staff of such places are themselves on the payroll, with the rank of officers. Entry to the polyclinics, hospitals and rest homes is possible only with a special pass.

There are two reasons why the KGB has these private, or 'closed', places for treating its employees, where the conditions and treatment are incomparably better than what is available to ordinary people. One is the need to prevent people working for the KGB being identified as such. The other is to avoid undesirable contact between the KGB employees and other members of the public.

Such privileges inevitably give KGB people a sense of their own exclusivity and importance as well as their superiority over the rest of the population. This has the effect of cutting them off psychologically and even physically from the Soviet people and turns them into an élite.

In the course of many years' work in Soviet intelligence and counter-intelligence, I myself experienced that sense of superiority over other people; it was as if their lives were spread out before us on a cinema screen; we knew, and they didn't, what the future had in store for them, and we would be amused at their efforts to keep from their families something that we knew about.

Today, unlike the 1930s, KGB case officers do not wear military uniform and in their dealings with people outside the service describe themselves as journalists, scientists or some other kind of professional specialist. This is not because Soviet people come out in a cold sweat at the mention of the KGB (as a matter of fact, they don't), but because they wish to conceal their true profession for security reasons.

Despite the fact that the KGB is still, today, as it was in the 1930s, an organization which can inflict severe punishment, the majority of Soviet people seem to be neither for nor against it. Their opinion of the KGB is formed by articles and films showing the security organs protecting the Soviet people from the subversive activities of the imperialists and the Western intelligence agencies.

For a case officer to be dismissed from the KGB is a major psychological disaster, primarily because he is deprived of his sense of superiority and power. This sense of superiority gradually becomes an integral and accepted part of his being, and anything that tends to threaten it or the failure of another person to acknowledge it provokes a bitter and hostile reaction, especially in case officers of limited intellectual capacity. This explains the quite unjustified severity towards dissidents displayed by some counter-intelligence officers, especially in the provinces. As for the camp guards and convoy troops (about whom much has been written by former Soviet prisoners) they belong to the very lowest category in the KGB, because their qualifications are not respected even by officers in intelligence and counter-intelligence. To confuse officers of the First, Second, Fifth and other Chief Directorates of the KGB with the sort of people staffing the prison camps is to misunderstand the nature of the modern KGB.

The KGB employs around half a million case officers

inside the Soviet Union and abroad and has at its disposal a vast network of agents, internal and frontier troops, and special commando units. The KGB comes directly under the control of the Politburo and Central Committee of the Party. It has never been and will never be an independent organization, but has always been and will always be the right hand of the Party leadership and the executor of its will. The last two chairmen of the KGB, Yuri Andropov and Viktor Chebrikov, have been members of the Politburo.

The present-day structure and organization of the KGB is, in brief, as follows:

The First Chief Directorate – intelligence
The Second Chief Directorate – counter-intelligence
The Third Chief Directorate – military counter-intelligence
The Fifth Chief Directorate – suppression of ideological
     dissidence
The Ninth Chief Directorate – provision of bodyguards for
     Soviet leaders
The Technical Department
The services responsible for surveillance and telephone
     tapping

The KGB's principal weapon for carrying out its intelligence and counter-intelligence operations is its *agentura* – its network of informers, people who have been recruited by the KGB and who carry out its instructions. Upon the quality of its agent network depends the success of all KGB operations at home and abroad.

The existence of a far-flung network of informers makes it impossible not only for any unofficial organization to come into being in the Soviet Union but also for any contact with foreigners to take place without the knowledge of the authorities, as I saw in the early 1950s, when I was working in the Second Chief Directorate in the department dealing with foreign diplomatic missions and foreign journalists accredited in Moscow.

Many years later, in 1979, returning from abroad I met a colleague with whom I had worked there. The question came up about dissidents who had left Russia, what they got up to abroad and how they fared. To tell the truth, while I was working in the TASS agency in Moscow I had heard very little about dissidents in the Soviet Union, because, like the majority of the Soviet population, I was not particularly interested in them. They were not very popular or well known, and Soviet people only learned their names after damning articles about them appeared in the press. But when I was working abroad I learned a good deal more about them, and I was curious to find out from my friend what the actual situation was with regard to dissidents inside the country. He told me that practically all the dissidents and those who shared their views were under surveillance by the Fifth Chief Directorate because their anti-Soviet activity did not represent a danger to the Soviet regime. It was true that the fuss they made abroad about various issues was something of a thorn in the side of the Soviet leaders, but it was not likely to have any tangible political results. What is more, my friend continued, in any group of five dissidents you could be sure that certainly one, and possibly two, of them were informers for the KGB, so that if the secret police were to receive orders to put an end to the dissident movement it would not take them more than an hour to round them all up. 'But,' he went on, 'we have no intention of doing that. We have already sent some of the more troublesome ones abroad, while others have gone to prison camps, and we need to leave the rest alone so that we can observe who next becomes a dissident.'

The KGB's later actions with regard to dissidents confirmed my friend's view: the dissident groups were broken up and some of their members arrested, with the result that today it is as naive to talk about a dissident movement in the Soviet Union as it is to deny that there is opposition – albeit unorganized – to the Party's domestic and foreign policy.

For what I term a society of automatic agreement there can of course be nothing more dangerous than the Western concept of freedom. That is why every foreigner who comes to Russia is regarded as a potential enemy. The Second Chief Directorate – one of the biggest and most important divisions of the KGB – is responsible for maintaining surveillance over all foreigners posted to or visiting the Soviet Union. The KGB's aim is to detect which of them is working for or is in any way connected with foreign intelligence services; to put a stop to their spying or other anti-Soviet activity; to prevent undesirable contacts between Soviet citizens and foreigners; to recruit foreign diplomats, journalists, businessmen and other foreigners stationed for a long or short time in the Soviet Union; to gather compromising material about foreigners for use in case of need; and to organize operations to compromise undesirable foreigners with a view to expelling them from the Soviet Union, either as a reprisal or when the Soviet leaders find it necessary.

The Second Chief Directorate also has a special service which deals with the screening of Soviet citizens who travel abroad to work in Soviet missions or as members of delegations. Whether a Soviet citizen will be permitted to travel abroad depends entirely on that service, and its decision cannot be overruled even by the Party *apparat*.

One of the most remarkable achievements of the Soviet regime is to have established a highly efficient system of surveillance over every Soviet citizen from the cradle to the grave. It is not an achievement that Soviet officials often boast about, nor one that they discuss much in public. There is in any case no need to talk about it to the Soviet population, because every single person is only too well aware of the way his every move is watched. The average Soviet citizen does not even object to being under constant observation: he has come to take it for granted.

Every adult member of the population has to have a labour book without which he cannot be employed anywhere and which records all his previous places of employment and the reasons why he left each job. Consequently it is easy to find out where he was working and what he was doing in the past and difficult for anyone to conceal any aspect of his career.

In addition every Soviet citizen has to carry an identity card which records all the places in which he has ever lived. A person arriving somewhere on holiday or visiting another town on duty or simply visiting a friend is obliged to report within three days to the nearest police station and obtain a temporary permit to stay. A breach of this regulation can lead to a fine or worse. No other document, such as an employment certificate or, as in the West, a driving licence, can take the place of the official identity card. Every Soviet citizen is well aware of the importance of carrying his identity card, because even if he commits a very minor offence – say, crossing the road where it is not permitted – the policeman will demand to see his identity card at once. Unless he has it on him, he will be detained by the police until his identity is established.

This system has been in operation since the very first days of the Soviet regime. The famous Soviet poet Vladimir Mayakovsky said he dreamt of a time when it would be sufficient for him to say he was Mayakovsky and he would be believed and would not have to produce a passport to prove it.

It is an unpleasant, humiliating system based on distrust of the individual. At the KGB school I was taught that one should see each person primarily as a criminal; even if he has proved he is not, one should then regard him as someone who had not yet committed an offence. The same attitude, but many times stronger, prevails in the Soviet police force, which has a far greater power to arrest any Soviet citizen than have the officers of the KGB. The police can even detain members of the security services for traffic offences or if one of them, under the influence of drink, commits an offence likely to lead to a breach of public order. Relations between the KGB and the police are, therefore, antagonistic, despite their professional collaboration. When KGB officers refer to the police they usually describe them as garbage. But though KGB employees have the chance of protesting their innocence if they are in trouble, the man in the street is powerless once he is in the hands of the police.

These are only the more obvious aspects of the system of control and observation over all Soviet citizens. There is another less well-known aspect of the system for which the KGB is responsible. Every Soviet person who is taken on for work involving access to secret information or who applies to travel abroad, even if he is an employee of the KGB, military intelligence or one of the governmental bodies, is carefully screened by a special department of the KGB. The screening covers not only the person himself but also his parents, his grandparents, his close relations, and the circles in which he moves, both past and present. All the KGB archives and police records are checked, and the person's neighbours are questioned. Consequently, without knowing why, even the most honest and loyal Soviet citizen may be refused permission to travel abroad or to take up a job because – for instance – his father or grandfather committed some minor offence, or because a neighbour has it in for him and has accused him, not necessarily of being 'anti-Soviet', but of being a bad family man or of drinking too much. Slanderous statements such as these might not be sufficient to ruin a man's prospects but they could easily swing the balance if the KGB had other doubts about him. If the KGB archives reveal that the person's relatives have had some connection with someone under investigation or, even worse, that they themselves have 'sinned', then his cause is lost.

This is why the business of preparing all the documents

necessary for travelling to a capitalist country has to be started at least six months before the departure, and to a socialist country at least three months before. When these preliminaries are complete the final decision is taken in the Central Committee of the CPSU, irrespective of whether the would-be traveller is a member of the Party or not. No Soviet citizen can travel abroad without going through this procedure, unless he happens to be a member of the Soviet 'establishment'. As they rightly say in the Soviet Union, the law is a spider's web in which only little flies get caught, while the bigger ones break through and fly wherever they please.

If an ordinary Soviet citizen wants to travel abroad on business or on holiday he has not only to go through the screening process to demonstrate his devotion to the Soviet regime; he must also have serious reasons for his journey, confirmed by his superiors at work and in the Party. But members of the Soviet élite and their children and relatives have no problems about travelling abroad on official business, more often than not travelling at the expense of the government – that is, of the people. They can go off to Western Europe or the United States on any excuse: to study, for example, the taking of the Bastille or the architecture of Venice, or even just to wander around Paris or Rome as tourists.

Similarly, practically every foreigner arriving in the Soviet Union, whether he be a diplomat, a businessman, a sportsman, a scholar, a journalist or a simple tourist, is caught up in the KGB's network on arrival and some remain under constant surveillance till the day of their departure. The surveillance is skilfully done, which is why some foreigners announce proudly that during their stay in the Soviet Union they were completely free to come and go as they pleased and suffered no interference. In fact they were all under observation.

It would, however, be an exaggeration to say that Soviet

counter-intelligence maintains continuous surveillance over every single foreigner who comes to the Soviet Union. Any professional intelligence officer knows that even a counter-intelligence service as well staffed as the KGB could not maintain the huge *apparat* that such total coverage would demand. It has to be selective in its choice of targets.

Before a foreigner who applies to enter the Soviet Union receives his visa he is carefully screened by the KGB on the basis of its vast records and of a report received from the KGB *rezidentura* in his country of origin. If the foreigner turns out to be 'clean' he may not be kept under constant observation, though he will be surrounded by informers. But if there is any doubt about him, he will be kept under observation until he leaves and, depending upon the KGB's plans, appropriate prophylactic measures or special actions may be put into effect, such as attempts to compromise, blackmail or even expel him from the country. This applies to temporary visitors as well as to foreigners on permanent posting.

From my own experience I can say that in our handling of foreign diplomats, journalists, businessmen and military attachés in particular, we were interested not only in rendering them harmless and in the possibility of recruiting them or using them as sources of information or even as agents of influence. We were also anxious to select from them suitable candidates for expulsion from the Soviet Union – for being compromised in some way, and then arrested and accused of engaging in some kind of spying or sabotage activity.

All foreigners stationed permanently in Moscow we divided into three categories. The first included the anti-Soviets – that is, people who disapproved openly of the Soviet system and made no attempt to hide their dislike of the Soviet leaders' domestic and foreign policy. Then there were the neutrals, those who did not voice any anti-Soviet views but at the same time who could not be classed as people sympathizing with the Soviet system. And finally there were the 'loyals', people who not only showed no signs of holding anti-Soviet views but who even considered the Soviet system to be progressive and who had an understanding attitude to Soviet policy.

In selecting candidates for expulsion, we paid special attention to the first two categories. By setting our agents on to them and recruiting the chance contacts they made themselves we aimed to gather as much information as possible about their work, their interests and their ambitions, in order to use these facts against them later. We also used the agents, with whom many of the foreigners had established relations of trust after knowing each other for years, to feed them with rumours and information to suit our cause or simply for the purpose of disinformation.

We also collected information about such candidates through other foreigners we had recruited and our own contacts and agents in order to prepare fat files on them. A particularly favourable occasion for attaching KGB agents to foreigners in the Soviet Union is when diplomats, journalists or businessmen go on trips to the Soviet non-Russian republics. Every foreigner, even if he is only a tourist, who visits one of the Soviet republics will be kept under observation round the clock and no contact he makes with the local inhabitants will go unnoticed. Later, if it appears to be worthwhile, the local person will be called in by the KGB and any further contact with the foreigner will be made under the direction of the KGB. Early in my career in the KGB and later in the 1950s when I was deputy head of a KGB department in Georgia I was myself responsible for keeping foreigners visiting Georgia under observation.

The principal candidates for being expelled or accused of spying were, and still are, diplomats, journalists and businessmen from the United States, Britain, France, West Germany and other capitalist countries. But there are also people from the Third World who voice anti-Soviet views or who maintain close contacts with representatives of American or Western European countries.

Operation aimed at the expulsion of a foreigner stationed in Moscow are carried out when there is need to rescue a Soviet intelligence officer or agent arrested abroad, or when it is deemed necessary to step up or initiate a campaign aimed at discrediting the activities of the intelligence services of the United States or the countries of Western Europe and the policies of their governments.

The question of whether a foreigner from Western Europe or especially the United States is to be exposed for some offence is decided at the level of the Secretariat and Politburo and must be approved by the General Secretary. Without such approval no such action by the KGB can be carried out.

Once the decision has been taken the operational plan is put into practice. The agent with whom the foreigner is on good relations or believes he has unofficial contact with is given instructions to take some secret documents to a meeting or, if that method has already been used, to leave them in a letter drop. The rest is, as they say, just a technical matter. The arrest of the foreigner presents no problem. If it is only a question of compromising and later expelling the person in question, the agent is arrested and later confesses that the foreigner tried to recruit him or use him for distributing subversive literature or collecting secret information. This sort of agent operates under a false name and his arrest is simply a put-up job. Occasionally of course such contacts are not KGB agents, and they themselves are under observation by the counter-intelligence service.

When members of foreign delegations visit the Soviet Union great efforts are made to get them to report favourably on their trip when they return home. Carefully planned programmes are drawn up by the host organization or, in the case of tourists, by Intourist, the Soviet state travel agency.

At the Union of Journalists I spent seven years drawing up such programmes for forty or fifty delegations a year, not to mention for a number of individual foreign journalists.

For the Soviet Union the tourist business is not primarily a source of income, since the number of tourists from the West is relatively small; it is mainly a means of conducting propaganda. Intourist's chief task, and the chief task of every organization entertaining foreigners in Russia, is to show foreigners Soviet life in the best light and to try to persuade them of the advantages of socialism over capitalism in all fields of activity. It is hoped that the visitors will pass the message on to their friends and perhaps write complimentary articles in the press.

This aim was prevalent in the days when I attended meetings of the Central Committee concerned with the spreading of propaganda among visiting foreigners. I recall a meeting at Party headquarters in the early 1960s at which Boris Ponomarev declared that propaganda could not be expected to show a profit in financial terms but that its political effect could often be impressive. It was a game worth the candle.

It is no exaggeration to say that the Intourist organization works primarily for the KGB and that the whole of its activity is under the control of the KGB. Among the huge staff of Intourist employees there are to be found full-time KGB officers as well as a large number of KGB agents working as guides and interpreters for tourist groups. At the end of each day all the intepreters have to report to the official in charge of the group, who in turn has to report to a KGB officer about the tourists' behaviour, their comments, their mood, their wishes, their political views, their efforts to make contact with any Soviet citizens – in fact, about everything the KGB might want to know. In the event of a tourist breaking away from the group he or she is immediately put under surveillance to discover any possible contacts with Soviet people or with other foreigners in Moscow.

The surveillance team is also watching for suspicious activities, such as the handing over of packets or books, the posting of letters (in which case the post box is immediately checked and the letter removed for examination), or attempts to photograph forbidden places.

If the KGB comes to the conclusion that the foreign visitor is engaging in undesirable activity it takes special steps to deal with him. Arrangements may be made, for example, for him to be detained on the street by 'ordinary' Soviet citizens who find him taking photographs and for him to be taken to a police station where his film will be exposed. Everything depends upon the extent to which the KGB considers the person concerned to be a danger to the Soviet regime. There are plenty of well-tried ways of dealing with a dangerous visitor. On every floor in every hotel there is a chambermaid on duty at her desk who is in fact a KGB informer paid to record all the comings and goings of foreigners and their visitors. If a foreigner leaves his room at an unusual time the duty informer immediately lets the KGB representative in the hotel know and the visitor is followed to his destination.

The principal concern of the Soviet counter-intelligence service is to maintain complete surveillance of the foreign embassies, consulates and other missions in Moscow and of the foreign correspondents accredited there. I was engaged on this work from 1953 to 1955 and played an active part in operations aimed at recruiting, compromising and blackmailing foreign diplomats and journalists and at establishing friendly contacts with them for subsequent follow-up by KGB men when they returned to their countries. Consequently I have a fairly complete knowledge of the methods employed by the KGB.

It is not only the diplomatic missions of the Western capitalist countries and the Third World that are kept under observation by the KGB: all the socialist embassies are similarly treated, especially those of Yugoslavia and Rumania, with whose governments and Communist parties the Soviet leaders do not see eye to eye on all questions. The KGB keeps diplomats from the socialist countries under observation in order to discover their contacts with Western diplomats; these are important for counter-intelligence and because such contacts might be useful for obtaining information and even for recruitment.

The KGB has at its disposal all the necessary financial resources and the most up-to-date technical equipment for conducting counter-intelligence work. Even back in the 1960s I was using, both in Russia and abroad, sophisticated apparatus developed by the KGB's Technical Department for listening to and recording at a distance conversations between people in whom we were interested. Since that time great advances have been made with such apparatus.

The monitoring service for listening in to people's private conversations – mainly telephone tapping – is a vast organization. It employs translators from all languages, from Hebrew to Swahili. All flats occupied by foreigners and all hotel rooms used by foreign visitors are equipped with bugging apparatus. The same is true of the more fashionable restaurants in which there are separate cubicles used for friendly meetings with foreigners.

The business of bugging has apparently acquired such dimensions in the Soviet Union that, on my last visit to Moscow in 1980, when I called on a very highly placed friend in his office for a private talk, even he turned on the sound of his television set as loud as it would go, giving me a knowing wink as he did so. And this was a man with the rank of a deputy minister who was listed in the Central Committee's *nomenklatura*.

Once they have been translated, the recorded conversations of foreigners are handed over to the appropriate departments of the KGB, where they are carefully analysed to determine the character, tastes, habits, moods and political views of the target, as well as his relationship with his wife. If he is very talkative the recordings may contain information of greater value. By observing the target and listening to his conversations the KGB hopes to hit on the best way of attaching an agent to him and then finding a favourable situation for recruitment, either on ideological and political grounds or by means of blackmail or just plain bribery.

The business of cultivating a foreigner posted to work in the Soviet Union actually begins long before his arrival. First of all, the KGB obtains the fullest possible information about him from the *rezidentura* of the First Chief Directorate in his own country. This will normally include information about his political opinions, his connections, his relations with his family, his habits and tastes, his drinking habits, attitudes to money, to women and so forth. He should, in the language of the KGB, arrive in Moscow 'quite naked' so that they can set about dressing him in other clothes.

The KGB is also responsible for conducting intelligence operations abroad. This is handled by the First Chief Directorate, which, since 1972, has had its headquarters not in the main KGB building on Dzerzhinsky Square, but in a specially built building at Yartsevo, near Moscow. This move from the centre of Moscow was dictated by the need to keep from the public view people who might be expected to work abroad under the guise of diplomats, journalists, representatives of commercial or other organizations, of Intourist, Aeroflot, or as staff at the headquarters of the United Nations Organization in New York and its agencies in Geneva, Paris and Vienna.

The First Chief Directorate also conducts counter-intelligence work among Soviet citizens abroad, keeps an eye on their contacts with local people, official and unofficial, as well as with members of other diplomatic missions in the country they are posted to.

The main task of people working for the First Chief Directorate, however, is the recruitment of foreigners for use as agents for the collection of information or as 'agents of

influence' who are in a position one way or another to
influence the policy of their government, to publish articles
containing disinformation, to spread rumours, and so forth.
People recruited in this way are also used to obtain secret
information about a country's political and economic situation, about its military potential and about statesmen and
public figures who are of interest to the KGB. The First
Chief Directorate also seeks to obtain examples or plans of
the latest inventions which are needed by the military-
industrial complex of the Soviet Union. The KGB also
recruits foreigners who may be of use in organizing demonstrations and riots and even acts of sabotage and terror in the
event of an emergency. Finally, the First Chief Directorate
is responsible for training experienced Soviet intelligence
officers for penetrating foreign countries as illegals. These
people live ordinary innocent lives, perhaps running small
businesses and the like, waiting for the day when they may
be called into action.

To provide cover for its intelligence operations the KGB
makes great use of Soviet embassies and international organizations which provide its officers with diplomatic immunity, so that the worst that can happen to any spies caught
red-handed is to be expelled from the country. For example,
a KGB colonel called Alexeyev was Soviet ambassador to
Cuba, and, subsequently, Madagascar. The TASS agency
also offers good opportunities, because correspondents are
usually free to move around, to make contacts with local
people and to extract information from them. For this reason
at least one-third of the TASS correspondents working
abroad are trained Soviet intelligence officers; many of the
other two-thirds, the 'pure' correspondents, are also obliged
to collaborate with the KGB. TASS has staff correspondents in practically every country in the world, but the most
important for the Soviet authorities are those in the West,
and there the agency has the most correspondents and most
KGB officers.

The TASS cover is also used by employees of the so-called Marketing Institute, which is not to be found in any official reference book but whose representatives are engaged in commercial and industrial espionage in the United States, Britain, France, Italy, Japan and the other industrially advanced countries.

In 1974, two years after I had returned to Moscow after more than five years as a TASS correspondent in East Africa, I called on my friend A. Baranov, Deputy Director of TASS, to discuss my next job abroad. There was a huge map of the world on his wall with little flags indicating where TASS correspondents were stationed. We began to look for a place for me in the English-speaking countries where the 'pure' correspondents were working.

'You've set me a difficult task,' Baranov said with a smile. 'Wherever you look, our "neighbours" are there already. Only Zambia is still free of them. You'd better go there before they grab that too.'

The 'neighbours' are, of course, the KGB. There are many countries in which for years now the TASS offices are staffed entirely by KGB and GRU officers. These include Iran, Turkey, Tanzania, Mali, Liberia, Ireland, Portugal, Spain, Malaysia and many countries in Latin America. In countries where there are two TASS correspondents, one of them is usually a KGB or GRU officer. On one occasion, just after the revolution in Angola, two GRU officers were sent there at once in the guise of TASS correspondents but without any journalistic training, and the KGB was quite upset at not having its own correspondent there. In the mid-1970s, when I worked at TASS, I used to meet the General Director, Leonid Zamyatin, daily. I was present one day when he agreed by telephone to allow the TASS correspondent in Dublin, Yuri Ustimenko, to be replaced by a KGB officer, because the situation in Northern Ireland was of such interest to the KGB. On other occasions, Zamyatin just as readily handed over Portugal, Spain and Brazil to the

KGB as well as some of the correspondents' jobs in TASS offices in London, New York, Washington and Paris. In other words, even a man of Zamyatin's importance was not in a position to withstand the demands of the KGB. In the Soviet Union it is sufficient to declare that you are working 'for the general cause' to defeat any 'local interests' that may be put forward.

The KGB also makes use not only of such magazines as *New Times* and *Asia and Africa Today* but even the Communist Party daily *Pravda* and the government newspaper *Izvestia* and any others that have correspondents stationed abroad. In Cuba for many years the *Pravda* correspondent was a KGB officer, Vladimir Paromonov, while the *Izvestia* correspondent in Spain in the mid-1980s was a KGB officer.

Even if relations between the governments of East and West improve, Soviet intelligence operations will not be reduced. Intelligence work and relations between states are totally independent of one another and it is a great mistake to confuse them. That was what I was taught at the KGB school and during my work in Soviet intelligence. So the KGB and GRU will go on sending their officers abroad in the guise of diplomats and journalists and Western governments will go on expecting them.

CHAPTER EIGHT

Counter-intelligence at Home

FOR NEARLY THREE YEARS, from 1953 to 1955, I worked in the Second Chief Directorate, in the department responsible for studying the diplomatic missions of the countries of the Near and Middle East. My own group, consisting of three people, dealt with the Turkish, Egyptian and Iranian embassies. We had dossiers on all the diplomats and non-diplomatic staff of these embassies, containing not only official information but also information obtained by agents of the *rezidentura* of the First Chief Directorate. The information in the dossiers was quite exhaustive; we knew all about these people's past lives, their sexual preferences, their habits, their attitude to money, and so on.

We usually did not need this information in order to identify spies or people likely to get involved in anti-Soviet activity, because in the great majority of cases we already knew who belonged to which organization. Where it was useful was in determining the possibility of our being able to establish contact with a diplomat, say, with a view to getting him to collaborate. We might even be able to establish such a relation of trust that he could be used by the First Chief Directorate when he returned home or went to work in other countries.

Our group also had to find ways of getting into the embassies in order to photograph documents, to steal ciphers and other operational documents, and to obtain information, to be reported to the Central Committee, about the political plans of the governments of the countries concerned, especially those relating to their links with Western countries.

To give some idea of how we set about carrying out our tasks, I will recount a few examples of operations in which I took part personally, but I shall have to alter certain names in the interests of the safety of the people concerned.

In the summer of 1953 a good-looking young diplomat, whom I shall call G., arrived in Moscow to work in one of the Near Eastern embassies. We knew even before he arrived that G. had no connection with the intelligence service of his own or any other country, that he was interested in literature and history, but that his main interest was European women. He was a bachelor, came from a prosperous family, spoke good Russian and, it appeared, had every prospect of having a successful diplomatic and political career. I was given the task of handling him.

The men keeping him under observation drew attention to the fact that G. liked visiting restaurants with eastern cuisine where he became friends with the waitresses – rather than with prostitutes, who were easy to find in the Metropole Hotel, where he was living until the department responsible for servicing the diplomatic corps could find him a flat in one of the blocks built specially for foreigners. This department, the UPDK, is officially part of the Soviet Foreign Ministry, but in fact it serves the interests of the KGB. We would make sure that diplomats found it difficult to obtain accommodation: we then offered to help them to solve the problem and thus established friendly relations with them. Unfortunately, all G.'s casual acquaintances, who were duly summoned to the KGB office on Kuznetsky Most and questioned, were unsuitable for one reason or another for use in our little game. So they were advised not to go on meeting G. because they might make it difficult to plant our agent on him.

Our observation of G. revealed that the restaurant he used most was the Uzbekistan, where he spent quite a lot of time perfecting his knowledge of Russian. So we decided to plant an agent of ours, a very attractive blonde (we know G. liked blondes), as a waitress there. She was to attract G.'s attention and get on friendly terms with him. Our interest in G. had increased because he had established good relations with British, American and French diplomats whom he met frequently. We reckoned he could be a good source of information about what was going on in those embassies.

I had no difficulty in fixing up our agent Marina with a job in the restaurant. I called on the manager of the restaurant, showed him my KGB identity card, and told him that it was essential to us that Marina should work there. I realized that it was not a good idea to have the restaurant manager, a rogue, aware of what we were doing, but he didn't dare to argue or ask any questions, and he agreed at once. I still don't know whether he actually had a vacancy. It was difficult to get a job as a waiter in a restaurant because in order to do so you had to bribe the restaurant management. In those days it was about 500 roubles; today it is much more.

Marina started work in the 'Uzbekistan'. She was a young woman who had not finished college for family reasons, and had begun to lead a dissolute life, picking up men and taking part in drunken orgies. She then met by chance a diplomat with whom she became intimate, which was how she was drawn into collaboration with the KGB. She had been working as a 'plant' for several years. Young, pretty and sexy, she had no difficulty in capturing the attention of men. G. proved to be no exception. The first time he visited the restaurant after Marina started to work there she caught his eye and he pressed her to spend the rest of the evening with him. Marina had been given a strict warning not to agree at once but to play the part of a respectable, decent young woman. She did as she was told, and it was only when we gave the word that she agreed to meet him and later to move in with him. In both G.'s hotel room and in the KGB flat, which Marina said belonged to a friend, we set up bugging apparatus and cameras concealed in the wall-clock, the radio and the mirror. All their sexual activities were recorded by the cameras. Such dirty work was necessary if we needed ever to discredit the young diplomat or force him to collaborate with us.

The affair that I am describing is not in any way exceptional: the same methods have frequently been used, and are still being used today, generally with success, and not only by the KGB. It was with the help of a KGB agent, the opera singer Lapshin, that in the late 1940s a woman employee of the American embassy, Anabella Bucar, was persuaded to defect to the Soviet Union. In the early 1960s Yuri Krotkov, a KGB informer, and others brought the French ambassador Dejean under control. Many diplomats and even ambassadors were compromised at one time or another. I have to admit that the KGB staff were contemptuous of the agents involved in such work, especially if they were male, although we found it impossible to manage without them. We considered ourselves to be higher in the social scale, and would never agree to do such dirty work, though it was permissible in the national interest to get others to do it.

The relationship between Marina and G. developed according to plan. G. was very upset because he could not obtain a flat from the UPDK and complained to Marina that he could not begin to live a normal life. The time had come to organize a chance meeting between myself and G. It took place in the Aragvi restaurant where I went to dine with my 'wife' Valya, another of our agents. Marina introduced me to G. as a member of the staff of the Institute of Oriental Studies, a friend of her brother who was away on business in the East. After some pointless chatter I asked him for his impressions of Moscow, the theatres, restaurants and life in general. G. said he liked living in the capital and had been

struck by the freedom he enjoyed and the things he had seen
after all he had heard about foreigners being followed, the
danger of being caught up in some unpleasant affair, and so
forth. G. was convinced that nothing of the sort was going
on: nobody was following him about and he was completely
free. But would he not get into trouble if his ambassador got
to know that he was meeting a Russian woman? I asked.

'Yes, I could expect some trouble from him. He has no
faith in Communists and, like our President, he fears them
and hates them,' G. replied.

'But you are not scared?' I asked.

'No,' he said. 'Because I have spent many years in Europe,
where I studied and graduated from university, where there
were Communists and Trotskyists and Fascists and goodness knows what else. But that doesn't bother me at the
moment. I like practically everything here: the only thing I
don't like is how slowly your civil servants work. For three
months now they have not been able to find me a flat, I still
haven't unpacked half my belongings.'

I looked surprised and asked him whether he would object
if I were to try to find out what was the matter. I had, I said,
some good friends in the Foreign Ministry who, though they
were not directly concerned with such matters, might be
able to help – not officially, of course. G.'s face lit up at my
suggestion. He gave me one of his visiting cards and asked
me to phone him if I needed anything from him.

I declined his invitation, saying that it would be incon-
venient for me to phone him at the embassy, because members of the staff of state institutions were not encouraged to
have close relations with foreign diplomats. What's more, he
might get into trouble himself. I told him it would be better
not to advertise the fact that we knew each other. G. agreed.
I said it would be better if he would phone me at the
institute, because a lot of foreigners called us up there and his
call would not make anyone suspicious. I then wrote down
on a table napkin a telephone number which appeared in the

telephone book against the Institute of Oriental Studies, though the telephone itself was on my desk in my office at the KGB. (The extremely efficient Second Chief Directorate can arrange to have telephones with the numbers of any ministries or departments and when necessary it can have embassy phones switched over to its own office. For example, on one occasion in 1954 a Crimean Tartar phoned the Turkish embassy and wanted to arrange to meet someone from the embassy to discuss a very serious and urgent matter. The Turk who answered him was apparently unable to decide the question himself and suggested that the Tartar should phone back in an hour. In exactly an hour the Tartar phoned the same number from the same call-box, but this time he was speaking, not to the Turkish embassy, but to me, who had to play the part of a Turkish diplomat.)

Anyhow, as we had agreed, G. rang me a few days later and I passed on to him the glad news that my friend had agreed to help, but on the understanding that complete secrecy would be observed. Within a matter of days he would be offered a flat. That was what happened and, as time went on, if my relations with G. could not be called close, we seemed to trust one another. More than once G. asked me to give him some idea of how he could thank my friend and me for the good turn we had done him. I tried to convince him that it had been done out of friendship and that no one expected any reward. Even so, when G. went on a trip to Western Europe he brought me back a Swiss Omega watch, which I recorded officially as government property and when our operation was over I handed it over to the KGB accounts department.

I continued to meet G. in restaurants with Marina and my 'wife'. As a specialist in Oriental affairs I could ask him questions about his government's aims in domestic affairs and various national-liberation movements – subjects which would not arouse his suspicions, especially as we talked in the presence of our ladies.

Once installed in his flat on the Kutuzov Avenue, G. decided to celebrate his move, and asked me and my 'wife' to have supper in his home. I turned down the invitation, saying that I would not want my connection with him to be revealed to anybody as the block he was living in was guarded round the clock by the police. G. agreed to celebrate somewhere else. Meanwhile, I suggested, it would not be a bad idea for us to meet and talk about this and that without our women.

We met in the Aragvi restaurant. The conversation moved gradually on to political topics and I began to ask G. about his government's policy towards the Soviet Union, America and other Western countries. I asked him to sketch me a political portrait of the President of his country, to tell me about his past, and so forth. Naturally, I did not ask these questions because we genuinely wanted to find out about the President or his government's policy, but so that G. would get used to hearing this sort of question. G. answered my questions in a relaxed manner and talked more openly every time we met. He told me about the diplomats he knew who were working in the American, British and French embassies, about the matters they discussed, and so on. This was not simply because I had done him a favour or was on the surface very open with him, criticizing some aspects of life in the USSR, it was rather because what we called the 'familiarity factor' was beginning to come into play : eventually even the most cautious person drops his guard and forgets that the person he is talking to represents a foreign state. The familiarity factor played a quite important role later when I worked in East Africa. My tennis partners, who included the President's assistant, took only six months to forget that I was a Soviet official and talked to me as openly as they did among themselves, so that I got to know some important facts. Some were about other politicians and the government's plans, while others concerned the President's private life, his relations with his wife, the rows they were having, his mistresses, and so forth. But you need patience and caution to use the familiarity factor properly, because clumsy behaviour or excessive curiosity can reveal your true intentions. This did not happen with G., however; he regarded me as an Orientalist and was quite ready to share with me his knowledge of matters that interested me. I was already well informed, from what G. told me, about the other members of the embassy staff, two of whom had also been drawn into our little game by my colleagues Mikhail Agazaryan and Nikolai Rakhmanov. This made it possible for us to check the information we were getting, and to judge whether our contacts were playing straight with us and whether they were ripe for recruitment.

One day in the spring of 1954 a Soviet citizen scrambled over the wall of the embassy where G. worked, a situation regarded by the KGB as an emergency demanding immediate action to establish who the person was and what were his intentions. This can be discovered through the official channels of the Foreign Ministry, but in this case it was decided to try and find out the identity of the man from G., thus killing two birds with one stone: first, to check to what extent he had become accustomed to me, and, second, in the event of his producing the necessary information, to establish a relationship of secrecy between him and me.

To make it clear to G. that something serious had happened I phoned him at the embassy, contrary to our arrangement, and told him it was essential that we should meet urgently. I told him to be at Sverdlov Square near the entrance to the Metro and that we would then decide where to go. Because this meeting with G. was so important it was decided that I should invite him 'home', that is, to a KGB flat, so that he should realize that the question we were going to discuss was serious (and, of course, so that we would be able to record the conversation). G. was genuinely surprised when I told him that we were to go to my home (where he had never yet been) because the matter could not be discussed in a restaurant.

Once we had settled down in the flat I told G. that the friend who had helped him with his accommodation had approached me with a request to discuss with G. a very important issue. If G. would tell us what we wanted to know, my friend and I promised him that not a single person in the world would ever find out where the information came from. I noticed that G. became very tense in anticipation of my question.

'It's like this,' I went on. 'We have learnt that there is a Soviet citizen hiding in your embassy. He climbed over the wall and was seen by the policeman at the gate, who asked your people to hand him back but they refused. The Foreign Ministry can, of course, send your ambassador a note of protest demanding the man's return, but that would only cause unnecessary complications between our countries and we don't want that. At the same time, once we know who the man is and what he is up to, my friend, who has an important position in the Foreign Ministry, can take the heat out of the affair and, instead of getting involved in official exchanges, the whole business can be cleared up in semi-official talks. But in order to do that we must know who the fugitive is and to what extent he represents a danger to us.'

G. didn't know what to do. It was awkward for him to refuse to give the information to me, but if he did so he would be breaking the laws of his own country. Seeing how undecided he was, I told him that I understood how difficult and delicate his position was, but that I wanted him to understand my situation. If I was unable to fulfil such a trifling request from my friend, G. might have some difficulties in the future and I would no longer be able to appeal to my friend for help. We knew that G. was planning to buy a car for himself in West Germany and to bring it to Moscow. To create bureaucratic obstacles over the importation and registration of the car would not be very hard for us.

Having taken a drink of brandy, no doubt to keep his courage up, G. then told me that the man who had climbed over the embassy wall had identified himself as an engineer working in an aircraft factory in the Ukraine. He had come to Moscow to contact a Western embassy with a view to defecting to the West. But all the Western embassies were so strongly guarded that it was impossible to get into them. He had found himself near G.'s embassy by chance. There was only one policeman on duty and the wall round the court-yard was not very high and easy to climb. He was asking for political asylum.

'Our ambassador has sent a telegram in cipher to our Foreign Ministry asking what he is to do,' G. said. 'True, the Ukrainian speaks very poor English, so that sometimes we don't understand him at all, and he behaves strangely, either from nervous tension, or from . . . I don't really know what. I am able to talk to him in Russian, and that is why the ambassador doesn't want to let me out of his sight, so that it was very difficult for me to get away from the embassy to meet you.'

I advised G. to tell his ambassador that it would be better for both our countries if the man were to be handed over to the Soviet authorities, since without permission from the Soviet government he would never be able to leave the Soviet Union, even in the diplomatic mail. With that we parted. G. followed my advice faithfully and persuaded his ambassador not to upset relations with the Soviet Union because of some disturbed Soviet citizen, who had not only ruined his own future but had put the ambassador in a delicate situation.

The Ukrainian was duly handed over, and G.'s conversation with his ambassador was recorded by our monitoring service and entered in his dossier.

G. continued to give me a good deal of information of interest to us, and we were able to keep the Foreign Ministry and Central Committee informed not only about his government's policies but also about individual diplomats in other embassies. We ourselves used this information to make contact with those diplomats and to determine their relations with Western intelligence services. At the same time, when we came to study the material produced by the monitoring service it became clear to us that G. was becoming ever more disillusioned with the Soviet system, and was beginning to understand that behind the socialist façade of freedom and equality the reality was the exact opposite. Nevertheless there was every indication that he would soon be ready for recruitment, though we could not be completely certain about it. For that reason the head of our department decided to carry out an operation aimed at compromising G., in order to bind him hand and foot.

Marina was told to act the jealous mistress and stage a scene which was to end in a quarrel and a fight. G. would naturally come out on top: we knew that he had more than once inflicted bruises on Marina. Marina carried out her task to perfection and the results of the row exceeded our expectations. I was really sorry for Marina when I saw her. Her face and body were covered in bruises and she had a broken rib. Not suspecting anything, G. prepared for a week's trip to Sweden on business and booked himself a seat on a plane. When all the medical certificates had been prepared concerning Marina's injuries, I phoned G. at the embassy and said I wanted to see him urgently. We met in the Aragvi restaurant at two o'clock in the afternoon. I had a gloomy expression on my face, to indicate that it was a serious matter. I told him that Marina, whom he had beaten up two days previously (at which G. sat up in his seat), had had, without saying anything to me or my wife, a medical examination and the report, with a statement by her, had been sent to the courts, which would then send a copy of the documents to the Soviet Foreign Ministry, since G. was a diplomat.

The deputy head of my department, Colonel Artem Davidyan, who had initiated the whole operation, told me that I was to hint to G. that it might be possible to settle the whole affair with the help of an influential friend of mine working in the Supreme Soviet, but that I could not guarantee anything. Davidyan himself was to play the part of the influential friend, since our bosses liked to complete an operation themselves, to recruit the foreigner personally and then report its successful conclusion to the heads of the KGB. We operatives were given all the tough preparatory work but appeared at the actual recruitment only as witnesses.

I had serious differences with Davidyan about the final trick played on G. I was opposed to the decision to compromise him, because, despite the doubts of my superiors, I had a strong intuitive feeling that G. could be drawn into collaborating without us having to compromise him. I was convinced it would leave a deep and unpleasant impression on G. and moreover turn him against me. In this I was proved right.

When I told G. about my influential friend he grasped at the suggestion like a drowning man at a straw, because he realized that, if he were summoned to court, his fate would not be decided there, since he enjoyed diplomatic immunity, but by his own government, which handed out severe punishment to people who broke the laws of the country and of the Muslim religion. We were also aware of this.

G. put off his trip to Sweden and a couple of days later we met with my 'influential friend' in 'my flat' where, following a very ample lunch, most of which was consumed by Davidyan, while G. hardly touched his food, I explained briefly to Comrade Davydov (as we called Davidyan) what my foreign friend's problem was. G. himself tried to tell Davidyan something, but Davidyan simply asked whether G. had indeed struck Marina, to which G. replied in the affirmative. Davidyan said it was a serious business but that he would try to help. To do so he would have to speak with his friends in the Foreign Ministry and the Procurator's office, who might ask him in turn why he was taking up the case of some foreigner who had committed a serious violation of Soviet law and nearly killed a Soviet woman.

'What can I tell them?' Davidyan asked, looking hard at G. 'Shall I say that you are a friend of a good acquaintance of mine or that you are just a good fellow? Or shall I say that you are repentant and that, with tears in your eyes, you persuaded me that you had made a mistake that you will never repeat? After all, you must know that Moscow doesn't believe in tears, and neither do my Moscow friends. No, there must be a more serious and substantial reason capable of persuading us.'

G., very tense and nervously clenching his fists, heard Davidyan out, apparently suspecting something but still not quite understanding what Davidyan was driving at.

Davidyan pursued his argument: 'As far as I know, you represent a country which has recently acquired its independence, having rid itself of the yoke of colonialism. But you are again threatened by imperialism, in the form of neo-colonialism. Your government is fighting imperialism, but the main force in the struggle against imperialism is the Soviet Union. Imperialism cannot be defeated by talk alone. You have to take action to fight it. In order to fight you have to know what the enemy intends to do tomorrow and who is helping him or is preparing to help him in the struggle against the progressive governments. I will not conceal the fact that these questions interest not only me but my friends as well, and if you agree to help us against imperialism, then I shall be able with confidence to tell my friends that we are also helping a worthy man and one who is our friend. If, however, you turn down my proposal it is hardly likely that I could be of any use to you.'

G.'s fate was decided. He was, as I have already said, a young diplomat and one who appeared to have very good prospects. We were not mistaken: he later became an ambassador and filled responsible posts in his country's Foreign Ministry and also in the office of its President.

Some time early in 1963 Norman Borodin, who was in charge of Tenth Department of the Second Chief Directorate and was responsible for handling foreign correspondents, called me at the Union of Journalists and asked me to meet him to discuss an important matter. We met in the restaurant of the journalists' club on the Suvorov Boulevard. This restaurant was known at the time as one of the best in Moscow, with a large selection of delicacies. The club was open only to members of the union and to people with special passes. It was my business to see that all the people working in the KGB section handling foreign newsmen were issued with passes to the club or with union cards enabling them not only to use the club themselves but also to invite foreign newsmen and diplomats there. But on such occasions Norman and other men working in the department would check the time of their meetings with me, so as to avoid any undesirable encounters.

We made ourselves comfortable in a private cubicle in which we usually entertained members of foreign journalist delegations and where the editors of the Soviet national dailies and periodicals used to get together. One such editor was Aleksei Adzhubei, who was such a frequent visitor that sharp-tongued newsmen had named the cubicle the *Adzhubeyevka*.

After several glasses of brandy and an ample meal Norman turned to business. He told me briefly that the KGB had been conducting an operation aimed at recruiting a Swedish woman journalist accredited in Moscow, whom we will call N. An experienced KGB informer, Valeri Lednev, who was on the staff of the newspaper *Soviet Culture*, had been attached to her. N. had apparently fallen in love with

Lednev, had quickly become intimate with him, and the couple were living practically as man and wife, but not officially registered as being married.

Lednev had been provided with a KGB apartment in Moscow and a cottage in the country near Moscow, where he and the Swedish journalist gave themselves over to their amorous delights. Lednev was, of course, not concerned with love-making so much as with carrying out the task set him by the KGB: obtaining political and other information and using N. for spreading disinformation and softening her up for the final act of the love story – recruitment.

The problem was, according to Norman, that, although N. was ripe for recruitment, she was having some doubts about whether Lednev seriously intended to marry her and whether he occupied an important enough position and had influential enough contacts. 'N. has seen you more than once at receptions and knows you are a leading journalist,' Norman said. 'Join us in the country for our New Year's party and then you can convince N. that Lednev doesn't lie all the time.'

On New Year's Eve all the people working for Norman Borodin gathered at the KGB *dacha* together with some people I didn't know from the department handling the Swedish embassy and others from the First Chief Directorate who needed to get to know N. personally. The evening passed off in a friendly and relaxed atmosphere. N. behaved with complete composure, as though she were in familiar company and despite the fact that Lednev adopted a rather coarse manner towards her, no doubt deliberately. Towards the end Captain Vladimir Krivosheyin (who was shortly afterwards to take his own life) proposed a toast to the happiness of Valeri (incidentally, a married man) and N. and to the success of our common cause. N. raised no objections and sank a full glass of vodka at one gulp.

N. knew perfectly well that she was dealing with the KGB, and had come entirely voluntarily to the point of being recruited. The operation was, apparently, successful.

After leaving Moscow Lednev continued to work for the KGB and even carried out responsible tasks outside the Soviet Union. He was a revolting character whom I always disliked; I felt like washing my hands after shaking his. He was not above playing the part of the lover–seducer and being photographed by hidden cameras in indecent poses with N. in the interests of operational necessity. But he was just as unclean and crafty a type in his own life, and as slippery as an eel. It was with much distaste and some surprise that I later discovered from my former colleagues that he acted as a secret courier between Leonid Brezhnev and Willi Brandt on the recommendation of Vyacheslav Kevorkov and the Chairman of the KGB, Yuri Andropov.

Similar methods were used to recruit many a foreign diplomat and journalist. Recruitment based purely on compromising a person cannot be guaranteed to provide 100 per cent success, any more than can recruitment based on a community of views concerning the policy of Western countries or on anti-Western tendencies, because in both these cases there is no certainty that the target will not later try to present what has happened to him as an act of provocation or that he will not change his political views. Consequently 'compromisation' is employed rather as a back-up to a recruiting operation. In the event that the target refuses categorically to collaborate, then the material assembled can be used to threaten exposure and expulsion from the Soviet Union.

In its dealings with foreigners, the methods used by the KGB depend on the personality and character of the foreigner and the aims being pursued. For example, a certain Roy Essoyan, an American citizen, Armenian by origin, arrived in Moscow as correspondent of an American news agency. According to material provided by our *rezidentura* in the USA, Essoyan was an experienced journalist and a clever and serious person. We also knew that he was fond of his family and that he had recently suffered a great misfortune: his son had died of poliomyelitis. Having considered a number of possible candidates to act as a contact with Essoyan the heads of the Second Chief Directorate chose me because I was from the Caucasus, spoke Armenian and could pass myself off as an Armenian. That the choice fell on me was due in no small extent to my good relationship with Norman Borodin. In the mid-1950s the work of handling foreign journalists accredited in Moscow was dealt with by a department consisting of about ten desk officers. By the 1980s, however, it had become a very important department headed by a general and having a network of agents in every organ of the Soviet press. These agents were planted on foreign correspondents with the object of either recruiting them or using them to obtain information of interest to the Soviet leadership or as channels through which to spread disinformation.

As deputy to the General Secretary of the Soviet Union of Journalists from 1957 to 1965 I co-ordinated the union's activities with this department and took part in a number of operations aimed at establishing contact with foreign journalists and recruiting them. The degree of success which the department had in its work of recruitment may be judged by the fact that Kevorkov and other members of his staff were on more than one occasion given military decorations by the Soviet government – decorations that are not easily won.

My acquaintance with Essoyan came about 'by chance' at one of the many receptions in Moscow. Since Essoyan was an Armenian we reckoned that my interest in him would not make him suspicious, since it was rare to have an Armenian as an American correspondent in Moscow and it was very pleasant for me, Gurgen Ovsepyan (as I was known then), an Armenian and correspondent of the paper *Soviet Sport*, to meet a compatriot in Moscow. Apart from that, the fact that I worked on a newspaper that had very little connection with politics was calculated to reassure Essoyan and give him no reason to suspect me of dirty work. I naturally carried a press card. In the course of getting to know Essoyan I started to speak in Armenian, to indicate that my interest in him was because of his Armenian background, but in fact he spoke practically no Armenian, while my English was inadequate for carrying on a conversation on everyday matters, let alone on political or other problems. A way out of this difficulty was found by providing me with a 'wife', Galya, who was a translator in the KGB's phone-tapping and bugging service.

After a few meetings with Essoyan I reported that the possibility of recruiting him either for ideological reasons or by means of compromising him seemed very slight on account of his political views, though it would be difficult to class him as anti-Soviet. It was decided I should carry on meeting him to establish really friendly and trusting relations with him and convince him that my intentions were sincere and disinterested. I came to like Essoyan a lot, both as a person and as an interesting interlocutor, and we soon began to speak frankly to each other. My 'wife' and I visited him in his apartment, discussed topics of general interest, and only rarely got on to political subjects. On one occasion when we were talking about the possibility of our meeting somewhere in the USA I expressed doubts about the likelihood of such a meeting, because *Soviet Sport* did not have a correspondent there and was hardly likely ever to do so. But I took advantage of the suggestion to ask Essoyan whether he would be prepared to meet any of my friends if one of them should be in the United States and if he would help them get to know the country and other newsmen. My friend would, of course, have with him a letter from me and perhaps some little gift.

Roy Essoyan replied that, although he did not speak Armenian, he had Armenian blood in his veins, and he would welcome a friend of mine in the Caucasian manner and would do everything in his power to help him. I don't think Essoyan suspected anything, because all our conversations took place through my 'wife' and were mainly of a totally neutral nature. His readiness to meet my friend in the USA confirmed this, and this was regarded as a definite success. It meant that, when Essoyan was in the United States or even in some other country, a colleague from the First Chief Directorate, working under cover of being a newspaper correspondent and provided with a letter to Essoyan from me, could get in touch with him and continue the contact with the object of using him for exchanging information or spreading disinformation, or as what is now described as an 'agent of influence'. In the end, however, my contact with Essoyan came to nothing because as a result of the disorders in Georgia in March 1956 I was sent to work in Tbilisi.

Our Middle and Near Eastern Department was considered one of the most successful at recruitment and at penetrating embassies. It was also the best off in terms of young and attractive women agents whose role I have already described. We used men as agents in making contact with foreigners, but usually only as an intermediate link before the operation was taken over by the desk officer or the *rezident*, who had a safe apartment at his disposal and several agents working for him.

For a long time such a *rezident* and recruiter was Mikhail Agazaryan, son of the murdered Secretary of the Communist Party of the Lebanon, who was brought out to the Soviet Union in 1944. Agazaryan spoke fluent French, Turkish and Arabic, could easily be mistaken for a foreigner – which is what in fact he was – and was clever, cunning and when necessary resourceful. He applied all these qualities to great advantage in his work with foreigners; they got along well with him, not suspecting his real job. The heads of the KGB used Agazaryan for recruiting foreigners 'under a foreign flag', that is, on behalf of a Western or other foreign intelligence service. Above average height, with eyes as black as olives and jet-black hair, and always wearing suits made abroad, Agazaryan passed himself off to foreigners as a representative of business circles in Turkey, Syria or Iraq, or as a businessman himself operating in a Western country. His 'legend' depended on the sort of person he had to work on.

There were times when Agazaryan was taking part in three or four operations at the same time, using different names and 'legends' in each case. This gave us a lot of trouble, because we had to keep a careful watch over his encounters with the various targets to exclude the possibility of his bumping into another of his contacts. For example, if Agazaryan was meeting a contact in the Aragvi restaurant, not a single foreigner would be allowed to enter. If necessary a notice would be put up on the door saying 'no room' and one of our men standing next to the door-keeper would admit only Soviet citizens. These measures were quite effective, and throughout the many years he worked with foreigners Agazaryan was never once exposed and enjoyed considerable success. For example, Agazaryan would recruit a Turkish diplomat while pretending to be a Frenchman working against the Soviet Union, or a Syrian diplomat under the guise of an American.

Agazaryan's success in the work was so impressive that, after some years working as a *rezident*, he was taken on to the staff of the KGB as a desk officer. Such agents are, however, very rare, and most of those we used lacked his talents.

In the past all the departments of the Second Chief Directorate, which were divided on a geographical basis, were involved in counter-intelligence and recruitment work. But today the Directorate has a special department to deal with the recruitment of foreigners, staffed mainly by people from the First Chief Directorate. The department was set up to make it possible to use the recruited or well-disposed foreigner after he had left the Soviet Union and was living abroad without a situation arising, as it had in the past, where the intelligence service was afraid to deal with foreigners recruited by the Second Chief Directorate because they doubted the quality of the recruitment. It was for that reason that, during my time, the majority of foreigners recruited in Moscow were never made use of abroad.

In describing these operations I do not want to give the impression that foreigners living in Moscow were always so naive that the planting of a KGB agent on them or the establishment of contact with them came about as quickly or as easily as I have described. We understood perfectly well that, however naturally and seemingly successful a plant was carried out, we could have no guarantee that the foreigner had not smelt a rat. For that reason we were inclined to prefer it when a foreigner made contact with a Soviet person on his own initiative. In such a case we took steps to recruit the Soviet citizen first and use him for our own purposes. If we did not succeed in recruiting him, as sometimes happened, or if he turned out in our opinion not to be suitable, then we had to persuade him, and if necessary to demand, that he should find a convenient excuse for ending his connection with the foreigner. Our proposal that the contact should be ended did not usually evoke any protest or resistance, so that we seldom had to enforce obedience.

I have travelled through practically the whole of the Soviet Union and had innumerable meetings not only with the middle echelon of Soviet officialdom but also with the ordinary people, and I can state with assurance, from my experience, that the majority believe the propaganda that any foreigner coming to the Soviet Union is probably a spy. That is why Soviet people take the view that only two categories of Soviet citizens will have anything to do with foreigners: those whose job it is to do so, and idiots. Idiots, because contact with foreigners that is not sanctioned by the KGB can have distressing consequences and may lead to charges of revealing state secrets or even of spying.

This general belief suits the authorities very well, because it acts as a hindrance to meetings with foreigners, whom they regard not so much as spies as carriers of Western influence which is harmful to Soviet people and undermines the propaganda aimed at persuading the people of the superiority of the socialist way of life over the Western way. Did those working in Soviet intelligence and counter-intelligence believe this propaganda? No, certainly not. We were in a better position than anybody to know who was who and what was what, but we did our duty as required by the Party leaders because we believed our work was for the good of the country.

Every Soviet citizen coming to the attention of the KGB because of contact with a foreigner had to be called in and questioned about his relations with him, and we had to evaluate whether there was any use to be made of the contact or whether it should be broken off. We would call on him or her either at home or, more rarely, at work, and introduce ourselves as Party officials so that the people around should not be suspicious. This was primarily because we did not wish to expose the person's possible future links with the KGB, and also to avoid involving him in any difficulties at home or at work, because when the KGB calls on someone an over-vigilant boss may use the visit as an excuse to get rid of a person apparently under suspicion.

Having shown the person concerned our KGB identity card we would reassure him that nothing serious had happened (otherwise he might have a heart attack, for which we would be responsible), then tell him that we had to clear up some matters and invite him to accompany us to Kuznetsky Most. Our initial approach was carried out in a calm and friendly manner, as was the questioning. We were strictly forbidden to shout or threaten, and in any case we were not inclined to. We mostly used persuasion and suggestion, although the people we were questioning did not always react kindly to us. I say this with authority, although it contradicts many accounts published in the West describing encounters with KGB officers, who are depicted as coarse, cynical and uncultured. This may have been true of operatives in other KGB directorates, especially outside Moscow, where the level of education and culture is not always as high as it should be, but it was not so in the Second Chief Directorate.

However, if we met with stubborn resistance and the person being questioned refused to take our advice or fall in with our demand that he or she should stop meeting the foreigner, we would warn him or her that we would be obliged to resort to measures of an educational or even administrative kind.

One such operation concerned a young scientist working in one of the Moscow institutes who had had frequent meetings with the counsellor in the Turkish embassy. I had him brought to my office, and once he had recovered his composure and was convinced that no one was intending to arrest him or put him in prison, I asked him to tell me how, when, where and why he had got to know the Turk, how many times they had met and what they had talked about. We already knew the answers to these questions, but this was the form the questioning had to take. It was 'questioning' and not 'interrogation', because only people under arrest are interrogated.

After he – let us call him Viktor Pavlovich – had told me frankly about how he got to know the Turk and his meetings with him, I asked him what interest he had personally in maintaining his contact with the Turk. None at all, he replied.

'Viktor Pavlovich,' I said, 'you are an educated person and you must realize that you cannot possibly have any interests in common with a foreigner, either professionally or personally. Moreover, you do not know who that person really is or what his real intentions are as far as you are concerned. You got to know him by chance in a restaurant when, to put it mildly, you were not entirely sober. So what? It could happen to anybody. But what was the point of exchanging telephone numbers and continuing the contact, especially since you are working in a closed institute and have access to secret work? Incidentally, did you tell him where you work?'

'No, as far as I remember, neither then nor afterwards did we touch on that question. We talked about things in general.'

'All right, but you know that Turkey belongs to NATO, collaborates closely with the United States of America, and is hostile to us. Can you exclude the possibility that your friend is connected with the American intelligence service or is working for Turkish intelligence?'

'No, of course, I can't.'

'Then what's the point of you, a Soviet person, getting mixed up with a foreigner about whom you know nothing, thereby exposing yourself to danger? Not because of us but because of him; we know that he is working for the Americans. He is a spy and is looking for Soviet people who are weak-willed enough to be used for gathering anti-Soviet information or even for spying themselves.' (This was pure invention, intended to give a certain sharpness to our talk, to inject some tension into the situation.)

'If you read the papers,' I continued, 'you can see that no foreigners ever maintain contact with Soviet people from feelings of friendship. They are usually pursuing some selfish ends and gradually, by pretending to be well-disposed and straightforward, lure a naive person into their cunningly set trap. Such a relationship can result in serious crime and then a belated repentance. It is our task, therefore, as a security service, to protect Soviet people from the encroachments of foreign intelligence services and to prevent them making fatal mistakes. That is the purpose of my talking to you now.'

'I understand and I give you my word that I will never

meet this fellow again,' replied Viktor Pavlovich. 'I'll go a hundred miles to avoid foreigners in future. Believe me, I had no personal interest in meeting this foreigner and I didn't tell him anything. I was, I suppose, led astray. But that's it, I'll never see him again. Do you believe me?' Viktor Pavlovich had seen the light.

'I believe you,' I said. 'We know you didn't tell him anything important, otherwise we would not be talking to you in such a friendly way. But don't be in such a hurry to break off relations with him. Let's think the situation over together and see whether we can't make use of your acquaintance with this foreigner in the interests of our country. He wants to out-smart you, but we can be smarter than he is. He wants to use you as a source of information, but with your help we will make use of him.'

'I'm not sure I understand you,' said Viktor Pavlovich.

'Take it easy, and I'll explain. Casual meetings between Soviet people and foreigners are dangerous, both for them and for us. But if they take place under our control they are no longer dangerous and can be of use to us. As a Soviet citizen it is your duty to help us to expose the real intentions of this foreigner. To do that you will continue your friendship with him, but under our control. You will have to be completely straight with us and follow our instructions to the letter. This is a serious matter, and if for some reason you can't help us, don't be ashamed to tell us but let us know why. Don't refuse to help us; such an opportunity is not entrusted to everyone.'

After some reflection Viktor Pavlovich agreed to help us, not because of the trust we had shown in him but because he was worried about his future prospects.

I then invited him to sign a document stating that he agreed to collaborate with the KGB and had been warned that if he revealed his collaboration he would be liable to punishment under article so-and-so, for revealing a state secret. I then suggested that he should choose a pseudonym so as to exclude the possibility of his being identified and to keep his collaboration with us secret. We agreed about how we would communicate with each other and then parted. He was now a KGB agent or informer.

The counsellor in the Turkish embassy would hardly be suspicious of Viktor Pavlovich, since he had not been planted on him: it was he who had sought out Viktor Pavlovich.

This case is typical of those in which we recruited Soviet citizens who had become friendly with foreigners and who had the right qualities for our purposes. But the system did not always work so smoothly and simply. There were sometimes cases where the Soviet citizens refused to collaborate with the KGB or even to break off their relations with the foreigners. In such cases – and they usually involved young women – we were concerned not so much that they might give away secrets or get involved in spying as that they could prevent us from planting our own woman agent on the foreigner concerned. We then had to resort to tougher measures, such as keeping them in the police cells for up to forty-eight hours or warning them that they might be deported from Moscow. For example, the daughter of the chief architect of the city of Moscow, Natasha Lopovok, was a girl of easy virtue who, despite being urged repeatedly to break off her relations with an Egyptian diplomat, for whom we had our own plans, went on meeting him. She also told him about being called in by the KGB and the warnings she had received, thus breaking the promise she had given not to reveal her contact with us.

We were formally entitled to charge her with a criminal offence, but we preferred not to. We summoned her father and asked him to help. After talking to us he sent her off to stay with relatives in Sverdlovsk in the Urals, where there were no foreigners.

It is not only direct contacts between Soviet citizens that are considered dangerous by the Soviet leaders and the

KGB. We had also to prevent contact with foreigners through third persons, if it might lead to a leakage of important or secret information. I have mentioned before our woman agent known as Sincerity. She was an attractive young woman but depraved and of an adventurous disposition. She had, on our instructions, established an intimate relationship with a Turkish diplomat whom we were preparing for recruitment by compromising him. All their love-making had been recorded on film. Sincerity, who was amazingly insincere and an inveterate liar and fantasist, announced that she had decided to break off relations with the Turk because she had just met a Soviet admiral who had declared his love for her and offered to marry her. The heads of the KGB were afraid that the admiral, who was talkative and liked to show off in front of women, might pass on some secret information to Sincerity, who was still involved with a foreigner. Sincerity's relations with the admiral had to be cut short.

At one of our regular meetings in the Moskva Hotel I asked Sincerity whether she felt any affection for the admiral. In her usual rather mocking manner she replied that her affections lay where there was money, a substantial position and comfort, all of which the admiral could provide. I was sceptical about the reality of this love affair, but a few days later Sincerity was seen meeting a vice-admiral in the Savoy restaurant by our agents. For once Sincerity was not making things up and might really break off relations with the Turk and so put paid to an operation to which the KGB attached great importance. As the officer responsible I was called in by General Oleg Gribanov, the deputy head of the Second Chief Directorate.

'What do you think?' Gribanov asked. 'Does Sincerity really count on that idiot of an admiral marrying her?'

'I don't know what the admiral is thinking about,' I replied. 'But Sincerity is determined not to let him go, so it will be difficult to get her away from him. She sees it as a magnificent opportunity to become a *grande dame*. It is use-less to threaten her, because she will only tell the admiral about her contact with us, and will ask him to protect her.'

Gribanov flushed with anger. 'If you can't cope with the little whore,' he said, 'I shall have to have a talk with this idiot personally. Have him delivered to me here in this office.'

The admiral worked on the naval staff, and it was no simple task to organize his 'delivery' to Gribanov. Even if I waved my KGB card at him he could go tell me to go jump in the river. After the arrest of Beria high-ranking officials believed, erroneously, that the KGB was a spent force.

A friend of mine, Captain Leontyev, also worked on the naval staff so I invited him to supper in the KGB's Dzer-zhinsky club, told him about my problem and asked for his help. Leontyev said that if we were simply to invite the admiral to call at the KGB building he would ignore our invitation. There was only one way, and that was an opera-tion in which he, Leontyev, could not take part. I under-stood what he meant. The admiral would have to be snatched somewhere in the street and delivered to Gribanov. I needed Gribanov's approval for such an operation, and when I asked for it, he said, 'Do it any way you like, so long as you get him here.'

I put the admiral under surveillance and tapped his private telephone. It was autumn and darkness fell early. The admiral lived on the Frunze embankment, which was practi-cally always deserted. From the phone-tap we learnt that he would be meeting Sincerity at eight o'clock in the evening at the Aragvi restaurant on Gorky Street. I decided to snatch him on the way to the restaurant. Normally when the admiral was meeting Sincerity he did not use his official car but took a taxi, and it was easy to have one of our cars disguised as a taxi.

As the admiral left the front door of the building our taxi started to move in his direction. He signalled it to stop, got into it and asked to be taken to the Aragvi. We followed in another car. The admiral became suspicious only when the taxi, having turned sharply into the side-street where the Aragvi was, suddenly shot off at great speed towards Kuznetsky Most and up the hill to the KGB building. The taxi-driver pulled up at No. 4 entrance, turned to the admiral and said: 'Here we are – we've arrived.' I opened the taxi door, showed the admiral my KGB card and invited him to follow me. As he was surrounded by several impressive-looking young men, he agreed.

'Am I under arrest?' he asked abruptly.

'No, comrade admiral,' I replied. 'You are invited for a talk with the general.'

Gribanov's office, like all offices of the top KGB people, was camouflaged. As you entered the ante-room where his personal assistant worked it was difficult to find the door to Gribanov's office, because it was disguised as ordinary book-shelves, which also served to make it impossible to hear what was going on inside. The office itself was spacious: wooden panelling covered half the walls giving a sense of solidity, while the wall-lights and a huge brass candelabra in the Stalin style gave the visitor an impression of crude power.

The admiral was in naval uniform. Gribanov, in civilian clothes, came from behind his desk with a friendly smile on his face, apologized to the admiral for this unusual way of getting to know him, and extended his hand. The admiral refused to shake it. Instead, he demanded gruffly to know what was going on. Gribanov invited him to sit down and explained that we had been obliged to resort to such an unusual method because, had we sent him an official summons, we might have damaged his reputation and given rise to false rumours. Apart from that, we did not want our meeting with the admiral to become known to anyone, because that might harm state interests. This was only a half-truth.

The admiral still understood nothing and sat there with a very arrogant look on his face. Gribanov then asked the admiral straight out, without any preliminaries, how serious his intentions were with regard to Nina (as he knew Sincerity). At this question the admiral shot up in his chair and shouted that that was his own private business and that he would not let anyone interfere in it. Gribanov paid no attention to the admiral's rough manner, and continued:

'Do you realize that Nina is living with a foreign diplomat and is simply making a fool of you? Apart from that, you, holding an important position on the staff of the navy and, incidentally, a married man, are not only violating the principles of Communist morality: you have unwittingly become involved through Nina with a foreign diplomat from a country hostile to us. At the moment, and I repeat – *at the moment* – we do not intend to take any steps against you so long as you break off your relationship with Nina. I cannot reveal to you everything we know about her and this foreigner, but you must believe me when I say that your relationship with her is damaging the interests of the state.'

The admiral did not listen to what Gribanov was saying, and started shouting that he didn't give a damn about our interests, that Beria's days were over, and that he would demand that the Party's Central Committee should take the necessary steps to put a stop to the KGB's contempt for the law and its interference in people's private lives. 'Unless I am mistaken, general, you and I will meet again in the Central Committee.'

'Very well,' said Gribanov. 'If you want to go to the Central Committee, so be it. I doubt whether the matter will go that far. But don't get angry with us if you come to regret that you didn't take our advice, which was given you with the best of intentions. You are free now, and I know you are in a hurry to meet the charming Nina.'

After the admiral's departure Gribanov instructed me to

draft a letter to the administrative department of the Central Committee to be signed by General Ivan Serov, describing the improper behaviour of the admiral and his refusal to carry out the KGB's request that he should end his connection with our agent, who had long been employed in the handling of foreigners and was at the present time maintaining intimate relations with a Turkish diplomat on our instructions.

The admiral's career came to a dismal end. He was dismissed from the navy, and when Sincerity learnt that he was no longer an admiral she simply dropped him and continued to work for us. The Turkish diplomat was recruited by us, not by being compromised, but for money. For that Agazaryan, Colonel Davidyan and I were awarded a month's salary as a bonus.

The stories that go around about the KGB's omnipotence are slightly exaggerated. At the same time the KGB can do things that would be quite impossible for any counter-intelligence service in the West. I will give a few examples.

If an attempt to recruit a diplomat or a journalist did not succeed it did not cause any ripples. But the penetration of a foreign embassy by illegal means could result in serious complications, and such operations were considered to be the most important and dangerous part of our job.

Our main target in Moscow was the Turkish embassy, because Turkey was a member of NATO and its diplomatic staff, headed by the ambassador, maintained close contacts with the American, British and French embassies. It was practically impossible for the KGB to penetrate those embassies, so in breaking into the Turkish, Iranian or Egyptian embassies, we hoped to find documents, notes of conversations and perhaps codes and code-books that would help us to have at least some idea of what was happening in relations between those countries and the West. Some Western diplomats had so little sense of security that they would throw into their waste-paper baskets scraps of paper with notes of conversations they had had with other diplomats and Soviet officials. These pieces of paper and other material were collected by the Soviet housemaids working in the embassies and provided us with a certain amount of information; on occasion we even utilized them when writing reports to the Central Committee. We were especially interested in sheets of paper left carelessly on writing desks, which appeared to have nothing on them but which still bore the impression of what had been written on the sheet above. But in terms of gaining important information nothing could beat an actual entry into an embassy.

After carefully studying the possibilities of penetrating the Turkish embassy we came to the conclusion that there was a 100 per cent guarantee of success. The heads of the KGB, after clearing the matter with the Central Committee, gave us permission to carry out the operation. I was included in the group which was to enter the embassy. There were three desk officers: the head of our section, Lieutenant-Colonel A. Kalabukhov, my friend Nikolai Rakhmanov and myself. Attached to us was Mikhail Agazaryan, who spoke good Turkish, two photographers, two specialists in safe-breaking and a technician who was to set up a bugging apparatus which was also intended to maintain radio contact with the man in charge of the operation, Colonel Artem Davidyan. We had no confidence in the 'walkie-talkies' of those days because of their poor quality.

The day chosen for the operation was a Sunday in summer, when embassies do not work and most diplomats who are not on leave go out of town. That summer there were only three or four diplomats working in the embassy; the rest were out of the country. The remaining diplomats and technicians at the embassy were sent invitations by various Soviet citizens and foreigners who were in fact part of our agent network. Thus the embassy counsellor, who was replacing the ambassador, was invited out by an agent of ours, a Turkish doctor who had been living in the Soviet Union for several years. All the streets around the embassy were kept under surveillance by special groups of agents, and all the traffic police were replaced by men from the security department. The embassy guard had long been collaborating with the KGB in return for money and had been told he would be guaranteed a comfortable living in the Soviet Union in the event of being exposed. He had agreed to let us into the embassy.

We went in one at a time on a signal from the watchers outside who were responsible for our safety. The operation lasted several hours. The safe-breaking specialists – one of whom, known as Old Vasya, had been in the trade since before the Revolution and had spent many a year in Soviet prison camps, but was now a reformed character – had agreed to use their talents for the good of the country. They opened most of the safes fairly quickly but spent a long time over the ambassador's safe, upsetting the timetable of the operation, but it was opened in the end. Agazaryan, Rakhmanov and I examined the documents taken out of the safes and desks, while the photographers, who were also expert at opening sealed envelopes, photographed the documents and returned them in exactly the same order as they had found them. Opening the cipher tables of the diplomatic code proved to be especially difficult. More than a thousand sheets of documents and notes were photographed, and new microphones were installed to replace the ones we had put in earlier which were obsolete or worn out.

Everything seemed to be going well when suddenly we received an alarming message: one of the members of the embassy staff who had been invited out had apparently sensed that something was wrong and told his host that he had to return to the embassy urgently. We began feverishly putting everything back in order. In the event of our not having sufficient time and one of the Turks breaking through the KGB cordon into the embassy we would pretend that we were ordinary thieves. But that was very much an emergency plan and the story was hardly credible.

Colonel Davidyan, directing the operation, took it upon himself to organize a minor traffic accident. The Turkish diplomat's car bumped into a private car. It was a trifling accident, but the driver of the private car demanded that someone from the traffic police should be summoned to establish who was to blame for the accident. An inspector arrived on the scene, witnesses were questioned, a report was drawn up, and so forth. The time we needed to complete the operation had been gained. Everything was put back in its place and we quietly left the Turkish embassy.

In the same way we penetrated the Egyptian, Iranian, Syrian and other embassies, for which we were rewarded with inscribed watches and the title of Honoured Chekists.

It is possible that some people, having read these lines, will frown scornfully and reward us with some unkind epithets. But I take a different view. The special services exist precisely to carry out such operations, which are intended to provide their governments with information necessary for their political aims and for the country's security. The work of intelligence, called by armchair critics 'espionage', serves the country of which you are a citizen and is in my view honourable work, difficult and not always devoid of danger.

CHAPTER NINE

···▬◆▬···

Frontier Intelligence and Working Abroad

MY WORK IN the Second Chief Directorate ended unexpectedly, when at the beginning of 1955 I was told that, as a former intelligence officer, I was being transferred to work in the newly created Tenth Department in the First Chief Directorate, which was in charge of the First Departments of the KGB in the republics dealing with frontier intelligence work. Colonel Aleksei Bochkov, whom I did not know, had been appointed its head. To tell the truth, I did not want to leave counter-intelligence, but the prospect of getting to know new people attracted me, and I agreed.

Colonel Bochkov explained that, because of the difficult political situation and the pressures of the cold war, the Party and government expected the Soviet intelligence service to organize a network of agents in the countries on our frontiers – Turkey, Iran, Afghanistan, India and, to my great surprise, China – which could be used for intelligence purposes as well as for sabotage operations in the event of war. The network could also be used for passing our agents deep into the interior of those countries and beyond them. The First Departments of the KGB in the republics did not, unfortunately, have sufficient experience in these matters, were unsatisfactorily inactive, and their proposals for action were generally very poor. Our department's job was to correct the situation and I was to be responsible for the First

Departments of the KGB in Georgia and Armenia, operating against Turkey and Iran.

I was advised to devote most of my attention to Turkey, since it was an ally of the United States. The Turkish intelligence service was particularly active, always trying to infiltrate its agents across the Soviet–Turkish frontier and into the Georgian republic. There was a rather special situation in this area, because before the 1917 Revolution the eastern part of Turkish Anatolia belonged to Georgia. After it was returned to Turkey many Georgian and Adzhari families remained there, but their relations were still living in Soviet Georgia.

The Soviet–Turkish frontier, like all Soviet frontiers, is guarded by the frontier troops of the KGB with the aid of modern electronic equipment and night-vision apparatus. Along the whole length of the frontier there is a strip, seven metres wide, of finely raked earth which is continually checked by the frontier guards to see whether any tracks have been left. (There are similar strips along frontiers even with the other Communist countries.) Apart from that there is a fine, practically invisible wire set along the whole frontier at a height of about thirty centimetres from the ground which if broken causes an alarm signal to ring in the frontier post; a light on a special map shows where the possible frontier violation has taken place. There are frequent false alarms, because the wire can be broken by wild animals, who do not recognize frontiers.

In spite of this technical equipment and the round-the-clock guard maintained by the frontier troops, the people living in the frontier zones of Georgia and Armenia found ways of visiting their relations in Turkey and Iran, and we knew this. Neither the Turks nor the Iranians made much effort to guard the frontier and were content to carry out occasional inspections of some sections in the daytime and to maintain a frontier post at points where the railway or the main road crossed the frontier. I asked a Turkish official why they had given up even inspecting the frontier in daylight. He replied quite seriously that his government hadn't the funds to pay for frontier troops and that there was no need for them to guard the frontier, since the Soviet frontier troops would not let anybody out or in. This was shortly after I had arrived in Georgia to examine the possibility of sending our agents across the frontier and was visiting the frontier posts in the Batumi region with Colonel Demurov, head of the First Department of the KGB in Georgia. The Turkish frontier official's reply told me that the frontier was open on the Turkish side.

But if the inhabitants of the frontier villages were able to cross the frontier, that did not mean that any outsider could also do so. Not because it was difficult to negotiate the frontier, but because it was practically impossible to get near it. Even today the appearance of a stranger in one of the frontier villages is immediately reported by the local people to a frontier post, because they do not want to spoil their relations with the frontier guards and have no particular sympathy for outsiders. Anyone trying to avoid the frontier villages will soon find himself in impenetrable undergrowth and marshland and be in danger from wild animals.

In spite of the difficulties, the Turkish intelligence service, unlike the Iranian or Afghan, tried repeatedly – and twice successfully – to infiltrate their agents across the frontier. We knew that these operations were being directed by a man called Akhmeteli, a Georgian by origin, who had left Georgia in the 1930s.

The First Department of the KGB in Georgia was given two main tasks : to neutralize the activity of Turkish intelligence in the frontier area by turning in or liquidating Akhmeteli, and to organize a network of agents on the Turkish side capable not only of obtaining intelligence information and documents but also of carrying out special actions and of infiltrating our agents deep into Turkey.

I spent nearly a month in Georgia and during my stay I

visited all the posts along the frontier between Georgia and
Turkey so as to have a clear idea of possible crossing places.
Then I studied the files on the informers we had living in the
Turkish frontier regions and prepared a detailed report on
the situation for Bochkov. It was not optimistic. The one
single plan put forward by the First Department, which, it
seemed to me, had been too hurriedly approved by the
Centre, had ended in failure. With the aim of turning or
neutralizing Akhmeteli the Georgian KGB had decided to
make use of his brother, who lived in Georgia. The brother
was surprisingly quick to fall in with the proposal that he
should cross the frontier illegally and carry out the KGB's
mission. With one of our agents acting as a guide he crossed
the frontier, got as far as Ankara, and then disappeared for
ever, recalling, no doubt, with gratitude the good turn the
Georgian KGB had done him, because he had long dreamt of
going to Turkey and joining his brother. We learnt about
this later from reports made by the KGB *rezidentura* in
Turkey. This allegedly 'successful' operation had been
directed by a member of the First Department of the Georgian KGB who was the nephew of the Chairman of the
Supreme Soviet of the Georgian republic. He, therefore,
received no reprimand and the matter was brushed under
the carpet.

Like every man in charge of an organization, Colonel
Bochkov wanted to show his leaders that he was not being
paid for doing nothing, but that under his direction the
department could almost achieve the impossible. Consequently his ideas and demands were often pure adventurism. I gained some idea of the pressure he was under,
however, when he told me one day that his superiors not
only demanded positive results from the frontier counter-
intelligence work, but expected him to capture people crossing the frontier illegally, not just Turkish agents but spies
sent over by the British and American intelligence services.
According to Bochkov, the department was also expected to

organize the passage not only of single agents but also, if the need arose, of whole sabotage groups trained to carry out special operations. (It had been decided to organize KGB special service units consisting of men from the reserve who could speak foreign languages, were trained in various special techniques, were physically fit, and had an impeccable ancestry.) On the Turkish side of the frontier we had to organize a network of informers whom we could trust and who had family connections in Georgia.

Apart from that, he said, it would not be a bad idea if we could snatch somebody from the other side, possibly two brothers from a part of Georgia called Adzharia, Turkish spies whom one of our agents had told us about, who were likely to try to cross the frontier into Georgia. So Bochkov ordered me to fly down to Georgia to organize the operation and to discuss with Demurov the possibility of bringing a man called Aga Khan, who was working for the Turkish intelligence service, over to our side. The man who told us about the brothers was a double agent codenamed Pikri who had been working for us for many years and had been recruited through his relations living in Adzharia. It was from his reports, which he deposited in secret hiding places near the frontier and which were picked up by our agent Kochakh, his nephew, that we had learnt of Khan's arrival in the frontier zone. Khan used Pikri's house in Artvin on the Turkish side for resting in and preparing to cross the frontier.

When I flew down to Georgia in April 1955 spring had only just arrived in the mountains. The weather was foul, and the rain, snow and thick fogs provided excellent cover for frontier crossings. We already had a good idea about where the two brothers were likely to try to cross – near frontier post No. 19, high up in the mountains. It was there that we organized an ambush. All the other frontier posts were increased in strength and the units used for pursuing and capturing illegal frontier crossers were brought to a state of alert.

The two brothers appeared silently and unexpectedly not far from where we were hiding in the undergrowth and we observed them through night-vision binoculars. We allowed them to penetrate about a hundred metres into Georgian territory and then, suddenly showing ourselves, ordered them to lie flat and put their hands behind their backs. After a moment's hesitation the two brothers opened fire. We did not return their fire but repeated the order for them to lie flat. They were in fact lying down already, in the hope of avoiding detection, but we could just manage to see them through our binoculars. The frontier troops had been ordered to take the two men alive, but the brothers put up a stiff resistance and managed to get back on to Turkish territory. Our troops pursued and killed them, bringing their corpses back to our side of the frontier. They were carrying no papers or documents and we never found out why they had crossed the frontier or whom they were going to meet.

A few days later the Turkish frontier guards requested a meeting at which they enquired whether we knew anything about two brothers from Adzharia crossing the Soviet frontier. They had been missing from home for several days and their families were worried. When we told them that we had no record of any frontier violations the Turks said pointedly that a few days previously there had been a furious exchange of gunfire at night. That, we told the head of the Batumi frontier unit, had been nothing more than some practice shooting.

When I returned to Moscow empty-handed I received an oral reprimand from Colonel Bochkov. Then he handed me an account of a conversation between the Turkish ambassador in Moscow and the first secretary of his embassy, whom the KGB regarded as a member of the Turkish intelligence service. The conversation, recorded by the KGB, was rather confused because, according to the translator, a radio had been switched on while it was taking place. It concerned a Soviet diplomat then working in the Soviet embassy in Ankara. The ambassador said he had received a report from his ministry that the Soviet diplomat, who was an Azerbaidjani, had been in touch with the Turkish counter-intelligence service and was about to request political asylum. The Turkish authorities had no intention of refusing him but at the same time did not want to upset their already complicated relations with the Soviet Union. So they had asked the embassy for its opinion about the likely reaction of the Soviet authorities.

A note from the Second Chief Directorate of the KGB attached to the account of the conversation said that the Soviet diplomat was a member of the KGB in the Azerbaidjan republic, that his name was A. Guseinov, and that he had been sent to Turkey to work in the *rezidentura* of the First Chief Directorate of the KGB.

The news that any Soviet citizen, especially a member of the KGB, is intending to ask for political asylum is regarded as a major emergency. Immediate steps have to be taken to prevent the defection. In every Soviet embassy and mission there is a special group of counter-intelligence officers whose job is to keep an eye on Soviet citizens abroad – for this reason I asked Colonel Bochkov why this case had come to our department. Wouldn't it be better to hand the matter over to the department directly in charge of intelligence work against Turkey and of the *rezidentury* in Ankara and Istanbul? Bochkov agreed with me and said that Colonel (later General) Sakharovsky, head of the First Chief Directorate, had apparently made a mistake: as Guseinov was a member of the Azerbaidjan KGB he had decided that it was a matter for us. There was no point now in redirecting the papers: I should get on to the appropriate department and agree on the urgent steps to be taken.

The Turkish Department went into a panic when I told them about Guseinov. They claimed that the record of the Turkish diplomats' conversation was inaccurate and an attempt to discredit a member of the KGB who was doing good work. I do not know what sort of reports Guseinov was sending from Turkey, but his colleagues had a good opinion of him. Anyway, an urgent telegram was sent in cipher to the *rezidentura* telling them to keep Guseinov under surveillance but in such a way that he would not notice it, and to give him so much work in the *rezidentura* that he would have no time to go into the city, until someone from the Centre arrived.

In the Soviet intelligence service, and possibly in other intelligence services too, it takes much less time to carry out an operation than it does to comply with all the red tape involved. First there is a letter to the head of department, then one to the head of the Chief Directorate, then one to the Chairman of the KGB and in some cases one to the Central Committee too. So the department had to work through the night to comply with all the demands of the bureaucracy.

The simplest thing would have been to instruct the counter-intelligence officers in the Ankara embassy to bring Guseinov and his wife out. But because his intention to defect was known to the Turkish counter-intelligence service, who were certainly keeping Guseinov under surveillance, we reckoned that if he and his wife were seen being taken out of Turkey in the company of members of the Soviet embassy the Turkish authorities might realize what was happening and take steps to wreck our operation. We did not want a repetition of what happened in Australia when the wife of the defecting KGB *rezident*, Vladimir Petrov-Proletarsky, was snatched from the hands of KGB officers by Australian counter-intelligence officers at Darwin airport in 1954. Consequently it was decided that three KGB officers, led by Lieutenant-Colonel A. Demin, should fly to Ankara in the guise of diplomatic couriers and bring the Guseinovs out.

In spite of the record we had of the Turkish diplomats' conversation we could not be absolutely certain that

Guseinov and his wife had decided to defect. So, as soon as our group arrived, Guseinov was to be summoned to the *rezidentura*, where Demin would tell him that we knew of his intention to seek political asylum and that he was to return to Moscow. It was hoped that such a blunt approach would catch Guseinov off his guard and make it difficult for him not to give himself away. Even if there were doubts about whether Guseinov was the man referred to by the Turkish diplomats he would still have to go to Moscow while the *rezidentura* looked for the real defector.

Guseinov was to be summoned to the *rezidentura* shortly before the departure of the plane to Moscow. He would be given an injection of a powerful drug that would render him semi-conscious and make him look very ill. It would require a further injection ten or twelve hours later as an antidote; otherwise he would die from heart failure. This was in case the Turkish authorities should seize Guseinov by force on the way to the airport. Approval for the plan had been given by Ivan Serov, apparently with the agreement of the Central Committee.

Two days after the recording of the conversation had been obtained the operational group flew to Ankara and brought out Guseinov, semi-conscious, on a stretcher. Demin reported that everything had gone according to plan. Guseinov had turned up in the *rezidentura*, and when he was asked point-blank when he was proposing to defect, he lost his head, went quite pale and very nearly fainted from fright. Realizing that he had no way of defending himself, he confessed everything. It remained only to seize his wife, which had seemed to be a relatively easy matter. But when Demin and the others arrived at the Guseinovs' apartment his wife, seeing who they were through a spy-hole in the door, guessed that her husband had been arrested. She leapt from the third-floor window and disappeared for ever. It later transpired that it had been her idea that they should seek political asylum. Demin was reprimanded by Serov for having let Guseinov's wife get away. Guseinov himself was condemned.

After this episode I carried on with my routine work supervising the First Departments of the Georgian and Armenian KGBs until one day we received a report that an officer of the Soviet frontier troops had been killed by a Turkish sniper as he went down from frontier post No. 19 into the valley. We took this to be an act of revenge for the death of the two brothers. Bochkov was beside himself with rage, not so much because of the murder as because there had been no substantial improvement in our frontier intelligence work at a time when the heads of our service wanted to see some concrete results. Akhmeteli was still beyond our reach; we had practically no channels for infiltrating spies across the frontier; and there was a great shortage of genuine Turkish documents for our agents going into Turkey.

The Soviet leaders could never forgive the Turks for having collaborated with the Germans during the Second World War, when the Soviet military command had to keep considerable forces in the Caucasus region in case Turkey entered the war on the German side. Nor had Stalin's plan to detach from Turkey the territories of Kars, Erzerum and Ardahan (which had been annexed to Turkey after the Russian Revolution of 1917) been forgotten. This was why we were instructed to organize a propaganda campaign directed against the Turkish government and aimed at encouraging the people of those regions to demand the return of the territories to Georgia and Armenia. This was made easier by the fact that Eastern Anatolia was the poorest part of Turkey, while the economic situation in Georgia and Armenia was much better, as the families and friends of Soviet Georgians and Adzharians knew very well.

In the autumn of 1955, as I was preparing to go off on holiday to one of the KGB's sanatoria on the shore of the Black Sea, I was summoned by Bochkov. He had other plans for me. I was to meet the informer known as Pikri on the

Turkish side of the frontier and discover whether he could guide our agent Bezhan to the town of Sivas, wait for him a day or so and then lead him back again to Artvin. That was the first job. The second was to find out if Pikri could lure Osman Iremashvili closer to the frontier. We knew that Iremashvili acted as a guide for Aga Khan, the agent we wanted to turn, and had more than once crossed the frontier successfully. Bochkov suggested that Pikri could tempt him with a smuggling proposition. If he agreed to come we would take him, arrange a meeting for him with his relations in Batumi and, of course, recruit him to our side. His family would bring him to his senses and we would warn him not to do anything silly. If Osman co-operated we could use him to try to catch Aga Khan himself, question him and then recruit him too.

Bochkov could see that I was sceptical. He explained that, once he had been with us, Aga Khan would never be able to persuade his bosses that he had been brought over to us by force. Even if he did persuade them, his career would nevertheless be at an end, because no one would ever trust him again. We, for our part, would explain all this to him and offer him good money for his services and even promotion in the service, because the Turkish or other agents would not only be able to cross our frontier but if necessary to go back again, and that would speak well for the success of Aga Khan's efforts. But if he did not agree then we would threaten to hand him back to the Turkish authorities as someone who had come over voluntarily to our side and had offered us his services in return for money. We would tell the Turks that we had turned him down because we didn't want to spoil relations with our Turkish neighbours.

Contact with Pikri was maintained through his nephew, our agent Kochakh, who was capable only of carrying out technical jobs, like picking up the semi-literate messages that Pikri left in hiding places near the frontier or handing Pikri money for his collaboration with us.

Bochkov's plan contained everything you might expect to find in a detective story, but we weren't writing thrillers : we were engaged in spying across frontiers. It was quite clear that Bochkov was not joking. 'You will understand,' he said, 'that we can't entrust such a delicate negotiation to Kochakh, although he's a good fellow and a brave one. This needs a professional, and that means you.'

I couldn't believe my ears. To send an intelligence officer illegally across a frontier to convey instructions to a double agent concerning an operation that might well turn out to be a flop was not just mad; it was criminal. Besides, I had already seen what Kochakh looked like when he returned across the frontier – covered in mud and utterly exhausted by the physical and nervous effort – and I had no desire at all to be in his place. I could have refused the job there and then but, whether out of bravado or from a sense of duty, or from a desire not to look a coward, I agreed to go with Kochakh to meet Pikri, not only to give him instructions but also to look him over and let him see that, if he tried to trick us, we would find him wherever he was.

In Batumi Colonel Demurov, Kochakh and I changed into the uniform of the frontier troops and with three soldiers accompanying us on horseback set off for frontier post No. 19. The uniform was necessary to avoid arousing suspicions among the people living in the villages near the frontier, among whom we could not exclude the presence of Turkish spies. The officer in charge of the frontier post treated us to a good meal with the traditional glass of vodka. His name was Ivanov, the commonest of all Russian surnames – a reminder that the majority of the men manning posts on the Soviet–Turkish frontier in Georgia and Armenia are Russians and Ukrainians, a measure of the Soviet leaders' lack of confidence in the peoples of the Caucasus, some of whom still live in Turkey and Iran.

Ivanov knew we were going to cross the frontier but was not told the reason for the mission. He and the head of frontier post No. 1 had been given instructions to organize diversionary manoeuvres on the sections opposite where the crossing was to take place, in case the Turks carried out a night inspection, which was most unlikely.

Led by Kochakh, I crossed in pitch darkness, dressed in peasant clothes and carrying only the traditional Caucasian dagger in my belt. We had no documents and no money. In the event of our being caught we would say that we had lost our way. All we had was two bottles of Georgian grape brandy, known as *chacha*, of which we had taken several swigs so that our breath would smell and confirm that we had been visiting friends and had lost our way. The *chacha* also gave us courage and warmth as we sat with Kochakh in a muddy hole covered with bushes, keeping watch on Pikri's house on the outskirts of the village.

We had to sit in that dirty hole throughout the next day, so I had plenty of time for reflection. I couldn't get out of my head the words Bochkov had said as he bid me goodbye. 'Listen,' he had said, 'if anything goes wrong they'll have your head and mine as well. I know who will have mine; I don't know about yours. You realize, of course, that the big bosses have not given written approval for your crossing. They are too scared of losing their jobs. They gave their blessing orally, but there's nothing in the file.'

The day passed without incident, apart from the fact that we were very tired from sitting and from the nervous strain. People go to bed early in the country, and as soon as the lights went out in the windows of the houses, Kochakh went across to Pikri's house and soon returned for me. Kochakh had told Pikri that I was from Dzhemal – that is, from the person for whom Pikri worked. Kochakh stood guard outside the house. Pikri's house was poor and bare, like those of most peasants in Eastern Anatolia. Pikri himself was also poor, which was probably why he was ready to risk his life working for us. It would have been ridiculous to suppose that he was moved by any ideological motives.

I could see that Pikri was very tense, so I decided to get down to business at once. I told him in general terms what we wanted of him and questioned him about Aga Khan and Osman Iremashvili. Pikri answered all my questions simply and clearly. When I asked him about the possibility of removing Osman Iremashvili, Pikri pondered the matter for some time, and I had the feeling that the idea did not appeal to him, but that he realized at the same time that he would be pretty well rewarded for his work. According to Kochakh, he didn't like Osman, though we did not know why. But that didn't matter – what mattered was to get Pikri's agreement, and that I did. We agreed that he would continue to communicate with us by means of the hiding-place and that he would have to let us know about the business with Osman – whom he would call Makhmud – at least two weeks before the two of them were due to arrive at the frontier. I set off home feeling satisfied with my efforts.

We were scrambling slowly up the mountain back towards the Soviet frontier, sliding about in the slippery mud, when suddenly, like a clap of thunder from a clear sky, there was an abrupt shout: 'Stop, who goes there! Lie flat, hands on your head, or else we open fire!' We flattened ourselves out in the mud without making a sound. It was a unit of Soviet frontier troops. Instead of reacting to the password I gave, they handcuffed us and took a sort of childish pleasure in taking our daggers away from us, obviously in the belief that they had captured some criminals or perhaps spies. When I asked them to call up frontier post No. 19 they took no notice and, jabbing us in the back with their rifle barrels, ordered us to march ahead of them. It turned out later that we had missed our way and crossed the frontier in the wrong place. Once we reached the frontier post we quickly established our identity and made contact with Demurov. He was pleased that I had liked Pikri. That meant a good mark for Demurov in Moscow.

Back in Moscow, I found Colonel Bochkov satisfied. 'I

ought to put you up for an award for having returned safely. But I'm afraid that, if I told them what you have been up to, we would be more likely to get a kick in the pants than a decoration. Therefore, Captain, we'd better not indulge in self-advertisement, because, as they say, modesty enhances a Bolshevik,' he said, with a laugh. But he showed his appreciation by having me made assistant head of the department two months later.

In the spring of the following year, on 3 March 1956, Colonel Bochkov informed me that I was to be transferred from his department in Moscow to Georgia. When he saw my reaction he tried to reassure me. He told me that there was trouble in Georgia (because of Khrushchev's anti-Stalin speech) and that General Serov had given orders that all the Georgians still working in the Moscow headquarters were to be sent to the republic to strengthen the Georgian staff and to help them to correct the mistakes in their work. Apart from that, Bochkov said, it seemed to the people in Moscow that favouritism and nepotism were widespread in Georgia even among people working in the KGB and that it would be a good thing to bring in outsiders in important positions. Bochkov told me that all the details would be filled in by the personnel department. He had tried to keep me in Moscow, but he couldn't go against Serov's wishes.

Next day I was received by Colonel Antonov, who supervised the work of the KGB in the Caucasian republics. Without a word he showed me a report drawn up by the head of the personnel department, Colonel Vasiliev, and addressed to Serov. It was a proposal to transfer a number of employees of the central *apparat*, including me, to work in Georgia. Antonov handed me the sheet concerning myself with an assessment of my work. In the margin there was a note by Serov written in blue pencil: 'Transfer to work in Georgia. In case of refusal transfer to somewhere else far from Moscow, and if he does not do well there sack him.'

I realized that my fate was already decided. I asked

Antonov the reason for such a stern decision, especially the threat of dismissal. Was my previous work that bad? 'Who knows what he is up to,' said Antonov. 'You know what Serov is like.' He told me to report directly to the Chairman of the Georgian KGB, General Inauri.

It said in the instructions that I was being sent to Tbilisi as deputy head of the First Department of the Georgian KGB and at the same time as head of the First Section. And so, after eleven years, I returned to Tbilisi, not to the peaceful Tbilisi of my youth but to a city seething with indignation.

On the morning of 6 March I reported to General Inauri, a former cavalry officer who had served in the Ukraine and knew Khrushchev, who had made him Chairman of the Georgian KGB.

The situation in the city was worrying, Inauri told me. The students at Tbilisi University were organizing a demonstration to protest at Khrushchev's speech about Stalin. In the little town of Gori, Stalin's birthplace, meetings were already being held at which Stalin's praises were being sung and his memory honoured. The students were being joined by intellectuals, factory workers and collective farmers. Inauri and Mzhavanadze, the First Secretary of the Georgian Communist Party, had appealed to Moscow for advice about what steps they should take. But Moscow had only suggested that the Georgian authorities should take their own decisions.

I asked Inauri if I could take a walk around Tbilisi to see what was going on. He agreed, advising me to be careful and not to take long about it.

Practically everyone knew about Khrushchev's 'secret' speech and, in the emotional way the Georgians have, they were discussing the charges laid against Stalin and openly criticizing Khrushchev and Mikoyan. With every hour that went by small groups developed into great noisy swarms of people. The situation was becoming alarming. There were reports that a stormy meeting was taking place inside the university, organized by a Committee for the Defence of Stalin's Memory.

Before I describe the subsequent events I must say something about the attitude of the Georgians to Stalin when he was alive and ruling the country. Stories to the effect that Stalin was regarded with special affection by the Georgians are far from the truth. Nor was it true that in his lifetime the Georgian republic enjoyed many privileges. For the Georgians Stalin was the same Stalin as he was for the Russians, the Ukrainians and the other peoples of the Soviet Union : he came to be idolized thanks to the efforts of Khrushchev and other Party leaders. He was not particularly admired or liked by the Georgians, chiefly because he had proclaimed the Russians to be a great people and by so doing had offended the national pride of the minority. Throughout his rule Stalin, apart from attending his mother's funeral, did not once visit Georgia. Moreover, Georgians could not forgive him for the destruction of the greater part of the Georgian intelligentsia during the mass purges of the mid-1930s.

So what happened after Khrushchev's secret speech? As we discovered later, Khrushchev's elimination of Beria in 1953 and the denunciation of Stalin as a petty tyrant and criminal were interpreted in Georgia as indications that Khrushchev and Mikoyan intended to humiliate and offend the whole Georgian people. People were indignant at the hypocrisy of Khrushchev, a man who had sworn devotion to the 'great helmsman' Stalin but vilified him after his death. In Georgia it is the custom to speak only good of the dead, however evil they may have been. The rumours that spread later, to the effect that the Georgians were intending to overthrow the Soviet regime and detach Georgia from the Soviet Union do not correspond with reality. I say this with some authority because I played a direct part in the enquiry into the causes of the disturbances in Tbilisi and other Georgian towns.

On 7 March the streets of Tbilisi were full of

demonstrators bearing portraits of Lenin and Stalin. Public transport had been brought to a halt. Offices, schools, colleges, shops and factories had all closed down. A state of anarchy reigned in the city. The Central Committee of the Georgian Communist Party had shut themselves in Party headquarters and did not show their heads outside. The KGB headquarters next door had been turned into a fortress with machine-guns mounted in the windows and all the entrances barricaded with sandbags.

On Lenin Square in the city centre, meetings were taking place at which the speakers – students, workers and intellectuals – were condemning Khrushchev and those who supported the views put forward in his speech. At the Stalin monument on the banks of the River Kura people were reciting poems dedicated to Stalin and singing Georgian folk songs which Stalin was supposed to have liked. There were attempts on the part of some Georgian nationalists to provoke a clash with Armenians living in Georgia, because Mikoyan, an Armenian, was attributed with having played a major part in the attacks on Stalin's memory. But the more level-headed speakers appealed for all who were against Khrushchev and his clique to unite.

The demonstrators then marched to Party headquarters and demanded that First Secretary Mzhavanadze should come out and give them his opinion of Khrushchev's speech. He did so, muttering something unintelligible, but was forced to leave the building and walk some distance at the head of the demonstration. The KGB could only stand and watch. Party members were sent in among the demonstrators to argue with them and calm them down. But if the Georgian Party leaders believed that they could restore a state of normality by peaceful persuasion, by now Khrushchev and the people in Moscow thought differently. 'Tank socialism' was brought into action. Russian tanks entered the city – and they really were *Russian* tanks, because the Georgian armoured division stationed close to Tbilisi was disarmed and surrounded by Russian soldiers and later disbanded altogether.

The demonstrators were not intimidated by the tanks and even tried to halt them, throwing portraits of Lenin and Stalin under their tracks in the naive belief that the tank commanders would not dare to run over the founders of the Communist Party. When the tanks ran over the portraits, the Georgians began to attack the tanks themselves. The tank commanders could not take that, and turned their tanks sharply to one side, breaking down light standards and crashing into shop windows.

It was all happening under my very eyes, and I had cause to reflect, for the first time in my life, on the essence of the socialist system. I stood beside a tank which had just knocked over a light standard, watching some young men who had rushed at the tanks and risked being run down. The tanks had halted and remained standing there while the demonstration continued. The buildings housing the Party, the KGB, the Council of Ministers, the main post office, the radio and television stations and the central telegraph office had all been taken over by Russian soldiers with automatic guns. The city was in a state of siege.

On the evening of 9 March more than a hundred thousand people attended a meeting at the Stalin monument. On their knees, the people passed a resolution addressed to the Politburo in Moscow demanding the dismissal of Khrushchev and Mikoyan and the appointment of Molotov as head of the Soviet state, since, according to rumour, he had opposed the speech and the criticism of Stalin.

Practically all the local staff of the KGB were out on the streets to observe what was taking place and report on the situation to their superiors. I was near the central post office, from where a fairly narrow street leads down steeply to the river embankment where the meeting was taking place. I could hear the sound of the crowd of many thousands moving ever closer. The officer commanding the detachment of troops increased the guard on the entrance to the post office when he saw the crowd approaching.

The crowd stopped about ten metres from the entrance. A representative of the demonstrators went up to the officer and, as we learned later, demanded that they be allowed in, because they had to despatch a telegram to Moscow. The officer, a lieutenant, refused, and at that point the crowd started to advance on the soldiers.

Perhaps one of the young Russian soldiers cracked under the tension or pressed his trigger by accident, but there was suddenly a burst of automatic fire which the other soldiers took to be a command to open fire. More than a hundred people were killed and more than three hundred wounded.

The KGB arrested more than four hundred people, but they were all released three days later. It was impossible to prove the existence of an organized anti-Soviet movement, since no such movement existed. The students who had spoken at the university meeting were taken off to Moscow to be questioned by Serov. The whole of Georgia knew and waited tensely to see what would happen to them. But they returned to Tbilisi a few days later and resumed their studies after having been warned against any repetition of such activities. Pleased at how quickly he had restored order in Georgia, Khrushchev refrained from employing further repressive measures against the students, not out of kindness but because he feared another outburst.

Such were the circumstances in which I started work in the Georgian KGB. In the summer of 1956 General Inauri informed me that I had been given the job of selecting men from the reserve who could be recruited into the KGB special service detachments that were then being formed. These were special commando units that were intended to operate in enemy territory in the event of an emergency. In order to select suitable candidates we had to go through the records of people of military age in all the military commissariats in Georgia, and then interview possible candidates personally. It was tedious work, but, according to General Inauri, the Centre in Moscow attached great importance to it.

Members of the new special service units had to be well trained, both physically and technically, to carry out acts of sabotage in foreign countries. They had to speak the language of the country in which they were likely to operate, be well acquainted with the local conditions as well as with the topography, the roads and the location of strategic military targets, above all the whereabouts of government and military offices, and the places were politicians and top civil servants lived. This information was in the possession of the KGB in embassies abroad and the special purpose units had to make use of it in their training.

With two subordinates dressed in regular army uniform I set out as representative of the headquarters of the Transcaucasian military district, with the rank of major, to go through the records in the recruiting offices in Tbilisi and the other towns and provinces of Georgia. We were due to complete the work by the summer of 1957. To tell the truth, there were few young men wishing to join the army, and we did not tell anybody, including the local recruiting officers, that they were to join the special KGB units. But if we came across a suitable candidate and he refused we would remind him of his sacred duty to defend the motherland, which had the desired effect.

In December 1956 I went to Moscow on leave and at the same time to ask the personnel department about the possibility of my returning to work, if not in the central headquarters, then at least in the KGB for the Moscow region, which rated in importance the same as a republican KGB.

Discussing this with Colonel Antonov, I said casually that I was ready to exchange my position as deputy head of a department for a job as an ordinary KGB officer in the Moscow region. Antonov understood perfectly well that it was hard for me to have to live on my own in Georgia, away from my family, and that work in a republican KGB was not to be compared in interest with work in Moscow. But he offered me no hope of a change : he said, in fact, that as long as Serov was Chairman of the KGB I had no hope at all of getting back to Moscow. 'There's nothing I can do to help,' Antonov said, but then added with a laugh : 'Why don't you get a bit tipsy and punch General Inauri in the face – you'd certainly get sent back to Moscow then, only in rather a different capacity!'

I had no intention of punching General Inauri, but something did happen that I could not have anticipated.

The following July I went to Batumi, where a member of my staff had prepared a list of possible recruits for the special purpose groups. I stayed at the only decent hotel there – the Intourist – which is in the centre of the town facing the sea. At dinner in the restaurant I found myself sitting next to a table at which were four young women speaking either Polish or Czech. They were, I learnt later, members of a group of tourists from Czechoslovakia.

Sitting at another table were three local men – Adzharians – one of whom was rather short and wearing a filthy jacket and a shirt that was in need of a wash. To attract the attention of the Czech girls he sent them a bottle of champagne via the waiter. There was nothing surprising in that, because it is one of the traditions of the Caucasian peoples, and my companion and I looked on with curiosity to see what would happen. I was wearing an ordinary suit of foreign cut and light-coloured shoes, which was unusual for that period and made it quite clear to the local people that I was a stranger. My companion went off to call on some friends, while two of the Czech girls and I decided to stroll along the promenade. It was late in the evening and there was no one about. We sat down on a bench to admire the reflection of the moon on the sea and listen to the sound of the waves on the shore.

Suddenly the three Adzharians who had sent the girls the champagne appeared in front of us. The little dirty fellow, who had already had plenty to drink, told me in broken Russian to clear off and leave their chosen girls in peace. I told him to go to hell and saw at once the flash of knife-blades in the hands of the other two. This meant they were not joking. The Adzharians are not only a hot-tempered people, they are also a little wild, and it means nothing to them to cut the throat of someone who gets in their way.

The girls were trembling with fright and chattering to each other in Czech. I could have walked away and that would have been the end of it. But then I would probably have cursed myself for the rest of my life for being a coward when I learnt what had happened to the young women whom I had left to satisfy the dirty little fellow's lust. So I drew the Makarov revolver that I always carried and fired without any warning in the direction of the little chap, but not at him. The other two Adzharians vanished but he was too scared to move. Determined to teach him a lesson, I forced him at gun-point to walk fully clothed into the sea up to his chin, which he did without a squeak. I don't know what happened to the Czech girls : I never saw them again.

I returned to the hotel, upset and angry at what had happened. A short while later, four policemen burst into my room and, in spite of my showing them my KGB identity card, led me off to the local police station. After explaining the affair to the duty officer I returned to the hotel and next morning took the boat to the seaside resort of Gagra to carry on with my job. We had hardly left the boat when we were met by the Gagra KGB who told me that General Inauri wanted me to call him immediately. I did so, and he ordered me to return at once to Tbilisi.

'What did I send you to Batumi for?' the general asked me as I stood before him. 'So that you could spend your time in restaurants with tarts, then fire your revolver in a public place and force a senior official, who found you in a disgraceful state on the promenade, to walk into the sea? Do you know who it was?' Inauri asked. No, I didn't, I said, and then asked permission to explain how it all happened, though I knew I would not be able to excuse using my gun on the promenade.

'That was the Minister of Education of the Adzharian autonomous region. So you can skip the explanations,' the general said. 'Five days' detention in the guard-room.'

There was nothing to say. There was no guard-room in the Georgian KGB, and I think it must have been the only instance in the history of that organization that a KGB officer was given such a punishment. What served as the guard-room for me was a cell in the internal prison.

When my five days were over I returned to my department, but I had decided that I could not go on working in the Georgian KGB. I asked General Inauri to dismiss me either on the grounds of a need for a reduction of staff or at my own request. The general was still furious and sent off to Moscow a proposal that I should be dismissed on the grounds of 'not being suitable for the service'. This was a terrible blow as it was the reason given when officers who had committed a breach of 'socialist legality', or who were 'Beria men', were dismissed. Since I was a Georgian I could easily be taken for one of the latter. But, thanks to Antonov, Moscow did not accept Inauri's proposal. In August 1957 I was dismissed from the KGB on the grounds of reduction of staff; that had considerable importance for my future career.

PART FOUR

The Media at Home and Abroad

CHAPTER TEN

Minority Peoples

IN THE COURSE of working in the countries of the Middle East I was made aware again of the two aspects of the nationalities policy of the Soviet leaders. Practically all Soviet officials abroad appear superficially to respect and admire the people of the country in which they are working. But among themselves they regard them with unconcealed amusement and contempt. Great-power chauvinism flourishes inside the Soviet Union, to be replaced by arrogant nationalism outside it. I am myself opposed to any manifestation of nationalism, be it British, French, Georgian or Ukrainian, because it inevitably gives rise to a superiority complex. I quote a friend of mine, Vladimir Getov, a graduate from the Academy of Social Science working in Soviet radio and television, who once shouted, 'We Russians, once so very backward, are now a great nuclear power. Who else could have done that in so short an historical period? Only we Russians.'

'What about the other peoples of the Soviet Union?' I asked. Had they not played any part in this achievement?

'All the rest are just little puppy-dogs,' he replied spitefully.

This attitude is perhaps not universal, but gives an indication of the chauvinism amongst leading officials.

This doubtless accounts for the widely held opinion in the West that the non-Russian republics, in particular the Ukraine, Georgia, Estonia, Lithuania and Latvia, are eager to break away from the USSR. Moreover, others believe that

in the event of war the non-Russian republics would welcome the American troops with flowers. Such views can be
held only by people who do not understand the nature of the
Soviet Union or by dreamers indulging in wishful thinking.
The nationality problem in the Soviet Union is far from
being solved and is a complex matter, but to talk of there
being antagonistic relations between the Russian and the
other peoples of the USSR is deliberately to misinform
world public opinion and the Western world. Neither
Lithuania, nor Estonia, nor Georgia, nor the Ukraine, nor
any other Soviet republic is striving to break away from the
USSR, because the great majority of the population were
born and grew up under the Soviet regime and do not have a
clear idea of any other system. Small groups of nationalists
and dissidents talking about secession do not reflect the
opinion of the majority of the people in those republics.

I would like categorically to affirm that in the event of war
all the Soviet republics will be fighting on the side of the
Soviet Union. I know this will not please some people, but
we have to face the truth.

The USSR is a huge multinational state embracing more
than a hundred different peoples and national minorities
speaking something like 130 different languages. They
include some who acquired literacy only after the Revolution of 1917 and others whose cultural history is centuries
old.

According to the Soviet Constitution all the peoples of the
Soviet Union are equal and enjoy identical rights, and this
provision is respected to a certain extent. All the republics of
the USSR have their own governments, their own adminis-
trations and social organizations, academies, institutes, universities and so forth. Both in the republics and in the
autonomous regions there are newspapers and periodicals
published in the language of the native population and the

teaching in schools is also conducted in the local language. At the same time there are also Russian schools, and the teaching of Russian is compulsory. But the existence of Russian schools and the compulsory learning of Russian is not in my view evidence of a policy of russification, because any multinational state has to have one common language in which the various peoples can communicate with each other. Nobody in the Soviet Union objects to this. The discontent arises from the fact that the non-Russian peoples resent the other measures aimed at increasing Russian domination. It began in the first days of the Revolution of 1917. The Revolution was carried out by the Bolshevik leaders, among whom were representatives of many other peoples, but it was Russians who overthrew the national governments in all the countries of the Caucasus and Central Asia and established Soviet regimes. It is also true that Russians were appointed by Moscow to the leading Party and administrative posts in the non-Russian republics, nominally to give them support but actually to exert control over the non-Russian governments.

Despite the fact that, today, all the republics have their own governments and civil services, any plans they may have for their economic or social development cannot be put into practice without Moscow's approval – that is, the approval of the *apparat* and Secretariat of the CPSU, in which the great majority of people are Russians.

The elevation of the Russians above the other, non-Russian peoples was encouraged in no small degree by a speech made by that great chauvinist Iosif Stalin, who paid special tribute to the 'great Russian people' and by so doing raised them officially to a dominant position and made the Russian the standard by which all other peoples were to be judged. Under Stalin, however, the Party leadership included Russians and Georgians, Jews and Ukrainians, Azerbaidjanis and Armenians, Estonians and representatives of other peoples, and that gave it to some extent an international character. But under Khrushchev and later under Brezhnev the leadership of the Soviet Communist Party became a Russian–Ukrainian monopoly.

Such a contemptuous attitude to the smaller peoples and the manifest lack of concern for their interests has given rise to a new wave of great-power chauvinism, carefully concealed and officially denied. However paradoxical it may seem, the fact is that, if Russians glorify and extol Russia to the Soviet population or even to foreigners, it is regarded as an act of patriotism; but if Georgians or Estonians permit themselves to sing the praises of their own national republics it is regarded as a sign of nationalism.

It was my lot to work in a number of large central organizations in Moscow and to witness examples of deeply ingrained and very widespread great-power chauvinism. For instance, Russians habitually use terms of contempt to refer to people from Central Asia and the Caucasus. The Jews are known as Yids, and people from African countries are black arses, and so on. To give an example, I remember an occasion on which my friend Colonel Arkadi Boiko in an outburst of frankness declared for all to hear that we would never allow the moustached and the *parkhaty* to get into positions of power again. The 'moustached' are the peoples of the Caucasus; and the '*parkhaty*' are the Jews; 'we' are the Russians. In reply to my question as to why he was so firmly opposed to the 'moustached' and *parkhaty*, Boiko replied that 'Only the Russians who have made and are still making history are fit to rule the state.'

Related to the question of the national minorities is that of the Jews. So much has been written in the West about Soviet Jewry and about the Soviet attitude to Israel that I think my own recollections may help to put the record straight.

When in the late 1950s and early 1960s I was working for the Soviet Union of Journalists I met the Israeli ambassador, a doctor of medicine called Orel. I was able to establish close relations with him, frequently visiting the Israeli embassy both for official receptions and on more private occasions. Ambassador Orel told me that he had agreed to take the job of ambassador because he was convinced that normal, if not friendly, relations between the Soviet Union and Israel, between which there were no fundamental conflicts, would be of great value, both to Israel and to the Arab countries. Orel argued that a change for the better in Soviet–Israeli relations would force the Arab nations, and the Palestinians too, to join in talks to resolve the conflict in the Middle East and put a stop to the bloodshed and terror. 'We have suffered enough,' said Orel, 'and we are sensible enough. We simply want peace for our people; we are also in favour of peaceful coexistence with all countries, both with the Soviet Union and with the United States, and I would like to believe that the Soviet rulers will believe me, as the representative of Israel, when I say that my government's intentions are not war but peace and the establishment of good relations with your country. If my mission to Moscow produces no results I shall be very disappointed. I shall go back to medicine.' And that is exactly what he did eventually.

I used to report these conversations to KGB General Gribanov, head of the Second Chief Directorate. We would analyse them and decide together on topics to be raised at future meetings. I also made detailed written reports which I sent to the International Department of the Central Committee. On one occasion I was summoned to the Central Committee headquarters to talk to the Central Committee Secretary Boris Ponomarev about my conversations with Orel. Ponomarev said he approved of my contact with Orel, but warned me not to give Orel any reason for supposing that there was going to be a change in Soviet policy towards Israel. Nor was I to support his views, even if they coincided with ours, since Orel understood perfectly well that I was acting in a professional capacity. 'Don't you turn into a Zionist under the influence of Dr Orel's sermons,' said Ponomarev with a malicious grin. He told me I was to turn the conversation to the question of the position of the Israeli Communist Party, which was being pressured by the Israeli authorities. I was also to affirm that the Palestinian people had just as much as right to set up their own state as the Jews had to have founded Israel with Soviet backing.

We in the KGB were first told about the foundation of the new state, at the end of 1947, by Colonel A. Otroshchenko, head of the Near and Middle East Department, in the course of an operational conference. It meant, Otroshchenko told us, that we were going to have a lot more work to do, and serious work at that, since the Central Committee and Stalin personally had given us the job of making sure that the new state would be a close ally of the Soviet Union and of persuading its future rulers that the Soviet Union could give them substantial assistance in creating an independent Jewish state and in protecting it from encroachments by Britain and the other imperialist powers. We had to bear in mind, Otroshchenko continued, that our number one enemy, the United States of America, would try to exploit the fact that there were a large number of Jews living in America, occupying important positions in the country's economic and political life and in close contact with Jews living in Palestine. We therefore had a great deal of work ahead of us resettling Soviet Jews in the future state of Israel. The great majority of them would naturally be people we trusted, many of them members of the Party. We were also faced with another task. We had to set up a network of agents to enable us to obtain information about everything going on in Israel and to influence and guide its policy in whatever direction we wanted. At the same time, Otroshchenko pointed out, Stalin's instructions about the need to maintain close relations with the Arab countries and to develop our influence over them remained in force, because the oil question was of first importance both politically and strategically.

What was meant by the 'oil question' was Stalin's decision that our network of agents and their influence in the countries of the Near East had to be so extensive and powerful in ruling and governmental circles that, if necessary, they could be brought into play to cut off supplies of oil and oil products to the Western countries, thus causing an oil crisis. This would result in economic and political complications, perhaps even in a real emergency with the threat of war. The policy of the Soviet rulers regarding Israel and the Arab countries, including Iran, has changed little since then.

I have to say that most of us working in the Soviet intelligence services would have preferred to have seen our government supporting Israel rather than the Arabs. Close relations with Israel would have been a great deal more useful to us for the purposes of gathering intelligence, in view of the close family ties between Jews living in the USA and in Israel. We used to joke among ourselves, saying that what was going to happen tomorrow in the United States was already known today in Israel. Our superiors agreed with us in principle but could of course do nothing contrary to the line laid down by the Central Committee.

Just how much help we had provided in the setting up of the state of Israel was quite clear to me, because following that conference in 1947 our work-load increased significantly. Every day we would receive lists of Soviet Jews who had to be checked in the KGB records to see whether we might use them for our purposes. The list of those planning to leave included representatives of all professions, including generals and officers of the Soviet army. On the basis of their personal and professional qualities they were recruited either for use as agents or for 'long-term settlement', to be brought into action in the event of an emergency.

Special groups of Soviet intelligence officers were formed to recruit, train and brief Jewish emigrants for intelligence work in Israel. They were headed by Lieutenant-Colonel

Vladimir Vertiporokh, who had just returned from work in the *rezidentura* in Teheran, and Colonel Aleksandr Korotkov, head of the Directorate in charge of 'illegals'. The success achieved by special groups can be judged by the fact that both Korotkov and Vertiporokh were awarded government decorations, a rare event in those days.

Nevertheless it has to be said that a clear majority of the Jews leaving at that time had nothing whatsoever to do with the KGB: they were, as they say, 'clean'. Many of them were given a course of instruction by the Party with a view to their preaching the virtues of the Soviet regime in Israel, but no real pressure was put on them. Statements made by some Jewish emigrés who have left the Soviet Union in recent years to the effect that something like one in four of the Jews emigrating had been recruited by the KGB are quite without foundation and could be made only by people having a very slight knowledge of intelligence work. On the other hand, it is unquestionably true that there are some KGB agents among the Jewish emigrés now living in the West.

Following the foundation of the state of Israel and the establishment of diplomatic relations between Tel Aviv and Moscow it was decided to organize a *rezidentura* at the Soviet embassy. One day after work I was walking to the trolley-bus stop with Vladimir Vertiporokh, who had been deputy *rezident* in Teheran, when, to my surprise, he asked me whether I thought he should go to Israel as *rezident* in the embassy. Without much thought I replied that of course he should go and enquired what doubts he had about it. 'In the first place,' said Vertiporokh, 'I already know those crafty Jews pretty well and I have a rather odd opinion of them.' He did not explain the nature of his 'odd opinion' but it was clear that he hadn't much sympathy for them. 'In the second place,' he went on, 'the work that the *rezidentura* will have to do is so serious and important that, quite simply, I am afraid of not being able to cope with it, and you know what that would mean.'

I tried to persuade him that he would be able to handle all the problems and that it was a very considerable promotion which could play a decisive role in his future career. I was genuinely fond of Vertiporokh, who with his blond good looks and kindly, easy-going character had earned the nickname of Uncle Volodya.

Whether my words played any part in his decision I do not know, but Vertiporokh agreed to become the first *rezident* of Soviet Intelligence in Israel. Apart from the fact that someone hostile to the Soviet Union threw a grenade into the courtyard of the Soviet embassy, Uncle Volodya did a good job and the *rezidentura* in Israel was considered to be one of the most effective, both in gathering secret information and in the recruitment of new agents. After his return to Moscow, Vertiporokh's work was highly praised both by the people in charge of the Soviet intelligence services and by the Central Committee of the Party: he was promoted to the rank of general, which rarely happened in those days in the KGB. Aleksandr Korotkov, who had worked on the Jews departing for Israel, was made a general too.

The founding of the state of Israel had a curious effect on Soviet Jews. Suddenly many of them wanted to leave the Soviet Union. At the same time it inspired others with the hope of being able to set up a Jewish autonomous republic in the European part of the Soviet Union, where the majority of Soviet Jews lived and still live. (True, there already existed a Jewish autonomous region with its capital, Birobidzhan, some 8000 miles to the east of Moscow. Not surprisingly, few Soviet Jews elected to move to so remote a place.) We received agents' reports from the Second Chief Directorate which indicated that members of the Jewish Anti-Fascist Committee, including the well-known Jewish actor and producer Solomon Mikhoels, had organized a campaign in favour of giving the Jews the Crimea, from which the Tartars had been expelled and which, as far as climate and location went, would suit the Jews, being a

southern people, far better than Birobidzhan. The writer
Ilya Ehrenburg, who was then head of the Anti-Fascist
Committee, was well aware of what Mikhoels and the others
were planning, but he refused to play any part in the business and even opposed it, and by so doing appears to have
saved his position and his life. In 1948, Mikhoels and his
supporters sent the Party Central Committee and Stalin
personally a letter requesting the formation of a Jewish
autonomous republic in the Crimea. This was the beginning
of the end not only for Mikhoels and the others but it also led
to a catastrophic deterioration in the position of all Soviet
Jews.

As Colonel Otroshchenko later revealed at a meeting of the
staff of the Near East Department, the Jews' request had
angered the entire Central Committee, the Politburo and
Stalin himself. They had interpreted the request as a sign of
expansionist tendencies on the part of the leaders of the
Jewish community, who had taken advantage of their positions in the Anti-Fascist Committee to establish contact with
Jewish anti-Soviet organizations in America and had practically become Zionists themselves. To tell the truth, most of
us listening to Otroshchenko had no idea what Zionism was,
but it was quite clear that this particular 'ism' did not fit in
with Marxism–Leninism. That meant it must be akin to
Trotskyism, and we were all quite sure that it was bad.

Otroshchenko told us that even Kaganovich, the only
Jewish member of the Politburo, had proposed taking serious steps to deal with the Zionist tendencies that were
developing among Soviet Jews. We then realized what all
this verbiage added up to: a fresh campaign was in the
offing, of which the Jews would be the victims. At the same
time we found it difficult to imagine what was actually going
to take place, apart from the arrest of those accused of
Zionism and contact with the Americans. After all, at that
time there were many Jews working in Soviet intelligence
and counter-intelligence, some of them occupying high posi-

tions, like Lieutenant-General Raikhman, head of the Second Chief Directorate, Colonel Gorsky, who handled the English KGB agents Maclean, Burgess and Philby when he was stationed in London, and Grauer, head of the Fifth Directorate.

The Jewish theatre, Jewish newspapers and Jewish restaurants in Moscow were all closed down. Then Jewish employees of all state bodies (there are no private ones in the Soviet Union) were dismissed on one excuse or another, not yet on a large scale but on the initiative of individual leaders. One of those arrested was Zhemchuzhina, the Jewish wife of Molotov, the Politburo member and Stalin's wartime foreign minister. Other Jewish wives of high officials were also arrested. The great majority of them ended their lives in prison camps.

But that was only the beginning: the campaign gathered pace. At the end of 1952, at a meeting in the United States Department, Colonel Raina announced that the counter-intelligence service had discovered an anti-Soviet terrorist organization involving a number of leading doctors many of whom were Jewish. The aim of the organization was to murder the Party leaders. We were given this information in confidence to encourage us to triple our political and police vigilance, but the whole Soviet population would soon learn about these 'murderers in white smocks'. When Raina read out the names of the doctors they all appeared to be Jewish; it seemed not so much a doctors' plot as a Jewish plot. That is the way it turned out.

Stalin and the people around him knew perfectly well that the affair of Mikhoels and the other Jews would prompt the counter-intelligence service to step up its interest in people of Jewish nationality, especially in view of the historically unfriendly relations between Russians and Jews. And they were not wrong. The case of the doctors became the case of the *Jewish* doctors, and eventually led to the persecution of all the Jews living in the Soviet Union.

Some Western accounts of the 'doctors' plot' have interpreted it as a plot by Beria against Stalin aimed at depriving Stalin of doctors who were loyal to him and replacing them with Beria's own stooges. This is an amusing idea, but nothing more. Beria was devoted to Stalin; he had carried out Stalin's wishes for many years and was on close, friendly terms with him. This was no secret to anybody who had anything to do with the top people or who worked in the KGB.

Apart from this, Stalin, particularly in his later years, not only had no faith in doctors, he was afraid of them, and his personal healer who provided him with medical aid was his secretary Poskrebyshev, who had been a medical orderly in the First World War and had some knowledge of medicine.

I found proof of this when I was working in the Georgian KGB in 1956–7 and came across a report made by the well-known Georgian professor of medicine K., who had treated Stalin for a bad cold he had caught while on holiday in the summer of 1945 in government dacha No. 9 in Abkhazia. When Stalin was cured he asked Professor K. how he could repay him. Professor K. begged Stalin to allow him to examine him at least once a year. The professor realized that Stalin's health was deteriorating. But Stalin said that he was absolutely fit and that he had his own particular physician, pointing to Poskrebyshev.

The real origin of the Jewish doctors' affair was to be found in the unofficial anti-Semitic campaign which had begun with the abolition of the Jewish Anti-Fascist Committee and the arrest and execution of many leading Jewish figures accused of Zionism, contact with the West and so forth. It was only natural then that Soviet counter-intelligence should devote special attention to Jews of all ranks and degrees. Agents were instructed to pay special attention to what their Jewish colleagues were doing. This situation was exploited by a violent anti-Semite, a woman doctor called Lidia Timashuk, a former KGB agent who had worked in the Kremlin hospital. By dint of great zeal and persistence she discovered that doctors working in the Kremlin had made a number of mistaken diagnoses and had consequently prescribed incorrect treatment, which had in some cases resulted in the death of the patient. Other patients had developed serious complications. Timashuk presented her findings – case histories and the results of laboratory tests – in the form of an agent's denunciation, accompanying it with her own inventions about a plot organized by the doctors against some Soviet leaders. The desk officer who controlled Timashuk sensed that the game was worth the candle and that if the case went ahead there was the prospect of promotion and medals.

The official explanation given in the Soviet press in 1953, after Stalin's death, that the whole affair was the responsibility of a senior investigator, Colonel Ryumin, closely assisted by his agent Timashuk, was not to be taken seriously. The fact is that no KGB investigator can arrest anybody, because that is not his job. The work of observing people under suspicion is carried out by the operational department and its desk officers who control the agents. No investigator in the KGB ever has control over agents. When the preliminary enquiries have been completed the desk officer applies to the prosecutor for a warrant to arrest the person under suspicion and hands the case over to a special group which carries out the arrest, searches the person's home and delivers him to prison for interrogation. As a rule the desk officer takes no part in the arrest. Once the arrest is made the file concerning the person under investigation is handed over to the investigating officer, who continues the enquiry to prove the arrested person's guilt.

The ultimate fate of the person under arrest depends upon the extent to which the investigating officer is objective in his judgements and upon his general decency and honesty. In fact, he is usually heavily under the influence, not only of the information produced by agents but also of the operational department which has been dealing with the case. The investigating officer's task is basically to confirm, by means of the arrested man's own confession, the agents' reports about his anti-Soviet or spying activities. That is why the main efforts of the investigating officer are not directed at seeking proof of the arrested man's innocence but at proving his guilt. I knew Ryumin personally, though we were not close, and I do not think he was an exception to this rule. In the case of the doctors, he did his duty valiantly and all the arrested men, Jewish and non-Jewish alike, confessed that they had tried to murder leading members of the Party and Government by giving them the wrong treatment.

The means used by Ryumin and his assistants to obtain the confessions is no secret because it was referred to in a confidential decree issued by Beria in March 1953 after Ryumin's arrest and the closing of the doctors' case. The decree said that the Lefortovo prison had a special cell equipped with frightful torture weapons: special devices for hanging people off the ground, rubber truncheons with a sprung steel core used for beating the soles of people's feet until they lost consciousness, various hooks and chains, and also desks with spring-loaded boards in them. These desks had been constructed to protect the investigating officer from an attack by the person under interrogation, but they were in fact used as an instrument of torture. The device could inflict a powerful blow in the stomach if the victim was standing up and in the chest if he was sitting down. It was said that several of the arrested doctors had died from such blows. Beria's decree said that before it was destroyed the torture chamber should be shown to all the desk officers as an example of what was impermissible in the conduct of interrogations. He stressed the need to observe 'socialist legality'.

To return to the 'doctors' plot'. Following the receipt of Timashuk's report the desk officer informed his superiors in the KGB and the Central Committee of the alleged conspiracy, as a result of which the whole network of agents was instructed to collect information about Jewish doctors, not only in the special hospitals but also in the local polyclinics. They were hunting the participants in the underground Jewish organization that was supposed to have links with Zionist circles in the West and whose aim was to undermine the Soviet system by killing off, not only leading officials, but ordinary people as well.

A KGB agent given such orders would certainly make every effort to expose the enemy. And if he could find nobody culpable he would be obliged to exploit the slightest error in diagnosis or treatment in order to concoct a report. He would not do this because he was dishonest, but in order to protect himself: if he did not produce the information required he could not be sure that he would not be accused of concealing information, because the KGB doctor working with him would in any case produce the necessary information to expose the Jewish doctor.

Rumours about 'doctor-murderers', as they were called in the press, spread throughout the country. People started refusing to consult Jewish doctors in whose hands they had been for years. It was the beginning of a terrible period for the Jewish people. All Jews in government institutions were dismissed – including those working for the intelligence services. Many Jewish KGB men were arrested and accused of spying, of having links with Zionists and of anti-Soviet activities.

One of those arrested was Mikhail Borodin, a close colleague of Lenin's and later Soviet adviser to Chiang Kai-shek. He ended his days in the KGB's internal prison. I was for many years on very close terms with his son Norman Borodin, who was also arrested and charged with spying for the United States. After four years in the internal prison, which he had used to look at from his office window, Norman Borodin was freed for lack of evidence, despite the exceptional efforts made by the investigator, Colonel Putintsev, to keep him in. Putintsev had been a friend of Borodin's.

It was not long before Putintsev found himself in the internal prison, this time under arrest for having violated socialist legality. He was sentenced to twenty-five years in a prison camp for his work on what was known as the 'Leningrad affair'. For some reason he was set free in 1955 or 1956. He and I lived in the same block of flats and on the same staircase; thus we met frequently though relations between us were cool. I could not forget his treatment of Norman Borodin. Norman himself forgave him and did not harbour any grudge against him, though he could have caused him a great deal of trouble if he had wished. Norman told me that Putintsev had behaved very cruelly towards him, not permitting him to sleep at night and submitting him to continuous interrogation on the 'conveyor' principle, in an effort to make Borodin confess that he had worked for American Intelligence, which he had never done.

On one occasion I found myself with Putintsev, celebrating the anniversary of the Russian Revolution in the home of my friend Lev Dogovichius, then the only Jew still working in the KGB – in the telephone monitoring service, because he was the only person left who could speak Hebrew. Dogovichius also lived on our staircase, on the seventh floor. After he had had plenty to drink, Putintsev's tongue loosened and he started to complain to me that he had suffered for having carried out the instructions of the Party and government. He told me he had been arrested as he left the court room in Leningrad where he had first appeared as a witness before the commission dealing with the rehabilitation of N. A. Voznesensky and the other Leningrad Party leaders who had been executed in Stalin's time for their 'anti-Party activity'. He was identified by other witnesses whom he had questioned and maltreated during the Leningrad affair. I asked Putintsev what Voznesensky's anti-Party activity consisted of and whether he really had been arrested because of his published writings, which were not pleasing to Stalin. Putintsev laughed and said that was all nonsense. Voznesensky and the other Leningrad Party leaders had sent a letter to the Politburo and to Stalin proposing that Leningrad should be made the capital of the Russian Federation (the central Russian republic of the USSR), on the grounds that all the other republics, except the Russian Federation, had their own capital cities. Stalin and the people close to him chose to regard this request as an act of separatism on the part of the leaders of the Leningrad Party organization – Voznesensky, Kuznetsov and others – and a sign that they wanted to throw off control by the Politburo. Relations between Moscow and Leningrad had long been complicated, each city competing for priority and exclusivity. Even today the Party organization in Leningrad, once the cradle of the Revolution, enjoys considerable advantages over the central committees of the Communist parties of the other republics. The leader of the Leningrad Party has always been a member of the Secretariat and the Politburo, and Grigori Romanov, whom Gorbachev recently threw out of all his jobs, appeared at one time to be a contender for the post of General Secretary of the CPSU. The fact that Voznesensky and his supporters had proposed making Leningrad capital of the Russian Federation had been known unofficially to employees of the KGB. Putintsev in his cups only confirmed that it was the main reason for the execution of Voznesensky and the others – the same as had happened to the representatives of the Jewish intelligentsia who had wanted to have their own republic.

By the end of 1952 the purge of Jews in the KGB, GRU, Foreign Ministry, the Central Committee *apparat* and other government organizations was complete. The exposure of the 'doctors' plot' and the dismissal of Jews from their work was carried out with the blessing of the Central Committee and its Secretaries, and we who were working in the security services were quite convinced that we were facing another Great Purge aimed at others than the Jews. The scale of the operation and the enormous number of agents taking part in it would have guaranteed the 'success' of the operation, had not Stalin died at the beginning of March 1953. He believed in the existence of a doctors' plot because, especially in his last years, he became excessively suspicious and fearful for his own life. As ever he reckoned: 'Better my innocent neighbour should die than I who have sinned all my life.'

It seemed on the surface that with Stalin's death the Jewish affair had come to a welcome end. The arrested doctors were freed. Colonel Ryumin, who had been made Deputy Minister of State Security, was executed, along with other participants in the Jewish operation. A little later the woman who had caused all the trouble, Dr Timashuk, was arrested and deprived of the Order of Lenin, the decoration she had received for her services to the Soviet government and her political vigilance.

But what about those who were dismissed? Were they invited to return to their jobs and did they receive apologies for the unpleasantness caused them? Nothing of the sort. Instead, confidential instructions were issued advising institutions to avoid taking on people of Jewish nationality for work in such organizations as the Foreign Ministry, the Foreign Trade Ministry, the TASS agency, the Novosti agency and Moscow radio and television, not to mention the KGB and the GRU. They remain in force to this day.

Statistics published in the Soviet Union and abroad giving the percentage of Jews taking part in the country's economic, cultural, scientific and political life compared with that of other Soviet minority peoples appear to contradict suggestions of any anti-Semitic prejudice on the part of the Soviet regime. Moreover Jews are often to be found among Soviet officials travelling abroad – such carefully selected and trusted people as Georgi Arbatov, director of the Institute of America and Canada; Aleksandr Chakovsky, author and editor-in-chief of the *Literary Gazette*, who always expressed his pride at being a Jew; G. Borovik, author and journalist who travels frequently in the West; Vladimir Pozner, a political commentator for Moscow radio and television, who is to be seen quite often on television screens in the West; and V. Zorin, another political commentator for Soviet radio and television, who was known as Brezhnev's court journalist. There is also General Dragunsky, chairman of the Anti-Zionist Committee, General Milshtein, the expert on disarmament matters, and the Soviet Deputy Prime Minister Dymshits, who has not been seen or heard of for some time. So the official view is that Jews in the Soviet Union are well represented and have nothing to complain about.

In reality the situation is different. To prove my point I will quote just two cases out of many that came to my knowledge, to demonstrate how far the Soviet regime is from resolving the problem of national minorities. Among Russians, and especially among Russian officials, anti-Semitism is accepted and not condemned. For example, if the head of a personnel office in a ministry or department were to refuse to employ a consultant, however able he might be, because he was a Jew, no questions would be asked. My good friend, S. German, in charge of personnel in the TASS agency, brushed an application for employment aside without even reading it as soon as he saw the reply to question 5, about nationality. I saw this happen more than once in the case of Georgi Vainer, who was unable for several years to find work at his own speciality and was forced to take a job as an electrician to avoid being classified as a 'parasite'. One of my friends asked me if I could find Vainer a job in the TASS or Novosti agencies or in the radio, which was where his qualifications could be best used. My position at the time in the Journalists' Union enabled me to have both official and friendly relations with the editors of all the principal media. So I called the Deputy General Director of TASS, Vladimir Khatuntsev and asked him to take Vainer on as an ordinary reporter on domestic matters. Khatuntsev agreed on the spot, though when he heard the name Vainer he seemed to hesitate, but promised to think of something.

He thought for some three or four months. In the end I phoned him again and asked him in a tone of genuine annoyance whether it was really so difficult for him to do me such a trifling favour. I pointed out that we did much more difficult things for him, such as including in delegations people whom he wanted to travel abroad. Khatuntsev took my point and said Vainer should report to the TASS personnel department the next day. I was then rung up by German, who wanted to make sure whether it was I who had asked for Vainer to be fixed up in TASS, because he had often hinted to me openly that I omitted to include him in a delegation of journalists going abroad.

Once I had reassured German, Vainer was able to start work with TASS the next day. Thanks to his ability as a writer his fortunes steadily improved, and Georgi and his brother Arkadi Vainer are now well-known authors in the Soviet Union. They have written a series of gripping detective novels out of which films and plays have been made, but as far as I know they are still unable to travel as tourists to the capitalist countries or to be published in the West.

An even sadder case was that of Bernshtein, who worked for me in the Union of Journalists in charge of the international department. He was intelligent and well educated and spoke English fluently, but he was never allowed to travel abroad, even to the countries of Eastern Europe, in a journalists' delegation. Later he left the Union of Journalists and took to translating works from English for various publishers. Everything was going well for him until the question arose of putting his name on a book. Publishers could not accept a translation made by someone called Bernshtein, so he had to get friends with good Russian surnames to submit the translation to the publisher as though it were their own work. The publisher, knowing perfectly well who had done the work, would then pay the fee to Bernshtein's friend, who would in turn hand it over to him. But it was the friend's name that appeared as translator on the title page of the book. In the end the publishers advised Bernshtein to change his name to something more Russian-sounding, which he managed to do with some difficulty, so that his translations now appear under the typically Russian name of Burakov.

Two examples of anti-Semitism may appear insignificant in a country as vast as the Soviet Union, but they reflect exactly the present state of the problem of the national minorities as it affects not only the Jewish people, but other non-Russian peoples as well. I am not Jewish, but neither am I Russian, and I have on many occasions had to experience the burden of what it means to come from Georgia, a nation defamed by Khrushchev in his day and treated by the Russian rulers in a thoroughly chauvinistic way. And it is not just the Georgians who are treated like that; the Armenians and other Eastern peoples are too. The appointment of Eduard Shevardnadze as Soviet Foreign Minister and of T. Menteshashvili as Secretary of the Supreme Soviet is not an indication of any change in attitude towards Georgians on the part of the great majority of officials big and small. As among the Jews, so also among the Georgians, Armenians and other minorities, there are always a few carefully chosen 'aborigines' who do not represent their 'reservations'.

A striking example of a Russian nationalist (though he is rumoured to be half Jewish) is Leonid Zamyatin, who is now Soviet ambassador to the United Kingdom. When in the early 1970s candidates were being considered for the post of chief TASS correspondent in London, Zamyatin, then General Director of TASS, flatly refused to agree to the appointment of an Armenian, Artem Melikyan. As chairman of the trade union in the TASS organization I was present at the discussion and I was astonished when Zamyatin defended his opposition to Melikyan by saying he had a moustache, that all Caucasians were lazy, and that they were interested only in eating and drinking.

I was very upset, not simply because, like most Georgian men, I also have a moustache, but because of the cynical manner in which Zamyatin decided the fate of an experienced journalist and a good man. After much persuasion by Vladimir Khatuntsev, Zamyatin, reluctantly and making it abundantly clear that he had been forced to yield, gave his approval to sending Artem Melikyan to London. He added that he was quite sure that Melikyan would not be able to cope with the work, but since there was no other available candidate he would have to have the job. Before Melikyan took over, the TASS bureau in London, headed by a Russian, had worked very badly. Under Melikyan it began to work better, but Zamyatin, vindictive and backbiting, never missed a chance of finding fault with the work of the London bureau, issuing a stream of instructions designed to disorganize the work of the bureau. Melikyan finally returned to Moscow without having completed the usual three years.

In spite of the fact that I had lived practically the whole of my adult life in Moscow and was regarded in Georgia as a russified Georgian whose first language was Russian and not Georgian, I always remained a Georgian in the eyes of the Russian rulers. This was not a point in my favour. I cannot therefore agree that the Jewish question is unique. When I was in Moscow in 1979 my friends were indignant that people in the West exaggerated the situation of the Jews in the Soviet Union. After all, the Russians were saying, the Jews had actually become a privileged nation in the Soviet Union, since they did at least have the chance of leaving the country, while other Soviet peoples had no such chance. For that reason, the great majority of Russians do not take kindly to the speeches and actions of the so-called dissidents of Jewish nationality.

CHAPTER ELEVEN

Union of Journalists

WORKING IN GEORGIA I had got out of touch with events in the rest of the country and learnt about them only through newspaper articles. It appeared that the situation was changing for the beter: people were voicing their thoughts more freely; covert criticism of Stalin's policy could be detected in speeches by officials; the Soviet leaders began to make a real effort to improve relations with Western countries; there was a slight lifting of the Iron Curtain which had for many years prevented democratic ideas from penetrating the Soviet Union. Khrushchev, having destroyed Beria and removed rivals like Malenkov from his path, took power in his own hands and began to play the part of the popular ruler. The creative intelligentsia, which included writers, poets, musicians and playwrights, were describing what was taking place as a 'thaw', and made the mistake of taking this performance seriously.

I have to say that neither then nor later did we in the KGB believe in any thaw or any democratization of the Soviet system, although our behaviour, like that of the Soviet population as a whole, became more relaxed, conversations became franker, and people were less afraid of being accused of anti-Soviet activity for some trivial reason.

In our view, Nikita Khrushchev and those around him were determined to show the Soviet people that they were better than Stalin had been and that they had a better understanding of the people and their aspirations. Without such a 'thaw' they could never have criticized the 'cult of personality' and exposed the myth – which they themselves had created – of Stalin's genius. I do not think they did this only for the benefit of the Soviet people. It was rather to affirm their own authority as progressive and popular leaders. No real change occurred; the domestic policy of the Politburo and the Party leadership remains unaltered to this day: there is still no freedom to voice one's opinions, to criticize the way the country is ruled, or to write as one pleases. As under Stalin, but in a somewhat milder form, the only freedom to write or criticize, make speeches or organize demonstrations is that which is sanctioned and approved by the Party leaders. That is why I never believed that Khrushchev was sincere in his proclaimed desire to change the totalitarian essence of the Soviet system. Behind Khrushchev's 'simple and clear' declarations about the need to 'correct the faults of the past' and to grant the people freedom and independence to create, there stood the counter-intelligence services of the KGB which, on instructions from that same Khrushchev and the Politburo, conducted a relentless struggle against anyone who displayed too much independence in creative, political or any other ways.

Paradoxically enough, the so-called 'secret speech' which Khrushchev made at the 20th Congress of the Soviet Communist Party at the end of February 1956 played an important part in my life, for the worse, as it seemed to me then, but perhaps it was for the better. (Why Khrushchev's speech 'Concerning the Cult of Personality and its Consequences' is still described as 'secret' is beyond my comprehension. How can one talk about it being secret when there were more than six hundred people present at the congress and when the whole country knew about it the next day?)

After my dismissal from the KGB I returned to Moscow in August 1957 on the opening day of the International Youth

Festival. It had been organized by the authorities to show that the Iron Curtain had been lifted. The Soviet population, convinced that a new era had arrived, greeted this event with tremendous enthusiasm. This was hardly surprising in a country whose people had for many years – in fact, since its foundation – never welcomed so many foreign visitors as on this occasion. But the rejoicing at the new freedom was premature. The Central Committees of the Soviet Communist Party, and the Komsomol, not to mention the KGB, had no intention of allowing Soviet boys and girls to mix freely with the foreign visitors. The so-called thaw turned into a very unpleasant experience for a number of Soviet young people. With assistance from the KGB, Komsomol officials set up flying squads to seize any young people, especially girls, who established 'impermissible' relations with foreigners. Members of these flying squads were provided with hairdressers' clippers with which they cut off a strip of hair from the heads of those who, from the Party's point of view, were on too friendly terms with foreigners. The victims of this treatment were thus prevented from appearing again in public. According to what I was told by Colonel Norman Borodin and Colonel Fedoseyev, head of department in the Second Chief Directorate, these measures were approved by Nikita Khrushchev. It is true that, once the festival was over, because of the many protests it received, the Party Central Committee condemned such actions as 'incorrect', but that was all. The offended and humiliated young people had to be satisfied with that.

At the time, however, these matters were of little interest to me, because I had a more important and more difficult problem: what I was going to do and how I was going to live. I had the idea that my experience of work in the secret police could not, unfortunately, be applied in any other branch of the economy or sphere of activity, but I was wrong.

At the end of August I had a meeting at KGB headquarters with Borodin and Colonel Fedoseyev. This was an important meeting, because it is difficult for someone who has been dismissed from the KGB to get a job elsewhere, for the good reason that no head of a Soviet institution wants to have looking over his shoulder a person who might still have contacts with the KGB and be acting as an informer. I have to say that the KGB seldom leaves its former employees in difficult circumstances so long as they have not been dismissed for some offence, revealed state secrets or have broken the rules of the service. In this respect my situation was satisfactory and moreover I had worked in the Second Chief Directorate.

Colonel Fedoseyev said he would inform Lieutenant-General Gribanov, who had succeeded Fedotov as head of Soviet counter-intelligence, that he intended to include me in the list of 'secret employees' of the KGB, which would make it possible for me to continue working in some Soviet institution and at the same time qualify eventually for a KGB pension.

Fedoseyev and Borodin kept their promises and, after informing General Gribanov, I was taken on to the secret staff with a salary of 2000 roubles a month, the equivalent of 200 roubles today. This was less than I had been receiving as a member of the KGB staff, but it suited me since I also had the possibility of receiving another salary from wherever I was going to be found a job.

'We need to work out some interim arrangement,' Norman told me. 'The fact is that, on the initiative of leading Soviet journalists and the KGB, the Party has decided to set up a Union of Journalists of the USSR. There will be a vacancy for a deputy to the General Secretary, who will be responsible for the union's contacts with foreign journalists and other press organizations in both the capitalist and the socialist countries. I believe that job would suit you well. But who gets it will be decided not by the union itself, but by the Propaganda Department of the Central Committee of the CPSU and by us. I doubt whether the Propaganda

Department will oppose our candidate, because they know perfectly well that the Journalists' Union's international contacts must be under our control and serve our interests.

'But we can't just shove you into the job like that. You'll have to work for a while in television as deputy editor of the international programmes. Ivanov, the head of the television service, knows about you already and has agreed to your appointment, all the more readily because we are expecting a visit by Dag Hammarskjold, the Secretary General of the United Nations Organization, who has asked us to let him appear on television. The people working on the international programmes know little about political affairs, unfortunately, and the editor, Sachkov, although he has a fine war record, also has a fine record for drinking and is busy turning all his employees into drunkards. I know it won't be easy for you at the outset, but you won't have to stay there long,' Borodin concluded.

I took a six-week holiday on the Black Sea coast and then started work in central television.

Early in 1958 Dag Hammarskjold arrived in Moscow and was put up in the Sovietskaya Hotel on Leningrad Avenue. According to Ivanov he wanted to appear on the television 'live', without showing us the text of his remarks beforehand.

'You realize that we can't possibly permit this,' the director said. 'Goodness knows what he might say, and we would have to answer for it to the Central Committee. So phone his assistant, then go and see Hammarskjold and persuade him that we must see the text before he speaks. How to do it you will have to work out for yourself, but do it in such a way that he doesn't get the impression that we are out to censor what he has to say.'

I phoned Norman Borodin and told him about the job Ivanov had given me; it had been agreed that all my meetings with foreigners would be co-ordinated between us. But Norman said that the KGB had no interest in Hammarskjold and that I should go ahead, so I duly made an appointment to see him. Hammarskjold was accommodated in a big three-room suite and there were bodyguards and KGB men on duty in the corridor. He received me cordially, making my task much easier. After an exchange of pleasantries I told him that it was essential for us to have the text of his remarks, not because we wished to know what he was going to say in advance but so that we could allot exactly the right amount of time to his speech.

Hammarskjold raised no objections, saying that the text would be handed to me by his assistant next morning. I said goodbye to him and had hardly reached the entrance hall where my coat was hanging when I found Hammarskjold already holding my coat for me and helping me on with it.

Hammarskjold's appearance on Soviet television went off without any complications, since the text of his remarks was shortened somewhat by the Party's Propaganda Department and a few corrections were made to it after I had delivered it to the Central Committee's headquarters on the Old Square.

My handling of Hammarskjold was well thought of – Ivanov thanked me and his approval played a certain part in my future career. In March 1958 Borodin asked me to go and see him in the KGB offices. When I arrived he scarcely allowed me to sit down.

'You must go at once to the *Pravda* offices to see Daniel Kraminov,' he told me. 'I have spoken to him about you and how we intend to make you deputy to the General Secretary of the Orgburo of the Union of Journalists. Gribanov has spoken about you to the deputy editor-in-chief of *Pravda*, Dmitri Goryunov, who doesn't object in principle to your being put up for the job but wants to meet you to make sure that you are as good as we've made you out to be. Speak to him straightforwardly and frankly within the limits of what's reasonable, but don't give the impression that you are desperate to get the job – let him persuade you you want it.'

That same evening I went to the *Pravda* offices. Kraminov

met me and took me straight to Goryunov, who, like Kraminov, was a deputy chairman of the Union of Journalists.

Dmitri Goryunov looked stern. Less than medium height, rather plump, and with a deep voice, Goryunov always appeared sad. He was to become one of my closest friends, one of the people I most respected in the upper reaches of Soviet journalism.

He asked me whether I understood anything about journalism or about the duties of a deputy to the General Secretary. I replied frankly that I had only a vague idea of what the job involved, but that if I were appointed I hoped to be able to cope with it. 'A self-confident fellow, I see,' said Goryunov with a smile. 'I've heard something about you,' he went on, switching suddenly to the more familiar mode of address, 'but, if you don't object, I will phone my friend, KGB General Z., in your presence. He knows you too. I'll just ask him whether they will recognize you as one of their men, because that is very important for our union.' I simply shrugged my shoulders. I knew General Z. through my work in the Second Chief Directorate and had discussed with him operations connected with foreign journalists and diplomats.

Goryunov picked up the receiver of his Kremlin phone and called General Z. Eventually he said: 'So you say he's one of yours,' and, looking at me, added, 'Then we'll take him on.' Then he put down the phone.

'We'll take you on,' Goryunov repeated. 'It all depends now on the Central Committee, because this appointment has to have its approval.' Nevertheless he and Kraminov congratulated me on being appointed to a job which opened the way for me to the top level of Soviet journalism and the company of people who play an important part in the formation of both the foreign and the domestic policy of the Soviet state.

Next day my appointment was confirmed and I became

Deputy General Secretary of the Orgburo of the Union of Journalists of the USSR.

The Chairman of the Orgburo of the Union of Journalists at the time was Nikolai Palgunov, the General Director of the TASS agency. He was a person with a wide general knowledge and a remarkable memory, a natural aristocrat who always wore a bow tie, even when he went to see Stalin. Stalin never even wore an ordinary suit, and regarded all neckwear, not to mention bow ties, as relics of the bourgeois past. It had been an act of heroism on Palgunov's part, and ran contrary to his nature. Normally he was far from being a hero and always preferred to play safe. The story was often repeated of how, when Palgunov was working as TASS correspondent in Paris in the 1930s, there was an unusually heavy snowfall. Palgunov did not dare to report this event on the basis of his own observation but sent a cable to Moscow saying: 'According to the French Havas agency, an unusually large amount of snow fell today in Paris.'

Palgunov was a representative of the Stalin school of journalists and was unable to adjust to the new tendencies in Soviet journalism after Khrushchev came to power, when there was a brief period of liberalization as a result of pressure by younger journalists. These included Alexei Adzhubei, Khrushchev's son-in-law, who made an effort to change the 'reinforced concrete' style of the Soviet press. Palgunov retired in 1960.

Adzhubei became editor-in-chief of *Izvestia*, and it was thanks to his influence on Khrushchev that some changes were brought about. The material published in newspapers and periodicals was more varied and interesting in content, new publications and publishing houses came into existence, and genuinely controversial articles were printed. But in the later years of Khrushchev's rule everything slipped back gradually into the old style, and after he was overthrown it all reverted to the way it had been. Soviet newspapers today differ only slightly in content and style from those that were published under Stalin, except for the absence of the excessively laudatory articles about the Party leader.

The Union of Journalists of the USSR is not a trade union of journalists but an organization which is supposed to improve the creativity of Soviet journalism and to extend and strengthen contacts with the journalists of other countries. In 1959 its leaders included Pavel Satyukov, the editor-in-chief of *Pravda* and a member of the Central Committee; Alexei Adzhubei, the editor-in-chief of *Izvestia*, another Central Committee man; Dmitri Goryunov, the General Director of TASS, also a Central Committee member; Boris Burkov, the Chairman of the *Novosti* agency, who was a candidate member of the CC; Mikhail Kharlamov, the Chairman of the State Committee for Television and Radio, who ranked as a member of the government; General N. Makeyev, the editor-in-chief of the newspaper *Krasnaya Zvezda*; and Shalva Sanakoyev, the deputy editor-in-chief of the periodical *Mezhdunarodnaya Zhizn*. The Union of Journalists thus played an important role in the Soviet political system in the fields of both domestic and foreign policy. Everything the Union of Journalists does was and is subject to the direct control of the *apparat* and Secretariat of the CC.

To tell the truth, I was not interested in the creative aspect of the union's work; my task was of a completely different kind. The secretariat of the union and the Propaganda Department of the Party had instructed me to organize an international department in the union and to draw up a plan for international contacts which would include invitations to foreign journalists to visit the Soviet Union and the despatch of Soviet journalists abroad. The object was not only to strengthen links with journalists' organizations in other countries but also to increase the authority of the International Union of Journalists, which had its headquarters in Prague and was effectively controlled by the International Department of the CPSU and the Soviet Union of Journalists. To make it appear independent the Chairman was a French journalist, Jean Maurice Herman, but the General Secretary, who in practice ran the show, was a Czechoslovak journalist and his deputy was a Soviet. This distribution of jobs made it possible to use the organization to take steps against the enemies of the socialist camp and to unite journalists in the fight against imperialism. After the mid-1950s a rival non-Communist organization had been set up in Brussels, covering a number of European countries as well as the United States. My job was to counter the influence of this new union.

In the eighteen months preceding the First Congress of Journalists in November 1959 I was able not only to organize the International Department but also to establish quite good relations with the editors of all the principal newspapers, as well as with officials in the Party's Propaganda Department, headed in 1958 by Leonid Ilichev, who later became a Secretary of the Party Central Committee. Before that he was head of the press department at the Soviet Foreign Ministry and played an active part in the work of the Union of Journalists.

Ilichev once told me that the Union of Journalists ought to be primarily a political and ideological organization, carrying out the policy of the CPSU in the Soviet Union and abroad. Much the same was said by the late Mikhail Suslov, when he was one of the most important Secretaries of the CPSU and regarded as the Party's chief ideologist. He addressed leaders of the Union of Journalists, including myself, before the First All-Union Congress of Journalists.

Like Mikoyan, Suslov, who was a key policy-maker until his death in 1982, was a cunning and resourceful politician who succeeded in holding on to his position under Stalin, then under Khrushchev and then under Brezhnev. It would be an exaggeration to say that he had any special knowledge of Marxism or that he made any contribution to its theory. His only achievement was to have invented the thoroughly unscholarly term 'advanced socialism' which in a later version – as 'mature' socialism – is still in use by the Party leaders. Although sickly (and with an unpleasantly feeble handshake), Suslov managed to survive for a long time both physically and politically.

In his speech he spoke at length about the crucial role of Soviet journalism in spreading socialism among the Soviet population and how it was fundamentally different from Western journalism, in which, as he put it, cheap sensationalism and anti-Sovietism financed by the capitalists prevailed, while the real problems of working people were scarcely reflected in the press. It was the usual propaganda speech, and I was surprised that Suslov should address highly placed journalists like Goryunov, Kraminov, Burkov, Satyukov and Adzhubei in such terms.

Our main task, Suslov stressed, was to bring about the creative development of Soviet journalism, to increase journalists' qualifications, and to continue the political education of the working masses. As far as the union's international activity was concerned, it must become an organization that would present and explain Soviet foreign policy to foreign journalists, especially those from the Third World countries who found themselves at the parting of the ways and needed help to take the way of 'non-capitalist development'. Suslov had doubtless played some part in producing this formula and it came to be widely used in official statements. Of course the term 'non-capitalist development' prompted the question: if not the capitalist way then which way? The Party ideologists apparently had in mind the socialist way, but they did not want to say so aloud for fear of scaring off Third World countries that had already heard about the consequences of socialist development in the Soviet Union.

Suslov was the first really important person I had come into contact with and I was amazed by the flat and monotonous style of his remarks and by the way he repeated the soulless formulae typical of the editorials in the Soviet press. It appeared that even Suslov, a Secretary of the Central

Committee, could not permit himself to use a more every-day, human language.

'You must be honest and modest Party helpers,' Suslov told us, 'restrained in your behaviour and manner of life. Only then will the people believe what you write and the accounts you give of our successes and shortcomings. And remember always that you are not "free" journalists but workers for the Party.'

I could see that Adzhubei, Goryunov, Kraminov and Satyukov, while paying apparent attention to Suslov and treating him with respect, were in fact laughing at him. It was the sort of talk that would have suited a factory meeting. As we left Suslov's office Goryunov commented bitterly: 'Now we know how to cure our political illiteracy.' Adzhubei, who detested Suslov, used much stronger language in his comments.

The Union of Journalists of the USSR had premises in a building on the Avenue of Peace, occupying the top two floors of a mansion that had belonged to the Russian poet Valeri Bryusov. The premises were not originally suitable for the purpose, but after some rebuilding and redecorating they were reasonably pleasant and comfortable. I had a large office with a long table for conferences and several telephones. The most important was the telephone known as a *vertushka*. Connected to a separate government telephone network with four-digit numbers, it gets you through directly to the General Secretary of the Soviet Communist Party, or at least to his secretary. The automatic switchboard for this network is guarded by the KGB. The telephone book is marked 'For official use only' and contains about ten thousand entries. It is kept in a safe so that unauthorized people do not find out numbers and use the *vertushka* themselves. In unguarded premises, the telephone itself has to be locked away. These strict measures were brought in after unauthorized people had used the telephone to get through to Secretaries and officials of the Central Committee *apparat* in order to make complaints or requests. It is practically impossible to reach ministers or editors of national newspapers on the ordinary telephone because their secretaries protect them from the public. But a call on the *vertushka* is answered by the important man himself. Moreover, even if you don't know the official concerned personally, you can ask him anything and expect a sympathetic and understanding hearing, since he realizes that he is dealing with one of his peers in the élite.

With the aid of the *vertushka* I used to help members of the union obtain apartments, jobs and vouchers for holiday homes, sanatoria and even places in hospitals. I myself acquired a new apartment through the intervention of Alexei Adzhubei, who simply wrote a letter to the Chairman of the Moscow City Council, Bobrovnikov. But I had difficulty in getting a telephone connected. I asked the telephone authority in my district to provide me with a phone in the apartment, but was told all the lines were being used and that there was a waiting list of three years. I really needed to have a telephone, so I called up one of the deputy ministers of communications on the *vertushka* : he assured me a telephone would be connected in the next few days. Two days later a whole brigade of telephone engineers descended on my apartment. The man in charge told me that all the lines in the underground cable really were being used, so they were going to provide me with a special overhead connection. Such is the power of the *vertushka*.

As well as an official car and its two drivers, my new job brought me the possibility of obtaining food, books and even theatre tickets without difficulty and without standing in queues. For a person living in the Soviet Union that is an extraordinary privilege. Nevertheless such benefits could not be compared to those I had had when I was working directly for the KGB.

Apart from a couple of girl interpreters, the International Department did not exist when I arrived, and my first job was to organize it. I was to co-ordinate the international work of the union with Daniel Kraminov, an experienced journalist and commentator on foreign affairs who enjoyed considerable authority with the CC. During the Second World War Kraminov had been TASS correspondent in Britain and attached to General Montgomery's staff. He spoke English fluently and had a fine grasp of international problems. After the launching in 1959–60 of the magazine *Za rubezhom* (*Abroad*), which is formally regarded as the organ of the Union of Journalists and publishes articles and commentaries taken from the foreign press, Kraminov was made editor-in-chief. Although he is a complex and difficult character, I liked his independent way of thinking and his self-reliance. He never bowed down before anyone, not even Adzhubei, who already had considerable power.

I remember seeing him order the rather tipsy Adzhubei out of his office after the latter had proposed that he should become a political correspondent on *Izvestia*, of which Adzhubei was then editor-in-chief. When Kraminov refused, Adzhubei said he could make mincemeat of him if he wished. Kraminov in fact kicked him out of his office. When we discussed how to handle foreign delegations he would take decisions himself rather than picking up the phone to refer to the Central Committee.

Kraminov approved the list of people I had selected to work in the International Department; I then took it to the Department of Agitation and Propaganda at the Central Committee, where I was received by the head of the department, Ilichev, and his deputy A. Romanov. At the meeting, I was asked to draw up a programme covering visits to the Soviet Union by delegations of foreign journalists and visits to foreign countries by Soviet newsmen. For each delegation of journalists we had to prepare a programme involving visits to industrial enterprises, schools, institutes, medical establishments and collective farms, as well as meetings in newspaper offices with Soviet journalists. If some special importance was attached to the delegation – for example, if it came from West Germany or America – then it might also be received by Soviet leaders.

'The Central Committee attaches great importance to this work,' Ilichev told us, 'because journalists who have visited our country can write about us in their own countries. Public opinion is formed by the mass media. We must dispel the belief in the West that there are bears prowling round the streets of Moscow and that Russians are savages with beards who gulp down cabbage soup out of their boots. Most important of all, we must persuade foreign newsmen of our desire to live at peace with all countries and, of course, of the superiority of our socialist system which has abolished unemployment, poverty and the exploitation of man by man.'

I had frequent meetings with Ilichev and he made a good impression on me. Short, rather plump, with a typically Russian round face and a way of speaking simply, calmly and with a sense of humour, he was very different from Party officials like Suslov and Ponomarev, although he had spent practically his whole life working in the Party. We often sat together at the Journalists' Club, where he would recount to such experienced newsmen as Goryunov, Kraminov, Burkov and Adzhubei how, in the late 1920s, he had written his first article for *Pravda* under the headline 'Fooligans from Sukharevka' instead of 'hooligans'. He cited this as a measure of his lack of education, but this had not prevented him from making a good career. Starting as a newspaper reporter, he became editor of *Pravda*, then head of the press department of the Foreign Ministry and a Secretary of the Central Committee from 1961 to 1965, and was then made a Deputy Minister of Foreign Affairs in the government, a position he still occupies.

I have the impression that Ilichev never sought to ingratiate himself with anyone – not even Khrushchev; Ilichev was not dismissed from his position as Secretary of the CC immediately after Khrushchev's downfall. He is intelligent, perceptive and quick-witted when necessary, and is well able to defend his own point of view. Most important, he is well acquainted with the realities of life in the Soviet Union, and not just from looking out of the window of a car. At the same time he is an orthodox Communist. When I knew him he enjoyed a drink (a practice now strictly forbidden by Gorbachev) and talked to everyone on equal terms without trying to impose his authority.

On one occasion the Soviet ambassador in Paris, Vinogradov, complained about me after I had spoken to him on the telephone; an official of the International Department was about to address a reprimand to me through the Central Committee. When I told Ilichev about it, he phoned Ponomarev in my presence and asked him what Vinogradov was doing in Paris apart from accompanying President de Gaulle on shooting trips.

Having obtained the blessing of Ilichev's Agitprop Department, I made an appointment with Norman Borodin to discuss how to organize counter-intelligence and intelligence work among the foreign journalists. It was impossible for me to conceal my KGB origins from the Soviet newsmen in Moscow, many of whom assumed at first that my duties included keeping an eye on them and their contacts with foreigners. This was not the case and slowly, after about a year, the Moscow newsmen came to accept me as one of them.

When I arrived in his office Borodin congratulated me on my appointment and said that General Gribanov wanted to see me. Still a comparatively young lieutenant-general, Gribanov was not particularly striking in appearance and had none of the stern and penetrating look that such people are credited with in fiction; indeed I was struck by his calm, friendly manner.

Gribanov also congratulated me and addressed me as a 'prince of journalism'. He had discovered that, when I was working in the First Chief Directorate, I was given the code-name 'Prince'. A Chekist was always a Chekist, Gribanov told me, and that my main task would be to facilitate the work of the KGB connected with foreign journalists.

I replied that I would do everything in my power to help, since I had not yet 'gone cold' and had not forgotten the rules of operational work, which were in my blood. Gribanov told me that Norman Borodin would keep in constant contact with me. He also suggested that I should take another KGB man into the International Department so that I would not have to spend time dealing with minor matters.

I pointed out that I had been approached for help by Gennadi Fedoseyev, who had recently been dismissed from the Second Chief Directorate for having, in a drunken state, fired his revolver at the ceiling of the Central restaurant, creating panic among the customers. Fedoseyev was now working under cover in the guise of deputy head of the Department for the Service of Foreigners. I had suggested making him head of the International Department in the union and Kraminov had already agreed. Gribanov did not object, though he thought I should keep an eye on Fedoseyev because of his tendency to drink too much. Gribanov also told me that the First Chief Directorate was interested in me and would soon approach me.

Oleg Mikhailovich Gribanov had been head of Soviet counter-intelligence for many years and it was under his direction that some successful operations were carried out involving foreign diplomats and correspondents, including Western ambassadors, one of whom was the French ambassador Maurice Dejean. Although Gribanov served the Soviet regime devotedly and honestly, like many others he was eventually thrown overboard and disappeared from sight. The reason for his downfall, and for the dismissal of a number of other counter-intelligence officers, was the defection to the USA in 1964 of Yuri Nosenko, who had been working in Geneva as a member of the Soviet delegation. Nosenko's father was, until his death, Minister for Ship-building in the Soviet Government and a close friend of Prime Minister Alexei Kosygin. Gribanov was held respons-ible for allowing Nosenko to defect, was dismissed from the KGB and relieved of his general's rank. People who are thrown out of such high positions usually break down com-pletely, become invalids or die shortly afterwards. Gribanov did not break down completely, but when I later saw him by chance I was distressed by the transformation in him.

In the autumn of 1965 I was drinking with a friend, another KGB man, Nikolai Tess, in the Crystal café on Kutuzov Avenue. We were chatting away when suddenly I saw standing at the bar a man whose face, though much changed, I recognized. It was Oleg Gribanov. Next to him was a young man who, I realized later, was a KGB man attached to him to ensure that in his present drunk and depressed state he would not get himself into trouble. I rose from the table and went up to him. The young man immedi-ately asked what I wanted. I replied that I had known Oleg Mikhailovich for a long time and was glad to see him. Hear-ing my voice, Gribanov looked round and I saw that he was drunk, but he recognized me and returned my greeting. I then asked him, stupidly, how was he getting on. He replied with a laugh that he was doing fine and asked what I was doing there. I replied that I had met an old comrade, another has-been. Gribanov replied that we were all has-beens.

I invited him to our table, but the young man objected. Gribanov brushed him aside and sat down with us. 'Don't give him any more to drink,' the young man whispered. We didn't really have much to say to each other. Swaying slightly Gribanov asked me if I remembered Yuri Nosenko.

'Of course,' I said.

'Well he's the one to blame for the fact that I'm reduced to nothing. If only I'd known, if only I'd known,' Gribanov kept repeating.

'Let's have a parting drink,' Gribanov said. 'Maybe this is the last time we shall meet.' So, without paying any attention to the young man's protests, I ordered whisky for us all. We drank in silence, got up from the table and said goodbye. And so, under the influence of drink and misfortune, Lieutenant-General Oleg Mikhailovich Gribanov, once the confident and proud head of Soviet counter-intelligence, walked unsteadily towards the exit.

By the middle of 1958 the business of organizing the Union of Journalists was complete and we started to receive delegations of foreign newsmen and individual journalists; soon we were dealing with as many as fifty of them every year. Whom we invited was decided in accordance with the interests of the Soviet government. For example, we invited a group of newsmen from Thailand not so much for the purpose of conveying socialist propaganda as of exploring the possibilities of establishing normal relations between the Soviet Union and Thailand. For each delegation we drew up a programme, approved by the Central Committee, which included trips around the country and visits to enterprises carefully selected to confirm the success of socialist economic planning.

We realized, of course, that the journalists knew very well that we would be taking them to specially prepared show-places known as 'Potemkin villages'. So when we discussed with them the programme for their visit I would ask them if they wanted to see the old-fashioned, backward enterprises and collective farms which did not come up to our expectations. If they did, we were ready to arrange it. But I thought it more important to show what we were aiming at and what we hoped to achieve, so that they would get a better understanding of the essence of socialism, which had transformed the backward Russian empire into a great modern state.

This trick worked amazingly well, because the foreign newsmen, being our guests, found it difficult to demand that they should be shown the back door of their host's house when they were being invited to enter by the front. Even delegations from West Germany, America, France and other Western countries did not quarrel with our proposals.

Another awkward issue was freedom of speech and the freedom of the press in the Soviet Union. To this constantly repeated question we replied that the accusation that there was no freedom of speech or criticism in the USSR was not true. Every Soviet citizen had the right freely to express his opinion and to make critical comments, which helped us to correct mistakes and shortcomings. We even welcomed such criticism. If, however, the criticism was malicious and was not aimed at helping us to correct mistakes, but was just a slanderous attack on the Soviet way of life and the Soviet leadership, then we rejected it. Everybody in the Soviet Union was free to support and to express his approval of the measures undertaken by the Party and the government which were aimed at boosting the country's economic development and improving the standard of living of the Soviet people. Are you able – we would ask the foreign journalists – to oppose the owners of your newspapers and magazines in the pages of their publications? Would your editor allow you to publish an article critical of his actions or his political views?

Your boss – we would tell them – is a private entrepreneur; our boss is the Communist Party and its Central Committee. Just as you support your boss, so we support our Party, the leaders of which are not capitalists, do not own private businesses or have private incomes, but direct all their efforts towards the good of the country and the people. It is not surprising if there are some people in the Soviet Union who are not satisfied, since there has never been a government or a social system that satisfied everybody. You know that better than we do, because in your countries half the population is usually dissatisfied with the government. But that does not mean the system collapses. We have a population of 250 million people, and if even 10 million of them are dissatisfied that is still only a pitiable minority.

After such a tirade the foreign journalists usually lost any desire to discuss questions of freedom or human rights in the Soviet Union. I used the same arguments when I was abroad and it always produced the effect I wanted.

The people appointed to accompany a delegation of foreign newsmen usually include, depending on the importance of the delegation, either an official member of the KGB staff or a trusted journalist with experience of work abroad, often a KGB informer. During a trip round the country the members of a delegation are kept under observation by the local state security, both to prevent any undesirable contacts with the Soviet people and to ensure the safety of the journalists.

Before the arrival of a delegation or an individual journalist we would have been briefed by the KGB *rezidentury* abroad. If we were told that a member of a delegation was working for or connected with a foreign intelligence service or was intending to gather information and photographs which might reflect badly on the Soviet system, he would be put under surveillance and special action might be required.

For example, when a delegation of newspaper editors from West Germany visited Irkutsk in Siberia one of them slipped out of a reception in order to photograph the old tumbledown Siberian houses and the muddy streets. While he was taking his pictures he was stopped by some 'ordinary' workers who asked what he was photographing. He replied, in Russian but with a foreign accent, that he wanted to have a record of an old Siberian house. The workers, KGB employees of course, seized him and dragged him along to the police station, where his camera was taken from him and his film exposed. The police held him for more than three hours in a very uncomfortable and dirty cell and released him only after I intervened. We had been warned by our *rezidentura* in West Germany that this man had connections with reactionary circles and intended to use his trip to the USSR for improper purposes.

Delegations of foreign journalists were usually provided with accommodation in what was then the new multi-storey Hotel Ukraina, situated on the bank of the Moscow River and Kutuzov Avenue, where there were also groups of buildings housing foreign diplomats, journalists and businessmen. All these buildings and certain of the rooms in the hotel are equipped with bugging apparatus and are kept under observation night and day by the KGB.

The resources allotted by the Government for looking after foreign journalists were enormous. The tables groaned under the weight of caviar, sturgeon and other delicacies and bottles of vodka, Armenian brandy and Georgian wine. The provision of so much expensive food and strong drink was motivated by a desire to show how well off and hospitable we were and to loosen the tongues of our guests. For every five or six foreign guests there were ten or even fifteen competent Soviet journalists invited, including a number of fairly strong drinkers, like Adzhubei, Goryunov and Burkov, as well as some, like Satyukov, the editor of *Pravda*, who were less disposed to drink.

The big booze-up in the Soviet Union started in the mid-1950s. Everybody was drinking everywhere : at receptions, when seeing people off on trips abroad, at the presentation of an academic dissertation, on the arrival of delegations and on their departure, or merely for the sake of drinking. Khrushchev and Bulganin drank, and so did Brezhnev and Polyansky, while the country's President, Klim Voroshilov, was constantly under the influence of drink, as red as a lobster. We all drank and we drank a lot, at the government's expense. Workers drank at their own expense; young people drank at their parents' expense, the peasants profiteered in fruit and vegetables and spent the money on drink; even women began to drink. Writers drank the proceeds from their works. I don't know whether people really believed a new era was dawning or whether drinking simply made life seem easier. What I do know is that statements by certain writers that drunkenness did not become all-pervasive until Brezhnev came to power are not accurate.

Of course we did not merely ply the foreign journalists with drink: we also conducted serious propaganda work among them, especially among those from the Third World. Every organization having contact with foreign countries was given the task of winning over to our side as many as possible of the countries of Africa, Asia, the Far East and the Middle East. For that purpose Khrushchev did not spare either effort or money. Five billion roubles were thrown away in Africa alone.

Work with delegates from those countries followed two main lines: among the journalists we tried to spread socialist ideas and extended material assistance to journalists' organizations and publications in the form of cameras, printing presses and so forth. At the same time the KGB recruited both agents of influence and people to spread disinformation and counter-propaganda.

Invitations issued to Western newsmen had a serious and complex purpose. We wanted both to influence them and to learn from them. For example, if an invitation was extended to journalists from Iceland we were told to impress them with the danger of having an American military base on their territory and of the need to persuade members of their government and influential political circles to take steps to get rid of the bases. But with a delegation from the USA our approach would be different.

In 1962 the union invited a delegation of more than a dozen American journalists. They were taken round the country by Yevgeni Litoshko, a former *Pravda* correspondent in the United States, and Vladimir Paromonov, a KGB officer who had served in Cuba. When the delegation was in the Black Sea resort of Sochi I was invited to join the party. I was informed by the International Department that the

Americans were experienced newsmen who were not easily convinced and who could not be suspected of sympathy for the Soviet Union. There was therefore no point in feeding them propaganda about the Soviet system, because they would not believe it. It would be much better to criticize American policy in order to find out their views on current events, which in turn might help us to foretell the future plans and real aims of the American administration, as well as the attitude of the journalists themselves. It was hardly likely that we would be able to make out the future policy of the American administration from the journalists but it could be useful to hear their views.

After the delegation had left I was told in the CC that articles and pictures had appeared in the American press and that the result of the visit from our point of view was satisfactory.

At one of the conferences held in the Central Committee offices Party Secretary Boris Ponomarev reprimanded us for paying too little attention to strengthening our business contacts with such countries as West Germany, Turkey, the Netherlands, Belgium and Japan. It was not very easy to establish contacts with them, and we tended to take the line of least resistance and invite delegations from countries of secondary importance that did nothing but ask for material and financial aid. But if the Soviet Union was to achieve her foreign policy aims, Ponomarev told us, our first priority should be to have influence and contacts in Europe.

Ponomarev's criticism was to some extent justified. We generally preferred to invite people from Third World countries or from countries like Italy, Greece or France with which we already had more or less satisfactory relations. Moreover, we were able to show better results from our work with delegations from these countries, which made us appear more effective.

My work in the union suited me, since I continued to be involved in operational work for the KGB while taking on new administrative duties, which included financial and management problems and dealing with a variety of requests from the journalists. This work was completely new to me and brought me into contact with a circle of people among whom I had lived when I was working in the KGB but from whose manner of life and way of thinking I had remained distant. What I knew about them I had gathered mainly from informers' reports and from meeting them when I had needed to make use of them in some operation.

The side of the union's work concerned with improving the contribution made by journalism to the work of the Party and with raising the professional qualifications of Soviet journalists bored me. Nevertheless, since I was likely to remain working in that field for many years, I had to study the basic principles. It was a painful process, involving a psychological transformation, but I managed it, and began to write articles for newspapers and magazines, usually under an assumed name, and to take part in radio and even television programmes. The Dean of the Faculty of Journalism at Moscow University, Yasen Zasurksy, sent me on a course of lectures on the fundamentals of Soviet and foreign journalism, which I found of great value later when I became a TASS correspondent abroad. After that I was even invited to give a course of lectures myself – on the work of foreign correspondents. Zasursky suggested that I should study for a doctorate, because he considered the content of my lectures quite sufficient for the purpose, but I regarded myself as a practical man rather than a theoretician and so I refused, only to regret it later.

CHAPTER TWELVE

·····━━◆━━·····

Information and Disinformation

THE FOUNDATION OF the Soviet Union of Journalists had coincided with resolutions passed by the Central Committee about increasing and making more effective our propaganda and counter-propaganda work directed at the USA and the countries of Western Europe. The Central Committee took the view that the ideological struggle was heating up and that organizations in contact with foreign countries had to make greater efforts in the field of counter-propaganda, which should be aggressive, persuasive and politically sophisticated. Counter-propaganda alone could not produce the desired ideological and political results; we needed new kinds of campaign against bourgeois ideology and its attacks on the socialist system. Active measures were to be taken to anticipate political and ideological acts of provocation against socialism by Western politicians, so-called Soviet specialists and members of anti-Soviet organizations. We would have not only to reply to the West's anti-Soviet attacks as we had done in the recent past, but to take steps to manipulate public opinion in the West, primarily in the United States, in matters of domestic and foreign policy. 'Active measures' involved the more effective use of international organizations which were under Soviet influence or had been set up with the Soviet Union's help.

At a meeting in the Central Committee conducted by

Mikhail Suslov we were told that the Politburo attached great importance to the new form of counter-propaganda. Properly organized, the 'active measures' could create in the countries of the West a political climate favourable to the Soviet Union and could help to weaken the Western governments during economic crises. Suslov said that special attention was being paid to relations between the United States and Western Europe. Our task was to prevent them forming a close political and especially military alliance.

On the same occasion Boris Ponomarev, the other CC Secretary present, instructed each organization to draw up a plan of action for propaganda and counter-propaganda and told us that the CC *apparat* would keep a careful eye on its outcome. He told Pavel Satyukov, the editor of *Pravda*, that much was expected of the Union of Journalists, because contacts with journalists were one of the 'active measures'. No one had better opportunities than the journalists to influence public opinion. Satyukov assured him of our co-operation, but it was not Satyukov but I who would have to carry out the work. Satyukov, Adzhubei and Kraminov were ideological leaders, while I was just a work-horse, along with others.

A few days later I was summoned by Ivan Agayants, head of the department in the First Chief Directorate of the KGB dealing with disinformation.

I had known Agayants since 1947, when I went to work in the First Chief Directorate against Iran. He was regarded as an experienced intelligence officer and specialist on the Middle East and especially Iran. He enjoyed considerable authority among members of the Soviet intelligence service because of his professional skills, knowledge and intelligence. He had worked abroad on many occasions, in both the East and the West, under the name of Avalov.

Agayants welcomed me and we talked at length about old times and the people we had known. There had been a lot of changes, Agayants said, 'and I would like to believe they are all for the better. But there is a difficult time ahead for us, because the CC has instructed us to extend our influence among leading people in Western countries. You have already heard about this at the meeting in the CC. But, while journalists have the job of conducting open counter-propaganda, our tasks are different. You have probably guessed why I invited you here.'

Agayants went on to explain : 'The Union of Journalists can be of great use to us. Our programme for counter-propaganda work is aimed at influencing public opinion in the countries of the West to our advantage and, if necessary, at compromising specific politicians and statesmen. We shall, of course, operate through our own channels, but it would be unforgiveable not to make use of the Union of Journalists and its contacts. We are hoping for results from our collaboration with you. The delegations of foreign journalists you invite interest us. We quite realize that it is impossible to recruit a serious journalist in a couple of weeks, unless he's the sort of fool we don't need, but to establish a contact that will enable us to use him in the future is feasible.

'In your position,' Agayants continued, 'you will not be able to give all your time to our business, and it's not necessary that you should. I would like you to persuade the secretariat of the union to appoint Pavel Gevorkyan as deputy head of the International Department of the Union of Journalists. [Gevorkyan had the rank of colonel in the KGB.] With him there it will be easier for you to carry out our plans, and you will be provided with information about every member of each delegation. What we aim to do with a particular journalist and how we propose to do it, we can discuss together. We need journalists not only from the West but also from the developing countries, so that we can use them and their publications for placing material damaging to the West.'

The 'active measures' required by the CC were to be conducted not only by the Soviet media but also by the

KGB. Department D, as it was then called, which was headed by Agayants, was given the job of getting the foreign press to publish articles containing disinformation, though this was a word we never used, calculated to mislead the public and create political instability. In addition, department D was to examine the possibility of setting up in the United States, Europe and the Third World newspapers, magazines and news-sheets which would be supported by Soviet funds but would appear to be independent or privately owned. I was to handle these matters, along with Pavel Gevorkyan.

It would, however, be an exaggeration to say that the International Department worked only for the KGB. Our main job was to project propaganda about the Soviet system and the achievements of Soviet rule, and to help to train and equip journalists' organizations in the developing countries. Foreign journalists received no real financial help, except in some cases the cost of the return journey to the Soviet Union, but each member of a delegation was given 50 roubles of so-called 'pocket money'. Delegations from the advanced capitalist countries paid their own fares, but the union covered all the expenses of their stay in the Soviet Union.

Before the foreign journalists arrived I would receive, through Gevorkyan, information about them provided by the KGB. Gevorkyan and I would then discuss how to neutralize any anti-Soviet journalist and how, and with whose help, to make an approach to others.

We also discussed the 'active measures' we could take while the journalists were with us, but our main task was to establish contact and see who could best be used to carry out our plan in his own country. We did not exclude the possibility of using a journalist to set up an independent newspaper or magazine to disseminate disinformation.

Such schemes were not so unrealistic as they might appear at first sight. I myself took part in the founding of such a newspaper which today has its own correspondents in many other countries and is actively employed to further Soviet policy and to discredit the work of the embassies of the United States and other countries. There is no lack of cases of successful disinformation work by the KGB.

In 1960 we were summoned again to the Central Committee. Boris Ponomarev told us once again that we were not devoting sufficient attention to such countries as Turkey, Ireland, Iceland, Belgium, Japan and especially West Germany. He said that, although the forthcoming visit of President Eisenhower might ease the problems between the USSR and the USA and ease the tense political situation in Europe, we must still concentrate on spreading our influence in the countries of Europe. Our efforts so far to establish better relations with West Germany had not met with success because revanchist elements were still influential, especially such politicians as Franz-Joseph Strauss. The Soviet authorities did not wish to see such men in power.

It was only later that I learnt from Alexei Adzhubei about the efforts that were made to improve relations with West Germany. By then Adzhubei had acquired a great deal of power and influence over Khrushchev, to the great annoyance of other members of the Politburo, especially the Foreign Minister, Andrei Gromyko. He told me that Turkey and the other countries were of secondary importance to the Soviet Union, but that West Germany was crucial because if we controlled West Germany we would control the whole of Europe and get rid of NATO. The Soviet Union could supply Germany with the raw materials it needed on condition that Germany remained neutral militarily and had close relations with the USSR.

Khrushchev tried quite openly to get the German politicians to understand that an alliance with the Soviet Union would produce much bigger results than collaboration with the Americans, who were far distant and did not understand European problems. The Soviet government agreed to the early release of all German prisoners of war and did not demand reparations. Khrushchev thought that Chancellor Konrad Adenauer would appreciate this gesture and would move in the direction of rapprochement, but this did not happen because there were powerful politicians in the ageing Adenauer's government who looked to the United States.

When I asked what was to happen to the German Democratic Republic, Adzhubei replied that the Soviet Union already had enough dependants and that East Germany was not to be compared in any way with West Germany in the sense he had been describing. Returning to his theme he said that the Soviet leaders considered that the most dangerous people in West Germany were Strauss, the Minister of Defence, and the press magnate Axel Springer, because one had the weapons and the other the mass media. Though it was unlikely that Springer would achieve power, Strauss's chances were real. 'This combination doesn't suit us, indeed it is positively dangerous,' Adzhubei said. 'Khrushchev realizes this, and at one time he was even ready to agree to the reunification of Germany, on the grounds that the union of the Socialist Unity Party in East Germany with the Communist Party in West Germany would be powerful enough to determine the country's domestic and foreign policy. Our German comrades were ready to fall in with this, but it didn't come off, and now it's too late. But if it's too late for reunification, it's not too late for separation – for distancing West Germany from the United States.'

I asked Adzhubei whether we were to invite Christian Democrats, socialist or neutral journalists from West Germany. After he had consulted Khrushchev, I was told to invite only the Social Democrats. Though Khrushchev strongly disliked them, they were the lesser of two evils. They were at any rate better than the Christian Democrats whom they were very likely to replace and it would do no harm to have some preliminary contact with them.

While Khrushchev was in power Alexei Adzhubei played

an important part in Soviet domestic and foreign policy, though both the Soviet authorities and Western sovietologists prefer to say little about it. After he married Khrushchev's daughter Rada, Adzhubei's career in journalism was meteoric. Still a young man, well educated and energetic, with some qualities of leadership, he rapidly advanced from being an ordinary reporter to being editor-in-chief of *Izvestia* and a member of both the Central Committee and the Supreme Soviet. He not only changed completely the look of *Izvestia* but he also facilitated the appointment of really capable journalists and editors to top positions in other newspapers and news agencies. They included such people as Goryunov, Burkov and Kharlamov. Adzhubei was no more talented than the others, but he enjoyed a freedom of action that they did not, and that made him an exception, as the Soviet public soon realized.

He was one of the first to write about Soviet people, not as though they were mere cogs in the wheels of the Soviet administration, but as individuals. It was on his initiative that an institute of newspaper and agency commentators was set up, which in the early days was even given the right to express its own thoughts and make its own proposals on political and international questions. Of course, the whole idea was soon dropped, because it met with objections from the *apparat* of the CC and the International Department, which were not ready for such free thinking and free expression. Commentators on *Pravda* and *Izvestia* today express their own suppositions and conclusions, but they have always been agreed in advance with officials of the Central Committee. At the time Adzhubei was a progressive who fed Khrushchev with ideas on both home and foreign policy, though he was more interested in the latter, and many of us believed that he intended to have himself made Foreign Minister. This might have happened if Khrushchev had not been overthrown in 1964.

I was on friendly terms with Adzhubei until 1963. After

entertaining foreign journalists in the Journalists' Club we would often sit over a glass of brandy and a cup of coffee – Adzhubei was very fond of drink – discussing political and other matters, and then Adzhubei would suggest going to the Lenin Hills, from where we could admire Moscow spread out before us. Sitting down on the grass and slightly drunk, Adzhubei would recite his own poems and those of Yesenin. Then he would suddenly pull himself together and say he had this or that to tell Nikita Sergeyevich. Once he said they ought to organize a meeting between Soviet newsmen and President Kennedy, and it was done. He went to the United States with Kharlamov, head of the Radio Committee, and they were received by Kennedy.

Adzhubei created a weekly publication called *Nedelya* (*The Week*). It was his idea that Soviet journalists should be awarded the Lenin Prize for the best reporting and commenting, and the Central Committee passed a resolution accordingly. The journalists who took part in preparing the book *Face to Face with America* about Khrushchev's visit to the United States were the first to receive Lenin Prizes. And it was on his initiative that Khrushchev and all the members of the Politburo attended the First Congress of Journalists and that the Union of Journalists become one of the important ideological organizations at that time. Adzhubei was present at all meetings of the Politburo in those days, although he was only a member of the Central Committee.

At the beginning of his ascent to power Adzhubei was friendly and easy to get along with, but he later became capricious and intolerant, ambitious and arrogant. His influence was strengthened by the attitude of the members of the Politburo themselves, who kow-towed to Khrushchev and supported his proposals knowing that many of them stemmed from Adzhubei. To oppose him meant opposing Khrushchev himself.

A minister who wanted to start some new building work or to re-equip a plant had to obtain permission from the

Central Committee, but Adzhubei had no such problems. At a meeting of the secretariat of the Union of Journalists the question was raised of providing financial aid for the construction of international journalists' centres in Algiers and Cuba. Such a centre had been built at Varna in Bulgaria in 1959. 'Why shouldn't we build an international centre in Pitsunda?' asked Adzhubei. We all exchanged glances, because a luxurious villa had just been built there for Khrushchev. Pitsunda is a little peninsula on the Black Sea coast of Georgia where there are ancient pine forests; it was classified as a prohibited area because Khrushchev had his villa there. Adzhubei told me to draw up a letter and a draft resolution and let him have it at *Izvestia* the following day. I did as I was told. Having read the draft and the letter addressed to the Deputy Prime Minister, Alexei Kosygin, Adzhubei telephoned him. 'This is Adzhubei,' he said, 'I have a request, Alexei Nikolayevich, that I've already mentioned to you. It's about Pitsunda. Nikita Sergeyevich has no objection, but we need a formal resolution. I am sending the draft resolution across to you with the Deputy General Secretary of the Union of Journalists. Can you see him right away? Fine. He will be with you in fifteen minutes.'

When I handed the resolution to Kosygin he signed it without reading it. Such was the extent of Adzhubei's power up to the removal of Khrushchev. There is no foundation to the rumours that they were not on good terms in the latter years of Khrushchev's rule. But on the day that his father-in-law was overthrown in October 1964 Adzhubei's career came to an end. He was dismissed from all his posts and put in charge of the features section of the weekly *Soviet Union*.

When our plans for inviting the editors of West German Social Democratic newspapers and magazines to visit the Soviet Union were complete I went to the International

Department of the Central Committee and discussed them with people in the German section. Our proposal was approved and a few days later, thanks to Adzhubei, the necessary resolution was passed by the CC. We invited about a dozen editors, headed by the editor-in-chief of *Vorwaerts*, Esko von Putkammer, whose father, General von Putkammer, had been a member of Hitler's inner circle. Esko von Putkammer had been taken prisoner by the Soviet army at Stalingrad and later became a member of the Committee for a Free Germany headed by Walter Ulbricht. By inviting the Social Democrats, who were then in opposition to Adenauer's government, we wanted to show that the Soviet Politburo preferred the Social Democrats to the ruling Christian Democrats.

The delegation of editors duly arrived in Moscow in, I think, May 1961. They were to be accompanied whilst with us by the deputy editor of the magazine *Zu rubezhom*, Pavel Naumov (later Chairman of Novosti), and by me, in charge of the Soviet journalists who were to meet them. At Agayants's request I included a KGB lieutenant-colonel, Yuri Tregubenkov, in the group of journalists. A month before the delegation arrived Naumov and I were summoned to the International Department to discuss the programme for the visit where, to our surprise, Boris Ponomarev himself joined us. He explained that, in spite of setbacks in relations with the Adenauer government, we were not giving up the struggle to make West Germany, if not an ally, at least a country not hostile towards us. He took the view that our future relations with West Germany might well depend on how skilfully we handled this delegation. We would have to make every effort, not only to convince them of our goodwill and peaceful intentions, but also to find out their foreign policy aims in the event of their coming to power. Apart from that, we should make the most of this opportunity to discredit the policy of the Christian Democrats and especially that of

Adenauer and Strauss who, contrary to the interests of Germany, both East and West, were moving ever closer to the United States.

I have never forgotten his final remarks, because they were unique. 'Tell them frankly,' Ponomarev said, 'that we regard Adenauer as a politician whose days are numbered, and Strauss as a follower of Hitler and as a revanchist who is harming the whole of Europe by his actions. Tell them that the Soviet government will be sincerely glad to see the Social Democrats leading West Germany and that we will give them all the backing in our power to get there. When you are talking to them, let there be as little propaganda as possible. Speak openly and sincerely, and then they will believe that our intentions are good and that our attitude to the Social Democrats has changed. They will begin to see the danger resulting from people like Strauss coming to power in West Germany.'

The importance attached to the visit by this delegation was clear from the fact that the Siberian highway Sverdlovsk–Novosibirsk–Irkutsk was opened for the first time for a foreign delegation.

After the meeting in the Central Committee I went to the KGB to discuss the visit. The meeting was attended by Agayants, by his deputy, Colonel Sitnikov, and by Yuri Tregubenkov. Sitnikov was a specialist on German affairs. Agayants repeated more or less what Ponomarev had said, but went into greater detail about Strauss.

'When you talk to the Germans,' he said, 'you can hint that we have information concerning Strauss's connections with the American intelligence service. Tell them they recruited him when he was in prison and that he now receives huge sums of money for the services he rendered them. He is more concerned with increasing his personal fortune than with a peaceful future for Germany. If you are asked what proof you have, you can say that we even have *documentary* proof, but that you can produce it only on the condition that it will be published in the West German press without the source being revealed.'

Sitnikov told us that there was one editor from Bavaria we had to watch out for; he spoke reasonable Russian, learned when he was a prisoner of war near Leningrad. Apparently he was close to Strauss. Sitnikov said that the KGB was already discrediting Strauss, through the press in West Germany and in other countries of Europe, but that it would not be a bad idea if one of the Social Democratic newspapers attacked him, not on the political front, but with accusations pointing to his lack of principle, his ambitions and his ties with the Americans.

Consequently when the delegation arrived we discussed Soviet–German relations, Adenauer, Springer, Strauss and even Hitler. My main conversations were with von Putkammer, with Naumov, a German speaker, acting as interpreter. We spoke frankly; I did not try to conceal our own shortcomings in industry and agriculture, both in Moscow and in Irkutsk, in the factories and on the farms. This approach produced results. Von Putkammer told me that when the delegation had arrived in Moscow they had been taken to a reinforced-concrete bunker at the embassy equipped for confidential conversations and warned that the Soviet authorities would feed them nothing but propaganda.

Herr von Putkammer was a good listener but he never asked to be shown our evidence about Strauss; in that respect my efforts were not successful. But soon after the editors' departure I learned from Agayants that the SPD leadership had held two meetings at which von Putkammer's reports were discussed, and that some SPD right-wingers had criticized von Putkammer for his gullibility. Agayants knew about this from his KGB agents in Germany.

I did not know how successful Tregubenkov had been with other members of the delegation; he was not a personal friend and such matters are never discussed at an official level. But I do know that the operation to compromise Strauss was ultimately successful.

My first proof came from Ponomarev early in 1963. At a secret meeting under his chairmanship the work of the so-called 'front organizations' was discussed. Somebody said that to achieve the desired goals in our ideological struggle what we really needed were large amounts of hard currency, since it was very difficult to find good collaborators who worked on a purely ideological basis. To this, Ponomarev rather angrily retorted that ideological work could never be materially profitable, it was an investment for the future. He claimed that money would be always available, provided there were enough productive ideas for its use. We never spared foreign currency, continued Ponomarev, when opportunities presented themselves. He cited our success in using *Der Spiegel* and (he then named another publication) to undermine so powerful a figure as Strauss. Mikhail Suslov repeated this claim later in the year at a confidential meeting of chief editors of central Party newspapers at which I was also present.

My second, and more detailed, proof came some years later. Colonel Arkady Boiko, a close friend with whom I had worked in Tanzania, was recalled to Moscow in 1970. When I met him again, in Moscow in 1974, he was in distress because the KGB had sacked him from an important job – apparently because of his drinking problem. What he told me was a revelation.

Having been recalled from Tanzania, Boiko was sent to Dresden to take charge of a top secret special *rezidentura* which the KGB had established there in the late 1950s. It was in Dresden rather than in East Berlin to avoid undue attention. The sole purpose of the *rezidentura* was to conduct 'active measures' against West Germany and Austria. It reported to no one except the Moscow Centre and specialized in planting disinformation material in the respectable media of German-speaking countries.

No Soviet national, said Boiko, would ever travel from Dresden to West Germany or Austria. The material was always carried by Westerners, via Switzerland or Italy or France. Local German journalists would thus be offered sensational stories not by strangers, but by their trusted friends or colleagues. Boiko named several publications and cited various success stories, but, he said, the biggest coup had taken place before he went to Dresden, when the *rezidentura* succeeded in using *Der Spiegel* to compromise Strauss.

Although there can be no doubt at all that the anti-Strauss campaign in *Der Spiegel* was launched on the basis of KGB-planted material, this, of course, does not imply any collaboration between the KGB and *Der Spiegel* : many respectable and politically impeccable publications fell victim to the KGB 'active measures' without knowing by whom they had been used.

Disinformation has always played a part in Soviet policy, and especially since the setting up of the Information Committee in 1947. The Committee organized a disinformation service, known as the Fifth Information Directorate, headed by Colonel Grauer. Its business was the preparation of disinformation material and the spreading of false rumours aimed at destabilizing the position of unwanted regimes and governments. Later it was given additional functions, such as the organization of sabotage, the incitement of disorder and other actions to undermine the stability of countries in the West and the Third World. Today every KGB *rezidentura* includes a representative of this department.

With the setting up of the Information Directorate of the Information Committee, the Soviet intelligence service, under the direction of the Secretariat and Politburo, began to organize disinformation on a regular basis, and it has been especially busy with this work in recent years. In spite of this, people in the West tend to exaggerate the amount of disinformation now circulating, both in printed form and by word of mouth. The preparation of disinformation material is a demanding and complicated affair, because pure disinformation unsupported by hard facts and without any documentary confirmation is quickly exposed and may well do more harm than good.

Disinformation is initiated either at the instigation of the KGB or on orders from the Party authorities, after which, with the help of journalists dealing with foreign affairs and connected with the KGB, and in the Department of International Information of the CC, it is brought up to the required level. Documentary disinformation, based on documents obtained by agents and on published material, is worked over in a department of the KGB and then, after being approved by the people in charge in the CC, is sent out to KGB *rezidentury* abroad for publication in the foreign press or distribution through 'reliable people', that is to say, agents of influence.

In the past disinformation work was the prerogative of the KGB and to a lesser extent of the Foreign Ministry. But today practically all government departments and public bodies having contacts with foreign countries play a part in it; in fact they are encouraged to take the initiative in such work.

In the mid-1960s a special group was set up in the Novosti agency, which is represented in many countries round the world, and Norman Borodin was put in charge of it. For the sake of secrecy the group was not based in the Novosti head office on Pushkin Square but in a building on Kutuzov Avenue, where disinformation material was prepared to be published in Novosti's official publications and distributed abroad by the staff of Soviet diplomatic and trade missions, by TASS and Novosti correspondents and, of course, by KGB and GRU officers.

Those responsible for spreading disinformation try to use mainly right-wing or at least 'neutral' publications. This requires not only trustworthy contacts and connections in political and journalistic circles, but also agents of influence in the same circles.

An article containing disinformation which has been placed successfully in the press abroad is usually picked up and printed in the Soviet press, so as to misinform the Soviet reader as well, and is broadcast by Soviet radio to practically all the countries of the world. A particular event is presented both to the Soviet people and to people abroad in the way the Soviet leaders wish, thus creating a general opinion hostile to a government not acting in accordance with Moscow's wishes. The aim is to present the impression that it is not only the Soviets who are opposed to that government but even right-wing media which could hardly be accused of sympathy for the Communist system.

Although it was difficult to discredit specific politicians of whom the Soviet Union did not approve, the Soviet authorities had some successes in this field – in addition to forcing Strauss to resign after his exposure in *Der Spiegel*. They were able to place disinformation in a number of influential newspapers in France, the United States, West Germany and Italy. For example, it was claimed by Ponomarev that the Soviets had made use of newspapers in Paris, Lyons and Marseilles to organize support for the future President of France, Giscard d'Estaing, during his election battle with Mitterand and his ally, the French Communist Party.

But it was not always possible to make use of the press in the West and the Third World for Soviet purposes, so the Soviet Union also took steps to set up its own newspapers and publications. In 1962 I helped to set up a newspaper in India which now exerts a certain political influence both there and in the Third World. Although Westerners eye this paper with some suspicion, people in most of the Third World countries take note of it and presumably believe much of what it says. The paper is recognized officially in a number of Western countries, where it has its own correspondents.

The bulletin issued by the French journalist Pathé is another example. For many years it supplied French politicians and statesmen with reports and features which Pathé had obtained from a KGB man working in the Soviet embassy in Paris. It was a long time before anyone suspected Pathé's connection with the Soviet disinformation service, and the material he published must have been to the advantage of the Soviet leaders and their policy.

There are two important factors which make it possible to exploit the Western press in the interests of Soviet policy – apart, of course, from the presence of agents of influence. The first is that the Western media can be in opposition to the government of their country, and the second is their love of sensationalism. Neither of these factors operates in the Soviet Union, where the press is controlled by the *apparat* of the Central Committee and serves only the interests of the Soviet leadership.

There is also some confusion in distinguishing between purely counter-propaganda material, diplomatic tricks played by the Soviet foreign service and disinformation. This is why many articles and statements defending Soviet moves or criticizing the policy of the West, in which facts and events are turned inside out, are taken by many people to be disinformation.

The fact is that disinformation is primarily concerned with large-scale objectives : obstructing a government's policy, provoking political conflicts between states so as to damage their relations, discrediting statesmen and politicians, organizing movements and events likely to upset a country's political stability, discrediting undesirable organizations (especially the intelligence services and people working for them), carrying out political and economic blackmail, and so forth. It is a complicated business which requires a lot of serious preparatory work as well as the means of distributing and publishing the material. Disinformation is not just a well-presented political lie – which is, incidentally, easy to recognize – but a compilation of facts and events which must not only be difficult to refute but which must result in serious consequences for the opposing side.

The most typical operation of this kind, and the most important one in recent times, was that aimed at influencing public opinion against the American administration's plan to produce a neutron bomb, which would destroy people but leave factories, buildings, weapons and so forth unharmed. Concerned that the Americans might produce such a weapon, the Politburo and Secretariat of the Party decided to organize a major campaign aimed at discrediting the American administration both in the Soviet Union and abroad. Every Soviet organization that had contacts with foreign countries and especially the Soviet mass media was told to expose the enormity of employing such a weapon. A major campaign was mounted to persuade foreign journalists of the great dangers involved in the American plan. At meetings with foreign journalists, both official and unofficial, Soviet journalists and KGB agents were instructed to say that if the Americans did not drop the idea of producing the neutron bomb the Soviet government would be obliged to develop such a bomb itself and that – and this was most important – in the event of a military conflict involving conventional weapons the Soviet Government would be forced to resort to atomic and nuclear weapons since it had no other answer to the neutron bomb.

General Borodin told me that he believed quite a few foreign correspondents and even diplomats were already opposed to the neutron bomb, and it was not difficult to persuade even the most reactionary of the foreigners of the inhuman character of such a weapon. Whenever we met foreign journalists we never failed to bring up the subject of the neutron bomb.

In the end, of course, we succeeded in turning public

opinion against the bomb and in persuading many politicians to oppose its development, almost certainly because of the reports they received from Moscow that the Soviet Union would use its nuclear weapons. That the campaign was successful was confirmed when the Americans finally abandoned the idea. I can state with confidence that we received considerable help in achieving our aim from the foreign correspondents whom we supplied with disinformation; I can also say that the Soviet Union was not incapable of producing a neutron bomb itself.

Another recent example of a very widespread but primitive form of disinformation, designed mainly for countries of the Third World and the discrediting of the United States and the CIA, is to be seen in a series of articles in the Mozambique newspaper *Noticias da Beira*, later summarized in *Izvestia* of 26 May 1981, under the heading 'Sabotage by the CIA'. The substance of the articles was broadcast by Moscow Radio to foreign countries. The articles claimed that from 1961 to 1976 the CIA organized 900 sabotage operations against politicians and governments of which the United States did not approve in various countries of the world. The primitive nature of this kind of disinformation is shown by the question that immediately arises: where did the people in Mozambique obtain such a wealth of information? Since Mozambique does not have any information-gathering centre or a worthwhile intelligence service, there can be only one answer – the information had been supplied by the Soviets, or more precisely the disinformation service of the KGB. But the KGB is only the instrument: the brain centre which plans and decides the purpose behind the disinformation is the *apparat* and Secretariat of the Central Committee of the Party, headed by the Politburo.

It may very reasonably be asked: how it is possible that the Soviets are able to operate so actively in the West? What about the West?

To this question I reply categorically that disinformation

work is a one-way street from East to West. This is due primarily to the difference in the two social systems. The Soviet Union is a country with a one-party system, broadly speaking a totalitarian state in which all the media are strictly controlled by the Party, which makes it impossible for any opinion differing from the official line to find expression. At the same time, the Soviet intelligence service, allied with the intelligence services of the Communist countries of Eastern Europe, has little difficulty in finding Western officials and journalists opposed to their own governments. Apart from that, if a Western journalist agrees for a sum of money (sometimes very substantial) to publish something the Soviet authorities want to see in print or to spread rumours about some public figure, he can put the money in his bank without questions being asked about where it came from. A Soviet journalist does not have this advantage, because Western currencies do not circulate officially in his country, and he is under constant observation by the Party, the security service and even his own friends and neighbours.

The year 1959 was an especially important one for the Union of Journalists and for Soviet journalism as a whole. In November of that year the First Congress of Soviet Journalists took place in the Hall of Columns in the House of the Unions in Moscow. It was attended by all the members of the Party leadership, headed by the First Secretary, Nikita Khrushchev. The Congress was also attended by representatives of foreign journalists' organizations from more than fifty countries.

Before the Congress opened the members of the Secretariat, of whom I was one, were invited to meet Khrushchev at the Central Committee headquarters. Khrushchev was full of life and good spirits and, it seemed to me, a little drunk.

'So what am I going to call you journalists?' he asked after

Adzhubei and Satyukov had explained how the Congress was to be conducted.

'Better call us the helpmeets of the Party,' said Adzhubei, and Khrushchev and the other leaders agreed.

The Congress passed off without any serious problems, and Khrushchev's speech made it clear that the Soviet leaders had promoted the Union of Journalists to the status of a direct assistant to the Party.

After the Congress there was a reception in the Kremlin to which all the newly elected members of the governing body of the Union of Journalists and the foreign guests – but not the foreign correspondents accredited in Moscow – were invited. Khrushchev and Voroshilov were late in appearing and they were both rather excited. Khrushchev proposed a toast which developed into an impromptu speech. He had some rather alarming news: 'Kliment Yefremovich Voroshilov and I have just returned from one of our armament factories. What we were shown there is simply unbelievable. The fact is that our scientists and military experts have created a fifty-megaton atomic bomb. It is so powerful that if it were exploded over Paris a third of the Ukraine and Belorussia would be wiped off the face of the earth. It is a colossal and very dangerous weapon. We do not intend to use it, but it will serve as a good warning to American imperialism and its satellites of what could happen if they try to destroy us by military force.'

When Khrushchev had finished one of his assistants came up to me and said that we must warn all the foreign guests that Khrushchev's speech was off the record and that they must not write about it even after returning to their own countries. They were all warned accordingly.

After the reception the members of the Secretariat gathered in the Moskva Hotel, where we had taken over a suite to serve as an office during the Congress. We set about celebrating our success. Adzhubei and the other members of the Secretariat were delighted that it was now the journalists rather than the writers who were out in front. After an enormous quantity of vodka had been drunk, Adzhubei began to criticize Stalin and in his usual sharp tone said it was time to wipe out all memory of him and to counteract residual respect that people might have for him by getting those who had been in the prison camps to describe truthfully their experiences. That was what Khrushchev wanted. We should seek out writers and journalists who had served terms in the camps and who had since been released thanks to Khrushchev.

'I think,' said Adzhubei to me, 'we ought to get you to deal with this matter. Your friends in the KGB can be of assistance. They know who was sent to which camp and when they were let out. This is a very serious matter, Ilya, and you must set about it in earnest. If necessary I'll talk to Shelepin [then head of the KGB] and he'll give the necessary orders. The Union of Writers will be given similar instructions.'

Some people may have taken this idea seriously, but it didn't interest me in the least. I reacted against it, because I knew what the department for fighting the intelligentsia was trying to do and that the desire to obtain further revelations was only a political scheme to re-write the past to suit Khrushchev's personal aims.

The drinking party went on for a long time. Sometime after midnight I was called to the telephone. It was Borodin's deputy, Major Slava Kevorkov, who was also a friend of mine and who was soon to replace Borodin. There was an emergency, Kevorkov said. 'What happened?' I asked. 'Has one of our foreign guests fetched up in the hands of the police or committed suicide?'

'Worse than that,' he replied. I couldn't think of anything worse. But his words sobered me up in a flash.

'An hour and a half ago,' Kevorkov said, 'Michel Tatu, Moscow correspondent of *Le Monde*, turned up at the central telegraph office and wanted to transmit an account of Khrushchev's speech at the Kremlin reception. At the tele-

graph office they refused to transmit his copy because there
had been no official report of the speech and no official text.
But that's neither here nor there – most important is where
did he get the information about the speech from? Our chief
[Shelepin] has been informed and has given orders that the
source of the story must be found at all costs.'

'It's easy to give orders like that,' I said, 'but where are you
going to look for the offender when there were so many
people at the reception – you can't interrogate every one of
them.'

We arranged to meet the next day.

I was genuinely upset; I had been in charge of the foreign
journalists and this was a failure on my part. When I
returned to the party, Adzhubei, seeing the anxious look on
my face, enquired what was the matter. I told him. Everybody gasped, but Adzhubei said calmly : 'Never mind, we
shall now have to publish the text of Khrushchev's speech
after editing it a bit, of course, though this wasn't our
intention.

The speech was indeed published, but it was unrecogniz-
able. In fact, it was entirely different.

When I appeared in Borodin's office the next day he told
me at once that he had good news for me. Very early that
morning two young men had turned up at the KGB on
Kuznetsky Most with what they said was important information. The duty officer had immediately informed the
KGB. The two youngsters, one of whom spoke French, had
been dining in the Aragvi restaurant the previous evening.
At the next table were sitting a man and a young woman,
both speaking French. The young man pricked up his ears
when the young woman mentioned Khrushchev and the
names of other Soviet leaders. The woman was giving an
account of some speech made by Khrushchev at a reception,
from which she had come straight to the restaurant. The
man she was with was questioning her about what exactly
Khrushchev had said and what had happened at the recep-

tion. Suspecting that there was something improper in all this, the two young men had decided to report the matter to the KGB, but had not done so at once because they had had plenty to drink.

They described the man they had seen, whom we recognized at once as Michel Tatu. He was one of the best-informed foreign correspondents in Moscow in his day, and we knew him well. He had been surrounded by agents from the first days of his stay in Moscow. But who was the woman? The chief suspects were the three French-language interpreters present at the reception. They were all instantly put under observation to establish what contacts they had with foreign correspondents. A day later it was reported that one of them, Larisa Kozlova, had spent the night with an Arab diplomat. Kozlova was the daughter of a retired KGB general, which made it hard for me to believe that she was our suspect. But she was. When I asked her why she told Tatu about Khrushchev's speech and why she had slipped away from the delegation to meet him, Larisa replied that Tatu already knew about the reception and had asked her to let him know what went on at it so that he could be the first correspondent to report it. 'I didn't think there was anything secret about the speech, and what does it matter whether Tatu gets to know about it today from me or tomorrow from the newspapers?' she argued. There was a certain logic in her argument if we overlooked the fact that she had heard the warning that Khrushchev's speech was off the record. Michel Tatu knew how to approach Soviet people and to obtain the information he needed for his work. He was surrounded by our informers, was watched constantly by the KGB, and from time to time was fed with pieces of information that suited our book.

Larisa ceased to work for us. I came across her by chance several years later in the Hotel Ukraine, no longer an interpreter but the wife of a rich Arab.

There was nothing exceptional about the case of Tatu and

Kozlova. The political vigilance about which the Soviet press is always talking has become second nature for most of the Soviet people. If they did not behave in this way neither the NKVD nor the KGB would have been able to gather such a quantity of compromising material about other Soviet citizens. When I was working in the Second Chief Directorate we used to receive so many letters, both signed and anonymous, about other people's views and behaviour that we hadn't the time to deal with them properly. Paradoxical as it may seem, it is not so much the KGB who create the atmosphere of suspicion and spy-mania in the Soviet Union as the vigilant Soviet citizens, and especially the old-age pensioners, of whom there are more than 50 million.

As well as entertaining delegations of foreign journalists I was responsible for organizing delegations of Soviet newsmen for visits to foreign countries. So many leading journalists wanted to travel abroad that we did not include KGB officers in these delegations. The people going abroad were told to spread Soviet propaganda and, when necessary, counter-propaganda, and they were advised not to shirk arguments with foreign journalists about even the most delicate issues, such as the attitude of the Soviet Government to the award of the Nobel Prize to Boris Pasternak or the missile crisis in Cuba. Members of delegations were, of course, invited to the International Department to be told how to behave. They would be allowed to accept invitations to appear on television programmes, since all the journalists were politically mature enough to defend the Soviet point of view on any question. I myself frequently had to lead delegations of Soviet journalists, to take part in public debates and polemics, and appear on radio and television programmes abroad, and I honestly do not recall an occasion when we suffered a political defeat.

We attached great importance to the International Organization of Journalists, which has its headquarters in Prague. It was, and still is, a means of spreading Soviet propaganda and also an excellent centre from which to obtain information about any foreign journalist or publication, as well as providing a channel through which to influence the media in the countries belonging to it. One of the permanent deputies to the General Secretary of the IOJ is always a Soviet official who has close connections with the Soviet embassy and the KGB *residentura* in Prague. Though he is formally responsible to the Soviet Union of Journalists, in practice he carries out all his duties under the direction of the International Department of the CPSU. He may freely visit any country belonging to the IOJ and check up on the work of the journalists' organizations. At the same time it is easy for him to make contact with newsmen who interest the Soviet Union and who may be willing to publish counter-propaganda and anti-American material and to place disinformation.

For example, Latin America was for a long time a blank spot on the map for us, particularly countries like Brazil, Paraguay, Uruguay and Bolivia. When Aleksandr Yefremov, the Deputy General Secretary of the IOJ in the early 1960s, returned from visiting those countries, the Soviet Union of Journalists invited over a number of Latin American journalists and we did out best to persuade them of the need for friendly relations with us. This paid off later, not only in changing the political climate in those countries, but also in giving us openings for appointing permanent TASS correspondents, most of them KGB officers.

The IOJ is chiefly funded by the Soviet Union and is a front organization for conducting Soviet propaganda and for carrying out Soviet policy. The material and technical aid provided to the developing countries and the training courses provided for their journalists enable the International Department to co-ordinate and direct the media in many though not all of them. That is why we opposed the formation of an independent news agency for the countries of Africa, since we were afraid that they might elude our influence.

The IOJ controls the International Journalists' Centre at Varna, Bulgaria, which is used for establishing contacts with journalists from both East and West. Though it is relatively cheap to stay there, when foreign journalists are invited from the West the IOJ usually covers the costs, because it finds it pays to do so.

The Bulgarian intelligence service is very active at the centre. A good friend of mine, Haralambi Traikov, former editor-in-chief of the newspaper *Zemledelchesko Znamya* and son of the former Bulgarian President Georgi Traikov, once said to me: 'You may be from the KGB, but our lads are no worse than you are at catching fish in Varna. Although we are a small country, there are many things we can do better than the big countries.' In practice the Bulgarian secret police co-ordinate their work closely with the KGB and use the Varna centre for recruiting foreign journalists. There was, of course, some exaggeration in Traikov's claim, because relatively few Western journalists take their holidays in Varna, but it would be a mistake to underestimate the Bulgarians. Their intelligence work is highly professional and active, both in recruiting foreigners and at organizing acts of terrorism abroad.

The IOJ also runs courses for journalists in Budapest, which are used by the Hungarian Communists for their own propaganda and for recruiting foreign journalists for intelligence and disinformation work.

My work in the Union of Journalists demanded a great deal of physical and nervous effort, partly because I was under constant pressure from the *apparat* of the CC, partly because I was always entertaining the delegations of foreign journalists and partly because the General Secretary of the union,

Pavel Yerofeyev, while happy to attend dinners and receptions, left the responsibility of the running of the union to me. Like all the other Soviet leaders, he would rather act as chairman or be seen on the platform at meetings, to impress both the journalists and his superiors in the Party hierarchy. This sort of leadership makes few demands on the great majority of Soviet officials while creating the impression that they are playing an active part in public life, for which they are rewarded with medals and slowly but surely move up the career ladder.

In those days I was naive and presumed that my hard work would be appreciated, but I was mistaken. Nevertheless I learned about many aspects of Soviet life which are concealed from most Soviet people. I was able to study the life style of the Soviet élite, the ever increasing corruption of its members, the fierce struggles for power at the top, the heavy drinking and immoral ways of the ideological leaders, and their utter contempt for the ordinary people, to whom they referred as 'cattle'.

It was clear to me that the socialist ideas promulgated by the Party leaders were not adhered to even by them. I eventually came to the conclusion that there would come a time when new Party leaders would introduce radical changes. I was not so naive as to believe that such long-standing practices could be halted by one swift blow, but I thought that some attempt might be made. I tried not to think about it very much. After all, I myself belonged to the privileged caste and it would have been foolish to complain about my way of life. In any case, I had little time for such reflections because working simultaneously for the union, the KGB and the CC, as well as attending endless receptions, kept me fully occupied.

One of the most enjoyable aspects of my work was meeting unusual and interesting people. For example, at a reception in the Dutch embassy in 1965 I got to know Father Nikodim, a well-known figure in the Russian Orthodox

Church, who invited me to visit the headquarters of the Orthodox Church at the monastery at Zagorsk. After an ample lunch in Nikodim's cell, he took me round the museum of the Russian Patriarch Alexius, who had recently died. I asked Nikodim whether he was not displeased that the Russian Church was in practice controlled by a state committee. 'Everybody knows that the Chairman of the Committee for Religious Affairs is employed by the KGB,' he replied, 'and therefore it doesn't bother us. It would be worse if we didn't know.' I then asked him if the state obstructed the Church's activity and used force to restrict the number of believers.

'That, if you'll forgive me for saying so, is a provocative question,' Nikodim said. 'Our seminary takes only young men who have already done their military service, because if they are called up from the seminary they are attacked and ridiculed, which damages them psychologically.'

'All right,' I said. 'But, as a Communist, I want to ask you another provocative question. Do you support the policy of the Communist Party which opposes you?'

'What policy do you have in mind?' Nikodim asked. 'Domestic or foreign?'

'Both,' I replied.

'All right. In the field of foreign policy we support the efforts of your Party to preserve peace. As far as domestic policy is concerned we support the economic efforts being made to raise living standards. But we are categorically opposed to the various religious sects which your Party confuses with the Orthodox Church. Your Party will never be able to suppress the sects by psychological means, but only by the use of force. We, the Orthodox Church, using the power of our religion, could, but your Party prevents us from doing so.'

I then asked Nikodim whether the Russian Church genuinely believed it could become a real ideological force if it was not opposed by the Communists.

'I would sound like a Party propagandist if I said yes,' Nikodim replied, 'but too few young people believe in God and fewer of them are attracted to the Church. They do not believe in anybody or anything: they are interested only in material possessions and in achieving goals that the Church considers sinful.'

He was not being entirely frank, but it was clear that he did not believe in a religious revival that would inspire the people and cause a change in the social structure. I agreed with him because the Soviet people have no special longing for religion. The fantastic theories of Solzhenitsyn, who underwent a sudden conversion to Orthodoxy, about Russia's spiritual renaissance have no foundation. The Church was separated from the state after the Revolution of 1917 but remains under the control of the Committee for the Affairs of the Church, which also supervises the activities of Muslims and Catholics. The Committee is usually headed by an officer of the KGB and includes representatives of the intelligence and counter-intelligence services. Soviet secret police have infiltrated the priests of the Russian Orthodox Church and other religious communities abroad not primarily as spies but to maintain a spirit of Russian patriotism. Their aim is not only to weaken the emigré communities but also to prevent religious emigrés being drawn into anti-Soviet activity. A religious environment can also provide favourable soil in which to recruit a believer convinced of the need to help his native land.

Stories about the persecution of religious believers in the Soviet Union are greatly exaggerated. The state does not encourage religion, forbids all forms of religious propaganda and efforts to attract Soviet people into the Church, and priests can be prosecuted for breaches of these regulations, especially if they attempt to involve children in religious practices. But few are arrested by the KGB or persecuted for attending Orthodox Church services or observing religious rituals. The persecution is confined to various religious sects, such as Baptists and Jehovah's Witnesses, to whom the Orthodox Church is also opposed.

Members of the Communist Party and the Komsomol are not permitted to go to church, to baptize their infants or observe any religious rituals, and if caught doing so would be punished, not by the KGB, but by their Party or Komsomol organization.

These matters are dealt with by the Committee for the Affairs of the Church, which works in close contact with the First, Second and Fifth Chief Directorates of the KGB. It stands to reason that, surrounded by such bodies, the Russian and other Churches do not enjoy complete freedom or independence, and are obliged, whether they like it or not, to support the policies of the Communist Party. I don't think Nikodim was actually working for the KGB, though he fiercely defended the interests both of the Church and the Soviet government at international religious conferences. He represented the coexistence of two contradictory beliefs: belief in God and belief in the superiority of socialism over capitalism, which explains why, when I asked my comrades in the KGB what sort of a person Nikodim was, they replied: 'He's a good fellow, but he believes in God.'

In the summer of 1960 a man turned up at the Union of Journalists saying that he was the former editor of the *Astrakhanskaya Pravda* and that he had just been released from a prison camp. It occurred to me that he might be writing a book about life in the camps of the sort to which Adzhubei had referred. I had already asked journalists who had spent time in the camps to write the book we wanted but they had all refused, saying that, after all they had suffered and seen, they could not risk such suffering all over again. Perhaps this one would be more compliant.

He was a man of more than medium height, thin and emaciated and with a sallow complexion. He was wearing a coat made from a very rough material. He lowered himself slowly into a chair and silently placed his documents before me. They indicated that he had been let out of a prison camp in 1956 because of lack of evidence to support a charge that had been brought nineteen years previously. He told me he had spent the four years since his release in hospital in Vladivostok. 'As you see, they have restored me to health,' he said with a grin, 'and now I want to get home to Astrakhan to see my mother.' I was moved by his reference to his mother, and I asked him to tell me his story, if he did not find it too difficult.

It was a simple and tragic tale. He had been working as editor of the *Astrakhanskaya Pravda* in 1936 when Anastas Mikoyan, then a member of Stalin's Politburo, arrived in the city. The local Party secretary organized a duck shoot for Mikoyan in the Volga delta and invited the editor to join them. By mistake he hastily grabbed one of his sporting guns that happened to be loaded with a cartridge intended for shooting wild boar or bears. Mikoyan's bodyguard and the head of the local NKVD discovered it when they inspected the guns and accused the editor of planning to assassinate Mikoyan. He was arrested and sentenced to death, but after he appealed to Mikoyan the sentence was commuted to twenty-five years in the camps. His wife, left with a three-year-old son, denounced him formally as an 'enemy of the people', thus saving her own life and that of her child. She had later married one of his friends and was still living in Astrakhan.

'My son is now twenty-six,' he said, 'but when I arrive in Astrakhan I shall never tell him that I am his father. Why should I wreck his life? But my mother is still there and she is expecting me. I do not feel well and I cannot fly. I have come to ask you to buy me a ticket on the river boat that goes from Moscow to Astrakhan. As soon as I earn some money I'll return it to you. I am so anxious to see my mother,' he said, with tears running down his cheeks.

I was moved by what he told me. It was painful to look at him and difficult to imagine all that he had been through. I told him he needed a couple of days' rest and some decent clothes and that we would buy the ticket.

The union's budget did not really provide for this kind of expenditure, so I had to break the rules. Our chief accountant nearly lost the power of speech when I told him what I intended to do and that he was to enter the expenditure as expenses involved in entertaining a non-existent Latin American journalist. It was lying in a good cause.

That evening I invited the editor to the restaurant in the journalists' club, where he told me what life in the camps was like and about the well-known Soviet journalist Mikhail Koltsov, and the Bolshevik and former friend of Stalin, Mdivani. It was a terrible story, far more realistic and impressive than Solzhenitsyn's *One Day in the Life of Ivan Denisovich*. 'Why don't you write about your experiences for the benefit of later generations?' I asked, saying that I could guarantee that his work would be published in Moscow. He thought for a while in silence: 'Who needs it?' he said. 'The people who have been through the camps know about life there. The people who sent us there are now in the camps themselves. Who knows what is going to happen tomorrow?'

A few days later when I told Adzhubei of my failure with this man he lost his temper, accused me of feebleness and asked why I hadn't brought the editor to him. 'You should have told him that Nikita Sergeyevich himself wanted to see such a book published,' said Adzhubei, still cross. I told him I didn't think I had the right to bring Khrushchev into it.

It was not long after this that *Ivan Denisovich* appeared. The story of how it came to be published is well known, but I am not sure that people know that the main role in getting it published was played not by Tvardovsky, editor of *Novy Mir*, but by Adzhubei. Whether Tvardovsky gave the manuscript of the book directly to Khrushchev is doubtful, but I know for sure that Khrushchev, who did not read it all, handed it to Adzhubei for his opinion.

Adzhubei told us in the club that he had found a man who had written about the prison camps in Stalin's time. Adzhubei couldn't remember the writer's name, but he said that, although the book was not of any great literary value and its language was not Russian but a sort of jargon, the theme was to Nikita Sergeyevich's taste and would complete the destruction of Stalin as a personality.

In September of 1964 I was due to deliver my plan for the union's international contacts for 1965. The Secretariat met on 18 September, and a few days later my wife and I set off for our holiday in the writers' holiday home in the Black Sea resort of Gagri. Staying in the sanatorium, which belonged to the Central Committee, we ran into Irakli Chkhikvishvili, the head of a section of the Agitprop Department of the Party and former editor of the Georgian newspaper *Zarya Vostoka*. He told me that they were expecting Alexei Adzhubei in Pitsunda where he was to join his father-in-law. 'We must give Alyosha a really good Georgian welcome,' Irakli said, and he invited me to join in.

On the evening of 12 October, the manager of the hotel came to my room to report on some strange goings-on. He said that the whole of Khrushchev's bodyguard had departed and that Mikoyan had arrived from Moscow to see him. It was said that they were going to fly to Moscow early the next morning. Obviously something very serious had happened – could it be war? Mikoyan had persuaded Khrushchev to break off his holiday and fly to Moscow for a meeting of the Politburo. All the members of the CC *apparat* who were holidaying in Gagri also took off for Moscow.

Adzhubei never reached Gagri. What happened, of course, was that Khrushchev was removed from all his positions on account of the 'state of his health'.

One of Khrushchev's assistants told me later that Adzhubei had turned up at the meeting of the Politburo, but Brezhnev – who was chairing it – told him to leave the building and not come near it again. At the beginning of the meeting Khrushchev had demanded the right to speak to the Soviet people over the radio so that the public should decide whether they preferred him or Brezhnev. By the end, he was a broken man : he begged the other members of the Politburo to allow him to remain for a short while as First Secretary of the Party and then, at his own request, to retire. The Khrushchev era was over.

Adzhubei was dismissed from the editorship of *Izvestia* and expelled from the Central Committee. Kharlamov, Chairman of the State Committee for Radio and Television, was also removed, and all the other leading people in Soviet journalism were under threat of dismissal. I was present when Satyukov, editor-in-chief of *Pravda*, was removed by Party secretary Mikhail Suslov. The principal charge against him was that he had permitted far too many pictures of Khrushchev to appear in the paper and so exaggerated his importance. When Satyukov pointed out that he had discussed and agreed the publication of all pictures of Khrushchev with Secretaries of the CC, Suslov said that on one occasion he had opposed the publication of four pictures in one issue of the paper and Satyukov had not listened to his opinion. Adzhubei and Satyukov were later expelled from the governing body of the Union of Journalists and other honorary positions. Adzhubei's departure marked the beginning of the decline in importance of the union. It has now become a haven for people who have been dismissed from their jobs because they were not up to them or for leading journalists in retirement.

In May 1965 Vyacheslav Chernyshev, the former Deputy Chairman of the Radio and Television Committee, was appointed General Secretary of the Union of Journalists. He had been removed from his job because of his lack of ability.

The time had come for me to think about my own future; I could not work with Chernyshev, knowing how stupid and limited he was.

I had a talk with the General Director of the TASS agency, Dmitri Goryunov, about the possibility of my getting a job as a TASS correspondent abroad, and then I went to the Agitprop Department of the CC and discussed the idea with Timofei Kuprikov. He was surprised at my decision and wanted to know my reason. I couldn't tell him that I considered Chernyshev a fool, so I told him that I was exhausted after seven years' hard slog.

I then talked to Yakovlev, the deputy head of Agitprop, whom I had known since the late 1950s when we were sent to Budapest together to attend an international conference of journalists. Yakovlev is an intelligent and very decent person, with whom I was on good terms. But although he could have satisfied my requests with a stroke of his pen, he calmly and politely turned his back on me, as befits a real *apparatchik*. I don't hold it against him, and I have reason to regard him as a decent person. After our discussion I went to work for TASS on the African desk and prepared to travel to Africa, a continent I had not yet visited. A new life was about to begin.

CHAPTER THIRTEEN

Working for TASS

THE TASS NEWS AGENCY – its full name is the Telegraph Agency of the Soviet Union attached to the Council of Ministers of the USSR – was set up in 1925 as a development of the Russian Telegraph Agency, known as ROSTA. Today TASS is the only news agency in the Soviet Union with its own correspondents throughout the Soviet Union and abroad who report on events in the USSR and on the more important developments in foreign countries. TASS is a huge organization employing more than three thousand people, with more than a thousand journalists in the head office on Moscow and some 350 correspondents working abroad in practically every country of the world. TASS has its own radio transmitters and receivers and a communications directorate employing about two thousand technicians.

TASS is organized into a number of chief editorial boards. There is one for foreign news, which has its own correspondents abroad, another with correspondents in all the republics and regions of the country reporting on domestic events, and a third one responsible for transmitting news and feature material by teleprinter to countries in the West and the Third World with which TASS has agreements for an exchange of information. From the day it was set up TASS has been performing the function, not only of a news agency, but also of a distributor of propaganda, counter-propaganda and disinformation. The Central Committee of the Party regards TASS as one of its ideological depart-ments. The KGB and, to a lesser extent, the GRU regard TASS as an excellent source of cover for their people work-ing abroad. Although TASS correspondents abroad do not enjoy diplomatic status and can therefore be arrested if they break the laws of their host country or if they are caught spying, the Soviet secret police use them to collect informa-tion of all kinds and to make contact with politicians and public figures in whom they are interested. In fact more than a third of TASS's foreign correspondents are secret service officers. Every KGB or GRU officer sent abroad as a TASS correspondent has to put in not less than a year working on the foreign news desk in Moscow and learning how to be a foreign correspondent abroad. There have been very few cases where a KGB or GRU officer has not made a success of his job and has had to be recalled. This may well be due to the fact that Soviet intelligence officers today are usually graduates, with a good command of their own language and two or even three others.

Paradoxical as it may seem, many a KGB officer em-ployed as a TASS correspondent has coped much better with the job than the 'pure' correspondent. For example, in the mid-1970s a 'pure' TASS correspondent in Spain was replaced by a KGB officer who was soon recognized to be one of the best foreign correspondents that TASS had. Members of the TASS staff know very well who's who among their fellow employees but may not discuss such 'official secrets'. To reveal the fact that a Soviet diplomat, correspondent or member of any other Soviet organization working abroad is a member of the Soviet intelligence ser-vice is regarded as treason and involves the immediate return of the person concerned to the Soviet Union.

KGB and GRU officers sent to work in TASS are not kept for long working on a desk in Moscow, whereas 'pure' cor-respondents have to wait for years for the possibility of going abroad, especially if it is to the United States, Canada or a

country of Western Europe, unless they happen to be children of privileged parents. One of the latter is the daughter
of Aleksandrov-Agentov, an assistant to the General Secretary of the CPSU, who has on two or three occasions worked
as a TASS correspondent in Western Europe.

The Central Committee has decreed that foreign postings
should be for not longer than five years, but people related to
or having good connections with top officials and intelligence officers can stay abroad for longer.

A TASS correspondent's duties involve more than sending a daily report to Moscow; he has also to draw up monthly
reports about the political and economic situation and sum-
maries of information gathered in private conversations in
government and political circles. These reports, usually
marked 'secret', are called 'mailers' because they are
despatched to Moscow in the diplomatic mail.

Ideally such reports are drawn up independently, without
involving the Soviet embassy, so that the account is objective. However, diplomats in Soviet embassies frequently
make the mistake, under pressure from the ambassador, of
painting an unduly rosy picture of the political situation in
order to make it look as though they have been successful in
improving relations with the country to which they have
been accredited. In order not to spoil their relations with the
ambassadors, TASS correspondents often agree the content
of the 'mailers' in advance with the embassy, altering 'facts'
that do not suit the ambassador. Thus Moscow often gets
embellished untruths or plain misinformation. I came up
against this more then once when I was working as a TASS
correspondent in East Africa and as a press officer with the
World Health Organisation in Geneva.

Most Soviet ambassadors insist that TASS correspondents show them their despatches before they are transmit-
ted to Moscow, a demand few correspondents can oppose.
This is presumably the reason why, in the mid-1970s, a
special desk was created in TASS, known as the operational

information desk, staffed by about a dozen journalists. They analyse the material from Reuters, UPI, Associated Press and Agence France Presse and draw up short reports about major events for a bulletin which is distributed three times a day to the members of the Politburo and Secretariat of the Party and to certain ministers. In the event of some exceptional development, like a *coup d'état*, the murder of a statesman or some violent anti-Soviet statement, a report is sent immediately to the Soviet leaders.

On the basis of reports provided by TASS correspondents and the main foreign news agencies TASS produces other bulletins, some of them marked 'secret' because they report statements and events of an anti-Soviet nature. The bulletins are distributed by KGB couriers to the national newspapers and periodicals, to the Central Committee, the Foreign Ministry, the KGB and GRU, the Ministry of Foreign Trade and organizations concerned with foreign policy.

TASS is the main supplier of information for Soviet newspapers and periodicals. The TASS news reports and bulletins, to which the Soviet media subscribe and pay for, make it possible for TASS to exist without overt financial support from the state.

Information about events taking place abroad is not subject to any censorship. The editor alone is responsible for the political correctness of the material. If any doubts about a press report arise it is referred to the *apparat* or Secretariat of the Party. Information about events in the Soviet Union intended for transmission to Soviet newspapers and to the radio for broadcast abroad is, on the other hand, subjected to a rigorous censorship, carried out by Glavlit, the body responsible for the censorship, of which a representative is always present in the TASS office.

Apart from straight reporting, the TASS agency conducts propaganda and counter-propaganda both inside the Soviet Union and abroad. For this purpose, in the early

1970s, a group of TASS political commentators was formed out of correspondents who had worked abroad. Their job is to write articles replying to statements made by the Western media or politicians, and this counter-propaganda is distributed, if necessary after reference to the *apparat* of the CC, to foreign countries, and broadcast over the Soviet Radio in foreign languages for the benefit of foreign listeners.

In that TASS is just as much an organ of the Soviet state as the Foreign Ministry, the KGB or the Foreign Trade Ministry, it differs greatly from the news agencies in the West. TASS correspondents are in fact civil servants. Statements published by TASS setting out the view of the Soviet leaders are not composed in the TASS offices but in the Ministry of Foreign Affairs and the International Department of the Central Committee of the Party.

I started to work with TASS in September 1965, spending three months on special courses to learn the principles governing information work while at the same time working as an editor on the desk dealing with African countries south of the Sahara. I chose Africa myself because I had never been there and because I would be working on my own. Then Dmitri Goryunov, the General Director of TASS, suggested that I should go to Ghana. My appointment had just been approved by the CC when Kwame Nkrumah was overthrown by a *coup d'état*, which prevented my departure. It was not easy to find me another country, because two-thirds of the posts in Africa were occupied by the KGB or the GRU, and many of the 'pure' correspondents had themselves only recently been appointed. But at last a country was found for me. It was Zanzibar. This exotic little island had recently attracted the special attention of the Soviet leaders and the International Department of the CC.

'Don't think that Ghana is more important for us than Zanzibar,' the head of the African sector, Manchkha, said. 'Zanzibar was always the gateway to East Africa, and it may well become a second Cuba – the revolutionary island of East

Africa. Our aim is to show the other countries of Africa, through the example of Zanzibar, the political and economic success that can be achieved by a country that takes the socialist path of development. And, of course, Zanzibar's strategic position is also not without importance for us.'

I realized later that Manchkha had in mind the possibility of using Zanzibar as a supply base for ships of the Soviet navy stationed in the Indian Ocean.

In spite of the importance attached to Zanzibar I was sceptical about its real value politically. I simply wanted to get to Africa, and I didn't care whether it was Ghana or Zanzibar. I read all I could about the country and came to the conclusion that it wouldn't be such a bad place to live in, and as for its importance for my future career as a journalist, it was all the same to me. I had had more than enough of responsible work, and I was delighted to think that I would be far away from Soviet reality. In this I was mistaken. The Soviet leaders really did attach great importance to the African continent and were determined to win it over politically.

The granting of independence to the countries of Africa and the emergence of new African leaders who had rejected the capitalist path and were mostly hostile to the West had created, in the opinion of the Soviet leaders, favourable conditions for spreading socialist ideas there and turning the African continent into a zone of Soviet influence. This was stated quite unambiguously by Suslov at a meeting I attended in the Central Committee. The object of winning over Africa was not simply to spread socialism on the Soviet model but also to obtain an absolute majority of votes in the United Nations Organization, of which the new African countries had become members. (Much later Suslov was to voice his concern at the fact that the African and other developing countries, now in a majority, were dominating the United Nations and were beginning to dictate terms to the great powers.)

In accordance with the principle that political influence

comes with the expansion of trade, the Soviet leaders, headed by Khrushchev, did everything they could to further economic relations with the countries of Africa. The Soviet government provided Africa with as much as five billion roubles a year in the form of interest-free loans, which were naturally attractive to the African leaders but which, as it turned out later, had a catastrophic effect on the situation of the Soviet Union itself. The Soviet government also started sending large numbers of military and other advisers to increase the military power of the African countries and to organize their economic growth on the Soviet pattern. Unfortunately they did not consider the history of the peoples of Africa or their national characters. The African leaders were at first pleased with Soviet military aid, but the economic advice they were given led to decline and disintegration rather than growth. The Africans were slow to see this but those of us taking part in the 'transformation' saw it only too clearly and informed our Soviet leaders. They, however, stuck to their dogmatic ideas of Marxism–Leninism and refused to listen.

Most of the African countries had single-culture economies and had a long way to go before they could become industrialized. The Soviet economists persuaded the African leaders that, in order to rid themselves of dependence on Western and other industrially advanced countries, they must create their own industry at a forced pace and abandon their single-culture system. Plans for the construction of industrial plants, designed to put an end to economic stagnation 'bequeathed to them by colonialism' and to create industrial–agrarian, economically independent countries, were presented to African leaders. Although it would be wrong to suggest that a single-culture economy is progressive, nevertheless many African countries, such as Zanzibar, the main supplier of cloves to the world market, and Ghana, the country of cocoa, certainly had in such crops a sure source of foreign currency. But once they had allowed themselves to be seduced by the proposals of the Soviet economists and abandoned their single-culture system, several African countries soon found themselves on the brink of bankruptcy.

Industrial plants need not only raw materials but also a skilled work force, and their products require a market. In Sudan, for example, a country which has several harvests of vegetables each year, including tomatoes, a factory was built to produce tomato juice. However, there was no demand for it among the local population or in neighbouring countries and the retail price was far greater than that for tinned tomato juice exported from Europe.

In Somalia a factory was built for the production of butter and other milk products. But it soon became apparent that there was not a large supply of milk and that the demand for milk products in Somalia and the neighbouring countries was limited. The requirements of the Somalian population could be satisfied by using a tenth of the plant's capacity.

Even the iron and steel plant built in Egypt was often unable to operate because of the shortage of raw materials.

In conversation with Soviet ambassadors in Sudan and Somalia I used to ask them why the Soviet Union spent money and handed over expensive equipment much needed in our own country which, instead of helping the developing countries, was doing them a bad turn. The reply I received from both ambassadors was absolutely clear.

The task that faced us, they told me, was not simply to provide the countries of Africa with economic aid but primarily to turn them into countries following the path of socialism and totally rejecting capitalism. To do that we had to create a working class, which could not be done without creating an industry. The working class was rated politically far above the peasantry. Once a working class had been created it would be possible to organize a Communist Party which would be the only party capable of taking power and leading the country along the path of scientific socialism.

The ambassadors rejected any idea of Arab or African socialism (and the new Euro-Communism); this was the strict party line and was adhered to in all our talks with African leaders and politicians. Such political adventurism could only end in disaster. After extending credits of five billion roubles a year to the countries of Africa, Moscow eventually withdrew them, suggesting more 'mutually beneficial' arrangements. The Soviet Government decided that armaments, almost free of charge and accompanied by military advisers, should be supplied as 'aid'. The weapons were usually obsolete and, although acceptable at the time to the Africans, were the cause of bad relations and in some cases – Egypt, Sudan and Somalia – of a complete break with the Soviet Union. Military aid was accompanied by political demands, on the fulfilment of which depended future supplies of ammunition and spare parts for the weapons.

The main factor which obliged the Soviet Union to quit many of the countries of Africa was its inability to provide either essential economic aid for industrial and agricultural development or the consumer goods and foodstuffs of which the Soviet Union was itself lacking. The African leaders dismissed theoretical plans for a 'prosperous socialism' in the future, and, to solve their immediate problems, turned to the West, which did not impose political conditions. Moreover, although many African leaders favoured an authoritarian form of government, once they understood the principles of scientific socialism they saw the danger of a partnership with the Soviet Union.

Time passed, but there was still no visa forthcoming for me from the Tanzanian Government. There was already a TASS correspondent in Dar-es-Salaam and President Nyerere did not wish to have another correspondent on the island of Zanzibar. The Soviet embassy informed us that it was unlikely that they would be able to change Nyerere's mind. So the International Department of the CC instructed the Soviet consulate in Zanzibar to apply direct to the government of Zanzibar for a visa for me. I was summoned some time later to Goryunov, who showed me a Zanzibar residence permit signed by the President of Zanzibar, Abeido Amani Karume, which gave me the right to live and work as a TASS correspondent in Zanzibar. But how was I to get to Zanzibar? I couldn't yet fly via Dar-es-Salaam because I had no Tanzanian visa and I would have been arrested for illegal entry. The only solution appeared to be for me to go on a merchant ship from the port of Kerch in the Crimea. This I did, and after a nightmare voyage on a battered old tub called the *Nezhin*, my wife and I arrived in Zanzibar in September 1967.

Before leaving Moscow I had been given three main tasks to carry out in addition to reporting the news: to establish contact with members of the American consulate; to keep an eye on the Chinese and assess their penetration into the countries of East Africa; and to find ways of discrediting the work of the American Peace Corps.

We needed contact with people in the American consulate to evaluate their attitude to the Chinese. The Americans had to be persuaded that the Soviet Union was not an enemy of the United States and that China was our common enemy. The Chinese leaders, guided by Mao Tse-tung's dogmatic teachings, were steadily increasing their military potential and extending their political influence over the countries of the Far East and Africa, thus creating a major political and military danger for the Soviet Union.

I had to work closely with the KGB *rezidentura* in Tanzania. I had discussed this in Moscow with the *rezident*, Arkadi Boiko, an old friend of mine who had been appointed to Dar-es-Salaam at the same time as I was sent to Zanzibar.

When I arrived in Zanzibar there were more than two hundred Soviet military advisers there and another hundred economic, agricultural, technical and other specialists. Even

I was surprised at the number of Soviet advisers in such a small island.

A year later, in September 1968, I was made secretary of the Combined Party organization, which came directly under the Directorate for Staff Abroad of the Central Committee. This Directorate is the ultimate authority for deciding which Soviet citizens may go abroad. It also decides whether or not to recall a Soviet employee if he has committed a breach of the rules it lays down. Those travelling abroad have to read these rules and sign a document saying they are aware of them and will adhere to them. They are restrictive: it is forbidden to visit restaurants or night clubs, to establish contacts with foreigners without informing the Soviet authorities, to sell any personal possessions, to make journeys without informing the embassy, and so forth. An exception is made for employees of the KGB and GRU, whose posting abroad to work under cover of Soviet embassies or other organizations is dealt with by the Department of Administrative Organs of the Central Committee, which is directly in charge of those bodies.

Rogov, the consul-general in Zanzibar, was a limited and indecisive person who was bent on enriching himself and had made his wife the consulate's chief accountant. His diplomatic activity consisted of nothing more than organizing receptions and delivering flowery speeches. For him, as for any Soviet ambassador in Africa or a developing country, the most important thing was not so much to persuade the leaders of countries following the non-capitalist path that the Soviet way of life was superior to the capitalist as to convince the Soviet leadership at home that they were producing results, even if that was far from the truth. In their efforts to convince the semi-literate African leaders, Soviet diplomats would tell them that before the Revolution of 1917 Russia was at the same level of development as the countries of Africa. On one occasion I could not resist asking Timoshchenko, the Soviet ambassador in Tanzania, whether Soviet diplomats had really forgotten that before the 1917 Revolution Russia had produced Mendeleyev, Chaikovsky, Rakhmaninov, Pushkin, Lermontov, Dostoyevsky and Tolstoy. Timoshchenko replied that if they told the Africans about such world-renowned figures they still would not understand what we were talking about, so that it was better to persuade them that we had been a backward country and that it was only thanks to the Revolution which overthrew the capitalists that Russia had become a great power.

Soviet advisers had persuaded the President of Zanzibar to give up exporting cloves, the island's main source of income, and instead to construct a huge port and organize tunny fishing on a commercial basis which would, according to the Soviet advisers, be more profitable for Zanzibar. In the end the port was not constructed because the contours of the sea-bed were too complicated and the construction work would have cost millions of dollars. It also proved impossible to fish for tunny because the little Russian motor boats were not fast enough to catch tunny and the Soviet Union could not supply the necessary nets. Meanwhile the cultivation of cloves had been neglected because Zanzibar believed Soviet propaganda that it was about to become a prosperous industrial island.

Zanzibar was reduced to a state of near-bankruptcy. Its President, who had four wives and had in the meantime built himself four modern villas, lost his temper and ordered the Soviet advisers off the island, leaving only the military, who had turned the Zanzibar army into what was, by African standards, a powerful force, capable, it was claimed, of occupying the whole of East Africa. Abeido Karume, his Soviet adviser Major-General Grigoryev and the Chinese military advisers who were in Zanzibar competing with the Soviets knew why such military might was necessary.

I eventually came to the conclusion that we would never succeed in making Zanzibar the 'island of revolution' to open the way for us into East Africa, not only because of the

Soviet diplomats' incompetence but also because of the corruption and thirst for riches that had seized the island's own
leaders. If it had not been for the natural beauty of Zanzibar
and the independent life I led there, I would probably have
asked to be recalled to Moscow because there was really
nothing for me to do. I had no wish to spend my time dealing
with Party affairs and sorting out squabbles among members
of the Soviet community, though that was what I had to do.

Establishing contact with members of the staff of the
American consulate was not difficult, and I was on very good
terms with the consul-general, Jack Matlock, an intelligent and well-educated man, fond of classical music and a
good Russian speaker. He had also learnt to speak Swahili.
In conversation with him and some of the American vice-
consuls I raised the question of their attitude to China. As
they did not appear to share the Soviet view I did not pursue
the subject. However, to establish the extent of Chinese
penetration into East Africa I obtained Moscow's permission
to make a trip through the countries of East Africa by car.
On my visits to Uganda, Kenya and Zambia I met not only
Soviet diplomats and members of the KGB and GRU
rezidentury but also local officials who all supplied me with
details about the number of Chinese officials in the country
and the reason for their presence. I collated this information
into a report to go to Moscow. When he had read it, Ambassador Timoshchenko exclaimed in surprise : 'But where did
you find so many Chinese? I drive around Dar-es-Salaam
and I don't seem to see any.' He was displeased with my
report, which had resulted in him receiving a cable from
Moscow not altogether to his liking. He reproached me for
wasting his time; he would have to write and excuse himself
to Moscow, instead of getting on with his serious diplomatic
work.

The International Department of the CC was interested in
the Chinese question not only because the Chinese were
gradually gaining political leverage in the countries of

Africa, and in Tanzania in particular, but also because Tanzania was a staging post for the supply of weapons to the national liberation movements in Southern Rhodesia, Mozambique and South Africa. The Chinese were making great efforts to replace the Soviet Union in this business. For example, they tried to persuade the Tanzanian leaders that they would be better off financially to employ Chinese advisers, since their keep cost only 450 shillings a month, whereas a Soviet specialist cost them 2000–2500 shillings a month. The combination of failure by the Soviet Union to develop industry and agriculture and the vigorous efforts by the Chinese led to the withdrawal of nearly all the Soviet advisers. I had warned Moscow that this would happen, but my opinion had apparently not been heeded.

During my trip around the countries of East Africa I tried to find out what I could about the work of the American Peace Corps, the attitude of the local leaders to it, and, as I had been instructed, I also thought about ways of discrediting it. I did not succeed in doing this myself because I could obtain no information about any subversive activity by the Peace Corps directed against the African governments. The Soviet authorities regarded the Peace Corps as one of the serious obstacles to the extension of Soviet influence over the countries of Africa. They also feared that the Peace Corps might undermine Soviet propaganda that the capitalist powers, the enemies of the Africans, had now changed tactics and, in the guise of friendship, were trying to re-establish colonialism. They were worried that the Peace Corps would conduct propaganda among the population, advertising the American way of life, and that some members of the Corps were recruiting Africans with a view to using them later for intelligence and subversion. Ambassador Timoshchenko and members of his staff often raised this question with President Nyerere and ministers in the Tanzanian Government. But, while the Tanzanians agreed in principle that the Peace Corps might have a bad influence on their country, they argued that they had no concrete evidence to show that the Peace Corps was engaging in subversive or any other improper activity, and so they could not decide to refuse its services.

One day in 1969 I had a call from Dar-es-Salaam in my office in Zanzibar. It was the KGB *rezident*, Arkadi Boiko. He wanted me to go to Dar-es-Salaam as a matter of urgency. I agreed, as long as I could take my wife.

I was surprised by the summons, because I had only just returned from Dar-es-Salaam, where I had taken part, along with members of the KGB *rezidentura*, in testing some of the new bugging devices capable of recording conversations at a considerable distance. I had been involved because my presence enabled them to take a room in a hotel without arousing the suspicions of the local counter-intelligence service.

Arkadi also made use of my frequent visits to Dar-es-Salaam as a cover for his meetings with agents. I would drive him around the city, drop him off in some dark side street, and then keep driving around, making sure that I was not being followed.

The day after I had spoken to Arkadi a little aeroplane flew my wife and me across the straits from Zanzibar to Dar-es-Salaam in a matter of fifteen minutes. Arkadi and some other friends from the *rezidentura* met us and drove us to a hotel in the middle of the city. Arkadi and I did not want to talk in the hotel room for fear of being bugged, so we repaired to the bar, where Arkadi told me that the Tanzanian and Ugandan leaders, who had succumbed to our pressure, were now on the point of taking a decision concerning the Peace Corps, but to do so they needed justification. It was the job of the KGB to provide them with one.

'The Centre has sent us an excellent article giving the names of all the people working for the Peace Corps who are actually past and present employees of the CIA,' Arkadi said. 'The Americans will not be able to disprove these facts if we can get the article placed in the Ugandan and Tanzanian press signed by an African journalist – or even unsigned, if the papers do not wish to reveal the identity of their sources. So now you understand why I invited you over.'

I said I did and I didn't. Why was I being involved, when there were other correspondents in Dar already?

'You live in Zanzibar,' Arkadi replied, 'and you are clean, whereas we are all well known here. Therefore you will be able to do it more easily than we can, because the person you are going to deal with may well know or suspect who we are and get scared.'

They were not very persuasive arguments, but I saw that Arkadi did not want to risk his own people unnecessarily. In addition, as I learnt later, the *rezidentura* was actively engaged in preparations for the *coup d'état*, in which several members of the government and some well-known Tanzanian politicians secretly opposed to Nyerere were involved.

I also realized that I would actually not be risking anything, because I had every right as a journalist to offer any local newsman or newspaper editor some 'sensational' material on the grounds that, as a Soviet correspondent, I couldn't publish my articles in the local media.

It was decided that it would be better in the first place to publish the article in a Ugandan newspaper and then, in a slightly different form, in a Tanzanian paper. It was no accident that we chose Uganda, because President Milton Obote was being supported by the Soviet Union and had received substantial sums of money, most of which he spent on maintaining his courtiers, on various forms of entertainment and on living in style. In return he was to play the part of an anti-Western and anti-American leader.

As soon as I arrived in Uganda I made contact with a member of the KGB *rezidentura* who introduced me to one of the influential newsmen who took an anti-Western line and who agreed to place the article in one of the Ugandan papers, as indeed he did. The Centre did not want the KGB *rezidentura* in Kampala involved in the affair, because the Peace Corps had been handed over to us in Tanzania.

The article we had received from Moscow was obviously a piece of disinformation, but it confirmed the connection between some of the leaders of the Peace Corps and the CIA, which supported our assertion that the Peace Corps was nothing but an instrument of American intelligence.

Getting the article published in Uganda turned out to be a straightforward business, but doing so in Tanzania was more difficult because President Nyerere and his government claimed to be neutral.

I was helped by the fact that I had recently concluded a contract with the Tanzanian Minister of Information to provide the Tanzanian newspapers with TASS teleprinters, and so I had got to know the editors of the papers. I used to call on them on my visits to Dar to ask what they thought of the TASS wire service, what use was made of it and whether they had any criticisms.

When I arrived in Dar I used this excuse for calling on the editor of one of the papers and, having disposed of the formalities, got down to business. When he told me that the TASS material suited his paper's needs I tried to look pleased, although I knew that not a single TASS report had appeared in his paper for a whole year.

Then I asked him: 'What do you know about the Peace Corps and what it is doing in Tanzania and other countries of Africa?'

He was quite taken aback and hardly knew what to say. I halted him with a sweep of my hand and placed the article before him.

'Just read that,' I said.

It was not a long article, but there was a fact in every line of it. Having read it through, the editor looked up at me in surprise and asked me why I had given it him to read.

I had been taught in the KGB's school in Moscow that if you mount a frontal attack there must be no evasive manoeuvres. So I replied that the imperialists, and especially the Americans, were our common enemies and we should fight them together. It was clear from this article that our enemy was the Peace Corps and that it had to be destroyed. Whether we would achieve that if the article were published in his paper I was not sure, but it was our duty to expose the true face of that organization, which was conducting subversive activity in his country, and I hoped that he, as a true patriot, would do what had to be done.

The editor rubbed his forehead with his finger and continued to study the article. I pointed out that a paper in Uganda had already published an article about the Peace Corps and that although President Nyerere and the people around him were not particularly fond of the Peace Corps they had no formal grounds for expelling it. It was possible, I said, that if the article were published in his paper it would help them to take the right decision. I knew I was talking nonsense, but in this case it worked.

'In the first place,' the editor said, 'I don't know where these facts come from. And secondly, space in the newspaper is filled for a long time ahead.' He was also talking nonsense, and I knew what he was getting at.

I assured him that the facts in the article were absolutely true, and that, as for the space, we were ready to pay for the article to be printed, as the French Consul-General had done in a similar case recently. The editor brightened up and asked whom we could name as the author of the article. I said they could decide that themselves, but that it could also be printed without a byline. Would a thousand shillings be acceptable to the paper? I asked, knowing perfectly well that the money would go straight into the editor's pocket. A day or so later the article appeared. As with the article published in Uganda, its contents were given to TASS, then published in the Soviet press, and then broadcast by radio in practically all languages, and thus entered the public domain. That was the beginning of the end for the Peace Corps in

East Africa. Uganda and then Tanzania (though not without some pressure by the Soviet embassies) refused the services of the Peace Corps, and other countries followed suit.

This piece of disinformation alone was not responsible for ending the activity of the Peace Corps in East Africa; it was part of a sustained campaign by Soviet diplomatic missions and the *rezidentury* to discredit the Peace Corps and its work.

My efforts in Tanzania were apparently well thought of in Moscow, since I was among the first TASS correspondents to be awarded the medal for Valiant Service, instituted in 1970 to celebrate the 100th anniversary of Lenin's birth.

In 1969 a new Soviet ambassador arrived in Tanzania. He was a nephew of the late Dmitri Ustinov, former Minister of Defence and member of the Politburo. Compared with his predecessor Timoshchenko, Ustinov was a relatively young man – only forty-five – much more up to date in his views and a more objective judge of the situation in Africa and of the possibilities open to the Soviet Union. He soon paid a visit to Zanzibar, where he had a meeting with Consul-General Rogov and me. We were naturally interested to know what plans the Soviet leadership had for Tanzania and for Africa as a whole. Ustinov said that the new Soviet leadership, headed by Brezhnev, had decided to abandon Khrushchev's policy and to establish more or less mutually beneficial relations with the African countries. That meant no longer throwing millions into a bottomless pit and trying to recover some of our expenditure. In Tanzania, Ustinov said, the Soviet leaders were worried about the penetration by the Chinese and the behaviour of President Nyerere, who seemed to be getting closer to the West. If there was a rapprochement with the West, the Soviet Union's money and effort would have been wasted. It was important for us to control Zanzibar, which might in turn restrain Nyerere.

Zanzibar was independent of the mainland in terms of

economic affairs and it had its own bank which held the foreign currency obtained from the sale of cloves. In spite of repeated demands by Nyerere that the money should be transferred to the State Bank in Dar-es-Salaam, the top people in Zanzibar refused to do so. We exploited this fact and the Zanzibarian leaders' striving for independence to exert a certain, though not very considerable, pressure on Nyerere.

At the beginning of 1970 I was suddenly transferred to Dar-es-Salaam. I was to continue working as a correspondent, covering events both on the mainland and in Zanzibar. When I arrived in the capital I found that the KGB *rezident*, Arkadi Boiko, most of the staff of the *rezidentura* and the TASS correspondent in Dar-es-Salaam had been called back to Moscow. The ambassador suggested that I should take over Boiko's apartment and car. This made it look as though I was the new KGB *rezident*, and that was no doubt the reason why, later, when I was appointed TASS correspondent in Zambia, the Zambian government refused to give me a visa.

My arrival coincided with the opening of a trial of a large group of Tanzanian politicians accused of taking part in a conspiracy against Nyerere's government. Ambassador Ustinov asked me to attend the open court proceedings to find out if the accused admitted links with Soviet representatives in Tanzania or indeed their involvement in the conspiracy.

Ustinov explained to me that it was perfectly natural for me to attend the trial, whereas to send one of his diplomats might give rise to suspicions about our interest. But I knew the real reason for Ustinov's concern: Boiko had been preparing a *coup d'état* which was supposed to replace Nyerere with a man closer to the Soviet Union and connected with the Soviet intelligence service. Having been educated in England, Nyerere had never inspired the Soviet leaders with confidence, and his links with the West were now growing stronger. The arrest of the participants in the plot was the reason for the sudden recall of Boiko and – just in case – of other members of the *rezidentura*, some of whom later returned to Dar when the accused did not confess to any connection with Soviet officials. Boiko's connection with Soviet intelligence was no secret in Dar-es-Salaam. On one occasion I was taken aback when I went into a shop belonging to an Indian businessman called Babla and he asked me: 'So where's your Richard Sorge then?' (Sorge was a Soviet spy executed in Japan in November 1944.) I replied that Boiko was not Richard Sorge and that he was on holiday in Moscow.

The courthouse in which the trial took place was strictly guarded and everybody attending, including accredited correspondents and diplomats, was searched by security officers. For nine days I conscientiously attended the trial and after it was over informed the ambassador, to his satisfaction, that the accused had not once mentioned the Soviet Union or even hinted at their contacts with Soviet officials in Tanzania.

I was not able to follow the trial to the end because I received a cable from Leonid Zamyatin, the new General Director of TASS, instructing me to go to work as TASS correspondent in Khartum, a possibility that had never occurred to me and which I did not welcome. It surprised me because it read like an order: 'The governing body of TASS considers it expedient that you should be transferred to Khartum to work as TASS correspondent because of the complicated political situation there and the necessity for having reliable information concerning the real state of affairs.' The reason given was Zamyatin's way of sweetening the bitter pill. I was given three days to reflect on the proposal.

I had known Zamyatin since the late 1950s, when he was first deputy head and then head of the press department of the Soviet Foreign Ministry. His life's dream was to become

Soviet ambassador to the United States of America. But he achieved a great deal in Soviet terms, thanks not so much to his talents as to his ability to keep his nose to the wind and to side with anyone who could be useful to him today and to drop or push under his friend of yesterday, not to mention anyone he regarded as a rival. It was Aleksei Adzhubei, then editor-in-chief of *Izvestia*, and Mikhail Kharmalov, then head of the press department and later Chairman of the Radio Committee, whom he had to thank for being appointed head of the Foreign Ministry's press department. But after the overthrow of Khrushchev in 1964 and the removal of Adzhubei from all his positions, Zamyatin, whom I had seen with my own eyes deferring to Adzhubei, announced that he really didn't know him very well.

As General Director of TASS, Zamyatin soon became extremely unpopular with journalists because the fate of those whom he did not like or who opposed him was of no significance to him. At the same time those who carried out his wishes without thinking or arguing became his favourites and were quickly promoted. This was not the case with Aleksandr Vishnevsky and Dmitri Postnikov, who both had their own views on things and were not afraid to voice them. Later, when Zamyatin became one of Brezhnev's courtiers, he got rid of his disobedient deputies.

But at that moment Zamyatin was my most important boss, and I found it hard to determine his attitude to me. I had heard from people who had worked under him in the Foreign Ministry that he was a very intolerant person, and that gave me cause for serious thought. I had spent some time in Khartum and I knew what its climate was like, and I had seen the filth and the poverty. I had no particular desire to go there, but there was no alternative. My wife and I came to the conclusion that, if I were to refuse the posting, Zamyatin, only just made General Director, would regard it as a threat to his authority since, significantly, he had signed the cable himself. Moreover, if I refused and returned to

Moscow I would be unlikely to be sent abroad again so long as Zamyatin was General Director. And so, reluctantly, I agreed to go to Sudan. That was in May 1970.

We arrived in Khartum in a frightful heatwave and amid clouds of dust. The TASS correspondent who met us was overjoyed at our arrival, which meant that in a couple of weeks he could leave the godforsaken place, where the heat, the dry climate, the dust-storms and the unbelievable filth made life very difficult for Europeans. The house in which the TASS correspondent was supposed to live was so appalling that my wife and I decided to live in a hotel until we could find better accommodation.

Fortunately, I was on good terms with the deputy director of TASS, Aleksandr Vishnevsky, a man of culture and independence of mind who could not stand Zamyatin. I sent him a cable asking for permission to rent a different house and office and received his agreement by return. A few days later I succeeded in renting a beautiful furnished villa from a Greek who had fled from the Sudanese Government to the West. Once we had installed air-conditioners we realized that it was, in spite of everything, possible to live in Sudan. Human beings can accustom themselves to anything, and we soon got used to the hot climate and even began to play tennis on the excellent grass courts of the former Royal British Club. On General Numeiri's orders it had been made into an officers' club and there was music every evening and gatherings of senior officers.

After getting to know the Soviet ambassador Nikolai Nikolayev and the embassy's counsellor Mikhail Orlov I set about studying the political situation. I was greatly helped in this by my translator Yakhia, who had been a Sudanese journalist and took an objective view of affairs in the country, unlike the Soviet ambassador and his advisers. The KGB *rezident* turned out to be a weak-willed drunkard who was dependent upon Ambassador Nikolayev, himself an intellectually limited petty dictator who misinformed the

Soviet Foreign Ministry and the Central Committee about the true state of the country so as not to expose his own inadequacy. The KGB *rezident* gave him full support in this, with the result that, soon after my arrival, he was recalled to Moscow to be replaced by Colonel Yuri Popov, with whom I got on very well.

The situation in Sudan was complicated. Unlike the other Arab and African countries, it had a powerful and well-organized Communist Party, led by Makhjub, who had graduated from the Higher Party School in Moscow and was committed to Marxist–Leninist teachings. After the *coup d'état* carried out by the Free Officers organization in 1969 General Numeiri seized power and, realizing the strength of the Communist Party and its influence over the trade unions, appointed five members of the Party's Central Committee as ministers in his government. The Soviet embassy immediately established close relations with them. Ambassador Nikolayev and Counsellor Orlov assumed that Sudan and its government were now in their hands and, bearing in mind that the Sudanese army was equipped with Soviet weapons and planes and advised by more than a thousand Soviet officers and technicians, the extent of Soviet influence certainly looked impressive. But that was not the whole truth.

The Communist ministers soon forgot about their attachment to the 'vanguard of the working class' and their 'sacred duty' to fight for the good of the people. They set about enriching themselves and soon turned into middle-class citizens with villas, cars, mistresses and all the other attributes of the *dolce vita*. This did not discourage Nikolayev from regarding them as Communists and militants and meeting them to obtain 'information', which he sent on to Moscow, assuring his superiors that all was well and under his control.

A different view of the situation was taken by Makhjub, the General Secretary of the Communist Party, who started a campaign against the government, which had promised to improve the people's standard of living, the medical services, working conditions and so forth. This criticism of the government's shortcomings did not please either General Numeiri or the Communist ministers, who then refused to obey the decisions of the Communist Party and set up their own rival Central Committee. Communist theory and practice demanded that such a move be denounced as anti-Party separatism, which is what Makhjub did. But Nikolayev and his advisers, who were well versed in the theory of Marxism–Leninism and the CPSU guidelines, did not follow suit and support him. For the sake of their own peace of mind they shut their eyes to what was happening, continued to support the Communist ministers and recognized their breakaway Central Committee.

There would be no need to explain all this in such detail if the actions of the Soviet ambassador Nikolayev and his counsellor Orlov had not led to such tragic events for the Sudanese people, who had not previously known bloodshed in political disputes.

I do not know how it came about, but it was rumoured among members of Makhjub's Central Committee that I represented the International Department of the CPSU Central Committee and that, disguised as a TASS correspondent, I had come to Khartum to sort out the situation in the Sudanese Communist Party. I first heard this from my translator Yakhia, but I treated it as a joke and paid no attention.

In January 1971 the Novosti correspondent Serov, who had the rank of Third Secretary in the embassy, said that a Sudanese working in his office had asked him to inform me that two Sudanese Communists wanted to meet me about an important matter. I told Serov I was ready to meet them in my office and that they should phone me in advance. A few days later two Sudanese turned up at my office and announced that they were members of the Central Committee of the Sudanese Communist Party. They had come to see me as the representative of the Central Committee of the CPSU. I told them that I had no connection with the CC of the CPSU and was certainly not its representative, but that I was ready to listen to what they had to say.

'We appreciate,' said one of them, 'that you can't admit to being the representative of the Central Committee, and we don't insist. In any case, we are bound to tell you what our General Secretary has instructed us to say in the hope that you will inform Moscow of our conversation.

'Our General Secretary has asked us to inform you that the attitude of the Soviet ambassador and the embassy towards the Sudanese Communist Party is unsatisfactory. We are in a very difficult situation. The Central Committee of our party is split. The ministers who were formerly members of the Central Committee have created a new Central Committee of a non-existent party and it is this which enjoys the active support of Ambassador Nikolayev and Counsellor Orlov. They completely ignore the legitimate Committee and its secretary Makhjub. This is causing great harm to the Communist movement in our country and is undermining the authority of our leaders and the confidence in them of the rank and file members.

'To remedy this situation we shall have to criticize the Soviet embassy and consequently the Soviet Union as well, although neither we nor our General Secretary want to. This is what we want you to tell Moscow. We assure you that only we direct the work of the Party organization everywhere, including the army. The breakaway ministers who have sold themselves to Numeiri have no standing. Unless this abnormal situation can be remedied the Central Committee will be forced to take decisive, even extreme, steps.'

I did not ask what these measures might be; it was

sufficient that I had been put in a delicate situation. As they left the two men showed me their identity cards to prove that they really were members of the Central Committee.

If I were to inform Moscow I would make an enemy of the ambassador, but if I did not, I would be committing a moral and political offence. So I chose the first course. I drew up an account of the conversation but instead of naming Ambassador Nikolayev I simply spoke of 'the embassy'. I sealed the envelope, into which I had put two copies, one for the International Department of the Party and the other for the General Director of TASS, and despatched it by the diplomatic mail which left once a week for Moscow. I gave a third copy to Nikolayev's secretary. The ambassador had no right to hold up my despatches to Moscow, especially since my report was marked 'Top Secret'.

After he had read my report Nikolayev's fury knew no bounds. He summoned me to his presence, strode about his office and shouted at me that I knew nothing about politics, that I was misinforming the Centre, and that I was a political illiterate who ought to be packed off to Moscow. After listening to his tirade I said calmly that as Soviet ambassador he had the right to send me back to Moscow, which would suit me very well, since it would give me the opportunity of describing what was going on in Sudan in greater detail than in my report. Nikolayev was struck dumb by what I said, apparently not able to understand how a Soviet employee could be glad to be sent back to his native land from abroad.

But Nikolayev did not send me back to Moscow. Instead, he and his faithful servant Orlov, whose father was some kind of a minister in Moscow, wrote at such length about me to the Foreign Ministry and the Central Committee that there was a thick dossier on me in the Cadres Directorate of the CC which I saw when I returned home. But I was not recalled, mainly because Leonid Zamyatin knew Nikolayev through having worked with him in the United Nations in New York and was well aware of his deficiencies.

In the middle of March 1971 a Deputy Minister of Foreign Affairs, Vasili Kuznetsov, arrived in Khartum in order, so I was told, to determine which of us was right and which was wrong. I had no doubt that the ambassador would be proved right and I told my wife to start packing our things. The main reason for Kuznetsov's arrival was that the 24th Congress of the CPSU was due to take place later in March and, because of Nikolayev, representatives of both Makhjub's Central Committee and the breakaway Committee had been invited. He and three assistants spent a week going through all my reports to Moscow, and the result was that Ambassador Nikolayev was recalled. I stayed on in Khartum. It was apparently the only case in the history of the Soviet Foreign Ministry in which a conflict between an ambassador and another Soviet official abroad had ended in the latter's favour.

Nikolayev did not leave at once, however, and while he was still in Khartum events took place that nobody had foreseen.

One day in June 1971 an excited Yakhia came running to me and said that a *coup d'état* had taken place, that Numeiri and other members of the government had been arrested, and that power had been seized by a group of officers led by Major Ali Ata, a member of the Central Committee of the Sudanese Communist Party. The coup had been quiet and bloodless. Life went on in its normal way in Khartum: there was no martial law or curfew. Major Ali Ata spoke on the radio and television and announced that a new President of the country, then in exile in London, would soon arrive in Khartum. Ali Ata himself stayed in the building of the general staff of the Sudanese army. Whether on instructions from Moscow or out of stupidity, Ambassador Nikolayev drove in the embassy limousine, with the Soviet flag flying on its wing, to the general staff building and officially recognized the new Sudanese government.

Yuri Popov, the KGB *rezident*, was in a state of great

confusion. The *rezidentura* had known nothing about the planned *coup d'état*, despite having informers among the army officers and in the Sudanese counter-intelligence service.

On the day the new President was expected to arrive from London, a counter-*coup d'état* took place, organized by the Egyptian military attaché who, with some officers who supported Numeiri, disarmed the soldiers guarding the officers and men of the Second Tank Brigade, loaded their guns and, in Soviet T-35 tanks, burst into the centre of Khartum and freed Numeiri. The city was turned into a battlefield. Meanwhile President Qadhafi of Libya forced the civilian plane carrying the new Sudanese President and his party to land and arrested them all, thus violating international laws.

Two tanks were stationed in front of the Soviet embassy and from time to time they fired blank shells to frighten the Soviet diplomats and the military advisers whom the ambassador had called in to defend the embassy. As a TASS correspondent I was allowed by the Sudanese authorities to move around the city. On several occasions I found myself in the crossfire, which was not very pleasant.

Once, near the embassy and in sight of Nikolayev and the Soviet diplomats who were shut up inside, I was dragged out of my car by Sudanese soldiers and had the barrel of a Kalashnikov gun poked into my chest and back. The soldiers' expressions were terrifying, and they had only just executed before our very eyes some Sudanese who had been thought to be Communists, which was why I had stopped the car. The same thing could have happened to me. But I caught sight of an officer and shouted to him that I was a TASS correspondent. He rushed up and ordered the soldiers to release me.

Numeiri spoke on the radio and called upon the people to kill all Communists and anybody close to them. Nobody would be punished for killing a Communist, he said. His order to kill, and a similar one made by Qadhafi, who turned up in Khartum, was carried out. Ali Ata and many officers and members of the Communist Party were murdered. Makhjub was arrested and hanged. A well-known Sudanese public figure who had been awarded the Lenin Prize for peace was also hanged, in spite of a personal appeal to Numeiri by Podgorny, the Soviet President. The Communist Party was physically destroyed and all the organizations and trade unions connected with it were dispersed. Numeiri put all the blame for the coup on the Soviet intelligence service, not realizing that in this case the culprits were Nikolayev and Orlov, because of whom Makhjub and his circle had decided to take 'decisive steps'.

Nikolayev is no doubt living in retirement and enjoying life quietly. But at the end of the 1970s his counsellor Orlov was working as Consul-General in Istanbul and may yet become an ambassador.

Disinformation is a very dangerous weapon. By misinforming his superiors in order to achieve his own aims and maintain an easy life, Nikolayev provoked the events in Sudan which caused the deaths of hundreds of people. Instead of putting Nikolayev on trial the Soviet leadership, displeased at Numeiri's changed attitude to the Soviet Union, found nothing better to do than to cut off supplies of ammunition and spare parts for the weapons and equipment they had supplied to Sudan, thus rendering them useless. Sudan was lost, and lost for a long time, perhaps for ever.

CHAPTER FOURTEEN

'UN Civil Servant' in Geneva

In June 1972 I handed over everything to the new TASS correspondent in Khartum and my wife and I returned to Moscow. It was pleasant to go home to our family and friends and to move into the new apartment we had acquired with our foreign currency, but we were disappointed to find the political and economic situation in the country far from healthy.

Every Soviet official who spends time working abroad tends to lose touch with life in his own country, despite the number of Soviet films that are shown in the embassies and the lectures and other propaganda measures organized by the Party abroad. From them I had gained the impression that the Soviet leadership under Brezhnev really had done something to improve matters. We had been told as much by Patolichev, the Soviet Minister for Foreign Trade, who had visited Sudan and had painted a picture of rapid and fundamental economic change.

The reality was different. The economic situation had worsened so that even essential foodstuffs and consumer goods were not available. On the other hand the press was constantly praising Brezhnev, who continued to give himself and his friends medals and titles. After the overthrow of Khrushchev we had hoped that his successors would stop talking about non-existent economic and political achievements, as Khrushchev had done when he spoke of how 'the present generation of Soviet people will live under Communism'. The new leadership had, it is true, abandoned talk of Communism and replaced it by 'advanced socialism'. Inertness and indifference, coupled with a passion for acquiring possessions by every available means, had taken hold of the entire population and especially of the élite.

Since we had returned from abroad we still had a supply of certificates equivalent to our foreign currency earnings which enabled us to buy food, clothes and motor-cars in the *Beryozka*, the special shops to which the ordinary Soviet citizen had no access. But our certificates soon ran out and we had to establish the right connections to go 'through the back door'. Having connections, or *'blat'*, as it is known, is of great importance in the Soviet Union. With *blat* at the top you can get a job working abroad, promotion or accommodation. With *blat* at a lower level you can obtain practically any food or drink, including whisky, gin and French cognac, and even clothes. Of course, payment is exacted in terms of services rendered.

For example, a friend introduced me to the manager of Moscow's leading provision store, still known by the name of its pre-Revolutionary owner, Yeliseyev. The shop has store-rooms full of mostly foreign provisions and drinks that are never displayed in the shop. The manager, Sokolov, told me with unconcealed pride that his customers included Brezhnev's daughter Galina, her husband, astronauts, ministers and other senior officials, including members of the Central Committee *apparat*. Sokolov was not interested in Soviet money; he said he had no need of 'wooden roubles'. What he did need, however, was some spare parts for his Volvo car, and he gave me to understand that, if I obtained the parts for him, his goods would be entirely at my disposal. I brought him the spares from Sudan, so that for several years I had no difficulty in obtaining the food and drink I needed. Galina Brezhneva and people like her did not, of course, obtain anything for Sokolov in return but, enjoying their protection, he was safe from interference by the police, who were supposed to be fighting crime.

Yuri Andropov, who was then Chairman of the KGB, knew all about the activities of Sokolov and his ilk, which were apparent not only in the retail trade but also among senior civil servants, all of whom were involved in immensely profitable underground deals. For example, Shchelokov, the Minister for Internal Affairs, was a friend of Brezhnev, and his deputy, General Churbanov, was married to Galina Brezhneva, both of whom made money by dealing in jewellery and precious stones. Then there was Andropov's own deputy, General Tsvigun, who was married to Brezhnev's wife's sister; he was also involved in their illegal operations. Tsvigun committed suicide. These men made use of their enormous power in the security services to send their agents abroad to acquire goods for themselves and their masters. After Brezhnev's death in 1982 many of his hangers-on disappeared from the scene. Churbanov lost his job in the Interior Ministry; Galina Brezhneva left Moscow; it was rumoured that Shchelokov committed suicide, and many lesser figures were dismissed or arrested.

But these were drops in the ocean by comparison with the scale on which bribery and corruption had penetrated the entire administration. There was even a sort of fixed tariff: the more important the official the bigger the gift. For people working abroad, returning to Moscow involved buying gifts for all the people upon whose patronage for another trip abroad or appointment to another job depended. We carted back not just suits, shoes, women's dresses and other accessories, but hi-fi equipment, the latest Japanese transistors, cameras, whisky, gin and so forth. We would have brought motor-cars as well, but our bosses did not rate that high; only the people round Brezhnev merited such expenditure.

The presentation of gifts, or bribes, was quite open, and if one was not given or if the recipients were not satisfied with it, they might very well express their displeasure equally openly.

Such malpractices, as well as widespread nepotism, the grim economic situation, the absence of the most elementary democratic freedoms and practices, and, in those days, the exaggerated praise of Brezhnev gave rise to serious discontent among thinking people. Discontent and criticism is still widespread among the working people and the farmers as well as among the intelligentsia, and has infected even people in important posts in the *apparat* of the Party, the KGB and senior officers in the Soviet army.

These critics are not to be confused with the dissidents, nor are they opposed in principle to the socialist system or in favour of capitalism. They do not aim to overthrow the Soviet leadership by force, because they realize it would not be possible. Unlike the militant dissidents, they know that making public statements opposing Party policy would lead only to tougher actions by the authorities. At the same time they realize that the present political and economic system has to be changed because it is acting as a brake on progress; it demoralizes people, depriving them of their individuality and turning them into obedient machines. There are hundreds of thousands, and possibly millions, of people who think this, and they constitute an unorganized movement in favour of the democratization of Soviet society. They reject any kind of help from the West and they do not seek publicity, but they are gradually moving the Soviet Union towards some sort of democracy. No one can say how long this process will take, but no one with personal knowledge of the Soviet Union can deny that improvements have taken place.

Of course, things have not moved as fast as many would wish and much remains to be done. But today some Soviet citizens may travel abroad as tourists; some have even been able to leave the country for good. People are no longer arrested and charged with a political crime for having told an anti-Soviet joke. And, at least among their own friends, people are no longer afraid to voice their own thoughts and opinions. This is due entirely to the reformers who are gradually undermining the dogmatic Marxism of the leadership.

On our return from Sudan in 1972 we had little time for engaging in such political debates : we had to make a new life for ourselves. First we took two months' leave, and my wife and I went to Sochi on the Black Sea coast and then to Hungary and Bulgaria. Then I took up my new post, in charge of the foreign news desk, in the TASS office. This involved checking, both for language and for political content, all reports from the various news desks and approving them for transmission by all the media, both at home and abroad. It was a nerve-racking task, because there is an unwritten law that TASS is never wrong and the man on the desk is held responsible for all mistakes. At the same time we had to keep an eye on the reports from the Reuter, AP, UPI and AFP agencies as a check on our own deskmen and the reports coming in from our own correspondents. GRU officers worked alongside us to evaluate anything of a military nature.

It was not a pleasant job, because it involved long hours for weeks on end and the constant worry of checking every story of any importance with the top people in TASS. I found it was boring, tiring and uninteresting, and longed to be posted abroad again, although I knew it might take the usual two, three or more years. The Central Committee reckoned it took that amount of time for a man to become re-inculcated into 'socialist reality', to study the latest decisions of the Party and speeches of its General Secretary, and then, rearmed with theory, to go forth again to foreign parts.

Another unpleasantness for me was that my new job brought me into even closer contact with Zamyatin. Aware that I knew a few things about him and that we had at one time been equals in status (he was deputy head of the Foreign Ministry press department when I was deputy General Secretary of the Union of Journalists), he was not very pleased to have me close to him. So he got his crony Desyatnikov to collect every bit of gossip about me (and about others too) so as to have ammunition against me in hand, and he was, according to his deputy Vladimir Khatuntsev, very glad of the opportunity that shortly arose to get rid of me by sending me to work in Switzerland.

Every morning Zamyatin, who in 1978 was made head of the International Information Department of the Party, issued instructions to the editors of the national newspapers and periodicals, the TASS and Novosti agencies, and the editors of radio and television news, about what they were to publish and broadcast concerning events in the Middle East, the policies of the American and British governments or the situation in Afghanistan or Poland. He also told them which events they were *not* to report if they revealed the Soviet government in a bad light. According to Zamyatin and people like him, Soviet people are not supposed to learn about such events.

What the Soviet press will publish about international affairs is now decided by the Department of International Information in conjunction with the International Department of the CC. In this way the Soviet leaders can be sure that there will be no unpleasant surprises in the press. There is nothing new in this; that was the way things were done even before the Department of International Information was set up. When I was working in the TASS agency on the foreign news desk I had to attend a briefing every morning at which we were told which international events to devote most attention to, what emphasis we were to give them and which ones to ignore altogether. I have to say here that this was not censorship, but political and ideological guidance. Articles and news items dealing with events abroad are not subject to any censorship. But if there are any doubts about doubts about the facts and their interpretation the matter is cleared up in consultation with the International Department, the Department of International Information or the Secretariat of the Central Committee.

In Moscow on holiday from Switzerland in 1978 I asked a friend working in the recently created Department of International Information, headed then by Zamyatin, why it had been created when there was already a Department of Agitation and Propaganda in charge of the press and an International Department in charge of foreign policy questions. My friend replied that the DII had been set up to co-ordinate foreign policy propaganda, because the International Department was overworked and unable to devote sufficient attention to the Soviet media's handling of foreign policy and counter propaganda, to which the Secretariat and Politburo of the CC attached great importance. The point was, my friend said, that we had to create the political climate we needed within the Soviet Union as well as fostering favourable public opinion abroad, and at the same time conduct active counter-measures calculated to neutralize and compromise the policy of the United States government and its satellites. The DII was working, he said, in close contact with its 'neighbours' (the KGB) in the field of counter-propaganda (that is, disinformation), especially with a view to compromising the military policy of the United States. This threatened the whole world but above all the countries of Europe. It was the most sensitive area for European public opinion, which was afraid both of us and the Americans. We had to convince them that it was American policy that constituted the main threat. That was why we had to reply immediately to every statement made in the West.

I believe my friend was right, because the Department of International Information consisted almost entirely of journalists dealing with international affairs and diplomats such as the former Soviet ambassador Falin, who is always writing very sharply worded articles against President Reagan's policy and that of his Western partners, notably West Germany.

The DII also took over the work of disinformation, which had been handled previously by the International Department, the KGB and the Foreign Ministry. The Department of Agitation and Propaganda was thus pushed into the background in the handling of Soviet propaganda and the press and retained only the function of co-ordinating publicity about domestic problems and questions of staffing. After Gorbachev became General Secretary in 1985 the DII was abolished and Zamyatin, who had headed the Department, was appointed ambassador to Great Britain. The Department's work was taken over by the Department of Agitation and Propaganda under Aleksandr Yakovlev, a Secretary of the Central Committee. Agitprop now plays a key role in foreign propaganda.

Despite having been made Chairman of the TASS trade union organization and a member of the Party committee, in April 1974 I was told by Vladimir Khatuntsev, the Deputy Director General of TASS, that the Soviet Ministry of Health had asked TASS to provide an experienced correspondent to work in the press department of the World Health Organisation in Geneva. I felt a great sense of relief.

'We have, of course,' said Khatuntsev, 'discussed this matter in the Central Committee and with your friends [i.e. the KGB] and agreed that you are the right man for the job. It's not a bad place to work – Geneva – and you would have the rank of counsellor in the diplomatic service. What do you think? Does it suit you?'

I told him I couldn't think of anything better and would be ready to leave for Geneva the next day. But secretly I was worried about how I would get along with all those medical experts and how I would cope with the job. After all, I had previously dealt only with political questions, not medical ones. Khatuntsev phoned the Deputy Minister of Health and asked him to explain to me what my duties would be.

A few days later I told Khatuntsev that I was ready to take the job on. Once the Central Committee had given the necessary approval, I set about reading all the medical books I could find and consulting my doctor friends, thereby acquiring enough superficial medical knowledge to enable me to get by.

Before leaving for Geneva I called on the Directorate for People Working Abroad in the Central Committee, where I surrendered my Party card and was invited for a talk with the head of the sector in charge of the United Nations and other international organizations. I was told that the Central Committee considered that we did not have enough influence in these agencies and that the Soviet representatives on them did not do enough propaganda work. As for the World Health Organisation, I was told, my job would be to obtain detailed information about how the WHO operated and about its relations with other countries, especially China. We had to try to change the direction in which the WHO was going, to increase our propaganda work, and to make active use of the WHO magazine *World Health*, a Russian edition of which was published in the Soviet Union. 'You will be participating personally in its publication,' the Party official told me, 'and it will depend upon your efforts and skill whether we succeed in using it for our own purposes and for increasing propaganda about the achievements of Soviet medicine and about our country in general.'

In the course of a farewell dinner, one of my high-ranking friends told me I would have to be careful in Geneva, because it was a happy hunting-ground for a crowd of sons, daughters, relations and friends of the Soviet élite, and what the Soviet mission ignored or forgave in their behaviour would not apply to me. I would have to be careful. 'You realize, of course, that Geneva is a place for the chosen few, and since you will be amongst them, pay no attention to what doesn't concern you.' Unfortunately, I was not able to obey my friend's advice.

It was spring when we arrived in Geneva and we immediately fell in love with the city. The day after settling into an hotel, I paid a call on Zoya Mironova, the head of the Soviet mission to the United Nations in Geneva for many years. Counsellor A. Orlov, representative of the Soviet Ministry of Health, was present at our meeting. She turned out to be extremely old, and though traces of her past charms were still apparent she suffered from the ravages of old age which had affected her memory. She would instantly forget the reply to her questions, which she would repeat over and over again. This happened in her conversation with me. But despite her failing memory, and the fact that her diplomatic staff made open fun of her, Mironova never forgot who was who or made the mistake of offending or sending back to Moscow an offender who was related to the élite at home.

Next I visited the accounts department, where I was told not to go through the WHO to obtain an apartment or for other administrative matters, because the mission would provide me with one and furnish it free of charge. My salary as a counsellor, paid by the Soviet mission, would amount to 2500 Swiss francs a month, from which I would have to pay for heating, water and other outgoings. Cigarettes, spirits and certain foodstuffs could be bought duty-free in the mission's shop. My salary from the WHO was 6700 Swiss francs, of which I had to hand over 4200 francs to the Soviet mission, which left me with only 2500. As the rent of the apartment, 1100 francs, was paid by the mission out of the WHO salary I handed over, my family and I were costing it a total of 3600 francs and the mission was making a clear profit of 3100 francs, enough to maintain a First Secretary and an apartment.

Every Soviet employee of an international organization was instructed – and I am sure they are still instructed today

– to seek opportunities for obtaining new positions that could be used, not only for professional and intelligence purposes, but also for reducing Soviet expenditure in foreign currencies. Every Soviet employee of an international organization has to surrender two-thirds of his monthly salary to the accounts department of the Soviet mission attached to the organization, and when he leaves for home all the money that has been paid into the pension fund for him has also to be surrendered. This enables the Soviet Union to reduce the size of its contribution to such international organizations and at the same time makes it possible to support employees of the missions attached to UNO without being involved in further expense.

Despite this exploitation, the Soviet people working in Geneva were far better off than they had been in the Soviet Union, even members of the élite. Consequently they were all trying – and are still trying – to stay on in Geneva (or in Paris, London, New York or even Khartum) for as long as possible, to amass enough savings and possessions to ensure a relatively comfortable life on their return to their socialist homeland. At the same time most of them think it their duty to talk about their yearning for home and about how tired they are of living in the capitalist world. I could understand that sort of complaint coming from people posted to Africa, but to complain about living in Geneva seemed to me like blasphemy. One of my friends, who had already spent five years abroad and was hoping for two or three more, kept saying he wanted to go back to Russia. I suggested that he should make an official request or get me to raise the matter with the Party Secretary. He brushed my suggestion aside, saying: 'I couldn't possibly do that: they would think I wanted to desert from the front line in the ideological battle.' He was no deserter – he hung on for another couple of years, taking home enough things to last his lifetime.

It is not a passion for acquisition that makes Soviet people who go abroad so greedy, it is the shortages at home. I don't condemn them for this behaviour because many of them do not know when they will get abroad again. All the same, I found it quite revolting, in the Saturday market on the Plein Palais – known to the Russians as Treasure Island – to see Mironova appear first to snatch up bargains after fifteen years in Geneva. What an example for the younger Soviet employees, who believe neither in God nor the devil, nor even in 'advanced socialism', but only in money and material goods. This passion also infected the top Communist officials who were supposed to set the moral tone. For example, Georgi Kondakov, the Secretary of the Party Committee and deputy head of the mission, who belonged to the *apparat* of the Central Committee in Moscow, had no hesitation about fixing his wife up with a job in the Geneva office of the Novosti agency and then in the World Meteorological Organization with the obvious aim of making himself rich. It was clear he did not believe in the 'bright future of socialism' under which he would have to live on return to Moscow. Aleksandr Kiselev, his deputy in the Party organization, was also interested in increasing his own wealth and eventually succeeded in having his wife employed as a translator of English in the WHO and later in the International Labour Organisation. Anything to get their hands on an extra franc. Kiselev even took steps to reduce the number of translators being sent from Moscow for conferences in Geneva so that this wife and the wives of other senior officials should have the work. The women didn't really know the English language, but they received the money, and the translations were done by the official Soviet interpreters in the WHO.

My next meeting was with Kondakov, who informed me that the most important tasks for all Soviet employees of international agencies was to collect every kind of documentary information, to record conversations with foreign colleagues on professional and political questions, and to establish contacts with representatives of the developing countries in order to counteract the influence of the West. It was most important to spread Soviet propaganda among the people we met and worked with.

'We shall assess your work,' Kondakov said, 'not by what you do for the international organization but by the quantity and quality of the information you obtain for the Centre in Moscow.'

With these instructions ringing in my ears I started work in the press department of the WHO. My first job was to find out how to get articles by Soviet doctors published in the magazine *World Health*. Then I had to get the WHO to agree that we could leave out of the edition published in the Soviet Union articles by foreign authors that contradicted the views of the Soviet Ministry of Health and the Science Department of the Central Committee. I succeeded in this by telling them that, unless they agreed, the print-run in the Soviet Union would be considerably reduced and might even be stopped altogether. I also succeeded in the course of a year in getting a number of articles by Soviet authors, including a propaganda piece about the Soviet health service by the then Minister of Health, Petrovsky, published in the magazine. As a result of these successes I was made a member of the Council for Propaganda in the Soviet mission. Such councils exist in practically all Soviet embassies. Apart from the ambassador, the Secretary of the Party organization and some senior members of the embassy staff, the councils include the correspondents for TASS, Novosti and the main newspapers and people in charge of Soviet organizations in the country. The purpose of such councils is to spread and improve Soviet propaganda and counter-propaganda, which when necessary is replaced by disinformation. The councils usually meet once a month to consider what has been achieved and where the community has fallen short. I had been a member of the Council for Propaganda in Sudan, so I was familiar with the work involved. But what I was to witness in Geneva exceeded all my expectations.

Geneva is, of course, exceptional in that a tremendous

number of foreigners, including members of various intelligence services, live there. But only the Soviet government permits itself the luxury of having more than 250 members of its political and military intelligence services in the city. When I was working there forty people at most were genuinely taking part in the work of the international organizations and attending their conferences, although the diplomatic staff of the Soviet mission exceeds 110 members. Who were the other seventy or more people with diplomatic status? They were employed to make contact with representatives of other countries, to gather information and recruit informers and agents.

During my stay in Geneva I had no contact with the KGB *rezidentura*. My colleagues in the KGB were worried that I might lose the job in the WHO. The American publicist John Barron, in his book on the KGB, had named me as a member of the Soviet intelligence service but, fortunately, the top people in the WHO had paid no attention. There was in any case no point in my being involved with the KGB because there were already plenty of our people in Geneva, occupying all sorts of positions. The most remarkable was Geli Dneprovsky who, not having been identified as a spy, had been put in charge of the personnel department of a division of UNO, so that he had his hands on the personal files of all its employees, with details of their origins, past employment and so forth : everything that every intelligence service needs and can spend months and years obtaining.

It is not just the KGB and the GRU that are engaged in collecting information and documentary material. All Soviet officials employed in international organizations, even one so seemingly remote from politics as the WHO, are drawn into this work. I could not conceal my amazement at a meeting of Soviet employees of the WHO to learn that some 900 reports running to several thousand sheets of paper had been sent to Moscow in the course of one year.

The reports consisted in the main of all the more important documents issued by the WHO in connection with medical and other problems. They were conscientiously copied by the Soviet employees on the photo-copying machines available on every floor of the WHO building (at the WHO's expense, of course) and sent with comments and notes to the medical institutes and the Ministry of Health in Moscow to speed the progress of Soviet medical science. Such activity is, of course, a blatant violation of the rules of the international organization, but that doesn't bother the heads of the Soviet mission who direct this activity.

The constant supervision and pressure on Soviet employees to obtain information forces them to find ways of resisting. In practice the preoccupation with gathering information leads to the creation of disinformation. Faced with the impossibility of producing all the material demanded, people start making up conversations they are supposed to have had with foreigners along lines they think will suit the Soviet mission and Moscow. For example, after the invasion of Afghanistan by Soviet troops we were asked to sound out our foreign colleagues' reaction. Every normal person realized that no foreigner was going to approve of the Soviet invasion, yet Moscow received several reports signifying approval of the developments in Afghanistan.

In the autumn of 1979 the Soviet mission received a secret document from the Central Committee concerning steps to be taken to combat Chinese expansionism and China's steadily increasing influence in world affairs. It was a long and sharply worded letter demanding action on our part against Chinese representatives and proposing steps to discredit their political and scientific ideas. Hardly a month had passed when a recently arrived employee of the WHO, G. Podoprigora, who knew no foreign language, wrote a detailed report about Chinese penetration of the WHO, which was highly appreciated in the Far Eastern Department of the Foreign Ministry. Consequently most of us reckoned that it didn't matter what you wrote about so long as you wrote something that had some claim to be serious and was likely to please your superiors.

D. Benediktov, the Deputy Soviet Minister of Health, who was a frequent visitor to Geneva, told us more than once that we must establish where the WHO was going and who was behind its general director Halfand Mahler, so that the Soviet authorities could determine a definitive attitude to the WHO. They had been trying to get Mahler to agree to make the WHO into a scientific centre which would receive all information about all the latest discoveries in medicine. This was much more important, Benediktov said, than taking part in the WHO programmes for the developing countries, which cost the Soviet Union money with no return in economic or political terms. In any case, we were in no position to compete with Western countries in this field because we hadn't the resources, the equipment, the medicines or the trained personnel.

At the same time Soviet employees of the WHO were instructed to find ways of getting as much as possible of the Soviet contribution to the WHO returned by setting up programmes of work that the Soviet Union could carry out. Apart from the financial aspect, the idea, though not properly thought through, was that if some of the developing countries could be persuaded to apply the experience of the Soviet health service this might make it possible to influence the politicians in those countries to change their political systems.

Special attention was paid by the Soviet mission to contacts with foreigners working in the international agencies. All such contacts had to be supervised by KGB officers responsible for carrying out counter-espionage work in the Soviet community. Every six months all Soviet employees of international bodies have to submit to the mission lists of the foreigners they know and with whom they maintain contact, with details of their official positions and any other information by which their potential use to the Soviet Union can be assessed. This is done not only for the purpose of exercising control over such contacts but also to enable the mission to have some idea of what Soviet employees can do if Moscow demands to know the reaction of foreigners to some move it has made.

In spite of these efforts the KGB is unable to exercise complete control over all the foreign contacts the Soviet employees have. Everyone has acquaintances he does not reveal to the mission. But if the KGB gets to know about such contacts and thinks they may have unpleasant consequences, the Soviet employee is warned and instructed to break off the connection. If he fails to do so he may be sent back to Moscow.

It is not only the clean Soviet employees who are kept under observation by the KGB's counter-espionage service. It also keeps an eye on people working for GRU, to whom similar disciplinary measures may be applied.

Every serious conversation with foreign colleagues has to be reported in writing, in a special room in the mission, on paper usually marked 'Secret'. The reports are handed in to the KGB officer in charge of the secret registry, who extracts matters of sufficient importance to send on to the Centre.

Conferences and Party meetings are held in premises which are equipped with special electronic devices making it impossible for anything to be overheard from outside; there is no possibility of any eavesdropping devices being set up by outsiders. Folders and attaché-cases have to be left in a special place in charge of the mission's duty officer.

In 1979 it was reported that a Soviet citizen working in one of the international organizations in London but visiting Switzerland on business had committed suicide in his hotel. His name was Panchenko.

From my friends in the KGB and GRU *rezidentury* in Geneva I learnt that Panchenko was an officer in Soviet military intelligence with the rank of major. My friends were quite convinced that, as had been announced officially,

Panchenko had indeed committed suicide when he was very drunk. At the same time they did not exclude the possibility that, as a result of his addiction to strong drink and consequently to women, he might have been hooked by a Western intelligence agency and, realizing that if his weaknesses and offences were to be discovered by the Soviet authorities he would be severely punished, he had chosen the best way out in the circumstances. Better a terrible end than terror without end, as they say.

That was what we thought, but the Soviet authorities thought differently and accused British intelligence and the Swiss authorities of reponsibility for Panchenko's death. To refute these charges the Swiss, assisted by some British criminologists, made a film for television which made it clear that Panchenko was not killed by Western 'special services' but had committed suicide. This version did not suit the Soviet authorities, in spite of the fact that there was documentary film which made it clear that Panchenko had cut his wrists in the bath. The Soviets insisted that British intelligence had murdered Panchenko because he refused to collaborate with them, and had dressed it up as suicide.

These accusations may have been convincing to the uninformed layman. But I had been told, even when I was at the KGB training school, that there were now poisons that left no traces after killing a man and gave the impression of death by natural causes, from a heart attack or food poisoning. Was it likely, so many years later, that British intelligence would kill a man in such a primitive manner? In October 1979 the film was shown on Swiss television, in spite of efforts by the Soviet mission to prevent its showing, and it was at that point that a piece of instant disinformation was brought into circulation – disinformation mixed with blackmail.

Even before the film was shown employees of the international organizations were summoned at various times to the Soviet mission and ordered, after the film was shown, to get into conversation with our foreign colleagues and tell them that we Soviet people were indignant at such a provocation being permitted by Western special services, to which the Swiss government had been too indulgent. The Swiss had an obligation to preserve a neutral attitude in such matters and to defend the honour and dignity of the representatives of foreign countries who were carrying out their international duties in Switzerland. We had also to say that Soviet officials were quite convined that Panchenko had been killed by British Intelligence and that documentary evidence of this would soon appear in the Soviet press. We were then to say with especial emphasis that we had learned from official circles that, after such an unfriendly act by the Swiss, the Soviet government intended seriously to raise the question of transferring all international organizations from Geneva to Vienna, because the Swiss government was apparently incapable of providing proper conditions for foreigners to work in.

The Soviet authorities never published any of the promised documentary evidence about Panchenko's murder, for the simple reason that there was none. But at the time the most important thing had been to disinform public opinion by means of rumours, to sow disbelief in what had been shown and then let time do its work. It was hardly likely that any Westerner would remember Panchenko for long, but the Swiss government would, in the Soviet view, remember the almost official warning and might well draw the appropriate conclusions. They may well have done so, since, a few months later, when I had defected and was already in London, I sent the Geneva newspapers a letter refuting the rumours being spread by the Soviet mission about me, but the Swiss authorities, apparently bearing in mind the Soviet leadership's warning, refused to publish the letter, indicating quite openly that it might upset their relations with the Soviet Union and the whole Soviet system.

*

My work in the WHO went smoothly and pleasantly. I carried out the tasks set me by the Soviet Ministry of Health satisfactorily and even registered certain successes, for which I received praise. It seemed as though everything was going well, especially after an international conference which the WHO organized on the subject of primary health services in the autumn of 1978 in Alma-Ata, capital of the Kazakh republic of the USSR. From the point of view of spreading propaganda about the Soviet health service everything went perfectly, because the three Central Asian republics of Kazakhstan, Uzbekistan and Turkmenia were turned into Potemkin villages for the benefit of the foreign visitors. The local journalists and even some officials jokingly thanked the WHO for having brought about something which they would not have been able to achieve in many years.

Before the conference took place there was, for example, practically no petrol in any of the republics. Cars and trucks stood for hours at petrol stations waiting for rationed petrol; the internal airlines were grounded; and there was not even any paraffin. The food shops were empty. But just before the conference opened, petrol and paraffin and food all became available, and in quantities never seen before.

The people most pleased were the doctors and medical staff. The modern aspect of the Potemkin village consisted of good medical facilities. In the central and local hospitals likely to be visited by the foreign delegates all the old medical equipment, the beds and the linen were replaced, the buildings were redecorated and the staff were specially instructed in how to talk to their foreign colleagues. 'We hope they don't take it all away again,' the local doctors said.

Of course, many of the foreign delegates, especially those from the developing countries, believed what they heard and saw and were probably ready to persuade the leaders of their countries to follow the socialist way in organizing their health services, not realizing that such a huge and costly show could be put on only by the Soviet system. I had the impression that US Senator Edward Kennedy, who was the conference's guest of honour, was greatly impressed by what he saw. But Soviet citizens are familiar with these spectacles on a national scale and they feel only a sense of shame.

After this success, my life took a turn for the worse. A new representative of the Soviet Ministry of Health with the rank of counsellor, A. Kiselev, a limited and vindictive person, arrived in Geneva and made life much more difficult for those of us working in the WHO. Eager to advance himself, he soon made his way into Mironova's good books and on her recommendation was 'elected' deputy secretary of the Party organization. He devoted all his efforts to taking care of himself and his superiors on their visits from Moscow. Unable to speak any foreign language, not only did he fail ever to appear in the WHO but he was unable, without the help of an interpreter, to make sense of any document. His appointment to such a post with such inadequate qualifications puzzled me and the other Soviet employees of the WHO, while his total incompetence, coupled with inordinate ambition, annoyed people and raised the question of whose fault it was that he had been sent to Geneva and whether there was any way he could be sent back to Moscow. The question was answered by a well-known Soviet doctor, a professor and academician, who came from Moscow on a short visit and told me that Kiselev was a protégé of Benediktov, the Deputy Health Minister. Kiselev had been working in the Academy of Medical Science in a laboratory handling rats and mice and then had started carrying papers round from office to office. Benediktov had written a doctoral thesis which had been rejected three times on the grounds that it had nothing to do with medicine. But Kiselev managed to persuade some academicians to approve it; the thesis, entitled something like 'Collaboration between the Soviet Ministry of Health and the World Health Organisation', was accepted, and Benediktov became a doctor of medicine. In gratitude he arranged for Kiselev to be appointed to Geneva, where no medical knowledge was needed. In this way the unsuccessful scholar became a diplomat.

The Soviet doctors working in the WHO were to some extent dependent on Kiselev and, knowing that he was Benediktov's protégé, tolerated his rude manners and stupidity. But I considered myself independent of him, since I was still employed by TASS. After we had crossed swords a few times our relations were practically broken off.

What annoyed Kiselev most of all was my outspoken opposition to the presentation of gifts to Benediktov and his party when they visited Geneva. Kiselev explained in advance what Benediktov wanted to take back from Geneva as souvenirs – usually carpets, Japanese transistors, tea or coffee services, watches, and so forth, and then told all the Soviet employees that they were expected to contribute between ten and sixteen francs. Admittedly the sum was not big, but the fact that the collection was made at all offended me, and on one occasion I refused to contribute the ten francs. I said that I did not object to planning who was going to provide meals for Benediktov and the other top people to save them spending their foreign currency, but to contribute money so that Kiselev could give presents, or rather bribes, to his bosses was something I refused to do. My objections were immediately communicated to Kiselev, who instructed Yarotsky, the secretary of our Party organization, to have a talk with me. No talk took place, because I told him the same as I had told the man collecting the money, and from that day no one approached me again for money for gifts. Kiselev, however, made no secret of his anger with me.

At the same time as this was happening I made some tactical mistakes in my relations with Mironova and Kondakov, not on a personal level but in official discussions about the spreading of Soviet propaganda concerning the Soviet system and Leonid Brezhnev. Without going into details, I can only say that my intention was to improve the quality of our propaganda and to save us from looking like idiots when, for example, we were asked by our foreign colleagues why Brezhnev had thought it right to award himself the Order of Victory or what were the literary and political qualities of the book that had been published under his name, or, more importantly, about the Soviet invasion of Afghanistan. I was opposed to letting Soviet employees get into discussions on these subjects at all, as we simply put ourselves in a silly position. Without realizing it I had earned myself three enemies.

My friends in the KGB *rezidentura* warned me that Mironova and Kondakov, to whom I displayed no hostility, were no friends of mine. They apparently disliked my 'proud and independent Georgian character', and were starting to believe the slanderous stories Kiselev was spreading about me. I did not take these warnings seriously and so provided the three with grounds for attacking me. The grounds were trivial, but the results considerable.

On 9 March 1980 a former member of the *apparat* of the Central Committee who had worked in the Asia and Africa Institute arrived in Geneva from Africa. I did not know him personally but I was asked to meet him and look after him. Although it was a Sunday I was pleased to talk to someone who had just returned from Africa. After lunch I took him round Geneva and showed him the sights. By six o'clock when we arrived back at his hotel we were both very tired, and after drinking a couple of glasses of brandy with our coffee we agreed that I would pick him up the next day and take him to the mission.

My car was standing at the entrance to the hotel. As I opened the car door I saw another car approaching and, so as not to block the way, I shut the car door, but so carelessly that the sharp edge struck me on the nose and made it bleed so badly that I had blood all over my face, my suit and my shirt. I pressed a handkerchief to my nose and set off for home, steering with one hand. I suppose I was not concentrating on what I was doing, because, as I turned out of the narrow street and looked to the left from where the traffic was coming, I paid no special attention to a quite strong bump but just went on my way without stopping. It was around seven o'clock in the evening and the streets were full of people, so that when I stopped at some traffic lights near the station a couple standing on the pavement saw the blood on my face and asked if I needed any help. I thanked them and told them I was all right. A few minutes later I parked the car near my house.

The house we lived in was occupied by other Soviet families, and as I got out of my car I ran into two KGB officers: Ivanushkin, the Vice-Consul-General, and V. Kopytin. They saw I was bleeding, and I explained what had happened. Ivanushkin took me by the arm and led me to the entrance. 'You smell of drink,' he said. 'Yes,' I replied, 'my friend and I drank a little brandy.'

Fifteen minutes later there was a ring at the door and when I opened it I found a policeman who, apologizing for the disturbance, asked me to report to the police station because I had bumped into someone's car at the road junction and the matter needed clearing up. I agreed, and the policeman left.

Because a Soviet citizen is not allowed to visit a police station on his own I phoned Ivanushkin and asked him to accompany me. Kopytin came too. To make sure that all the rules were observed I asked my wife to phone Colonel Pochankin, the head of the KGB counter-intelligence group, and inform him of events.

When we arrived at the police station we discovered to our surprise that the duty officer knew nothing about the affair, and that the policeman who had called on me had gone off duty.

Next day I went to the mission. After I told Pochankin what had happened he inspected my car and could not detect a single scratch on it, so we wondered how I could damage another car without even scratching my own. We then went to the police station in my car and talked to the policeman who had called on me the previous evening. He explained, somewhat apologetically, that I had caused slight damage to an old Mercedes belonging to an Arab butcher whose friend had written down my number and reported it to the police.

Pochankin asked the policeman three times whether the Swiss police would prefer charges and was assured that they would not, but he asked me to settle the business of repairing the Arab's car as quickly as possible because he was making a fuss and kept phoning them. I went straight to the office of my insurance company and filled out the necessary forms, admitting that I was to blame. The insurance agent phoned the Arab and assured him that his car would be repaired in the next few days, as indeed it was.

I then went to the mission and wrote out a complete report on the affair for Mironova and Kondakov, pointing out that everything had been settled. Pochankin handed my report to Mironova and told me that all was well. The incident seemed to be over. Then Kiselev, determined to exploit the affair against me, sprang into action and, thanks to the sclerotic state of Mironova and his close relations with Kondakov, he succeeded. Mironova was shown an affidavit from the Swiss police concerning an accident caused by a son of an important father who, on New Year's Day 1980, had been drunk while driving and had damaged six parked cars. Unlikely though it sounds, Mironova, possibly prompted by Kiselev and Kondakov, believed that the affidavit referred to me and did not take the trouble to read it properly.

There was nothing I could do but appeal to Pochankin to intervene on my behalf. To be fair, I have to say that he tried but was not successful. He then agreed to go with me to Mironova, and he informed her formally, as a representative of the KGB, that the Swiss police had not drawn up any documents concerning Dzhirkvelov, that the incident would not have any consequences for the mission's relations with the Swiss authorities and that Dzhirkvelov's further stay in Geneva would not lead to any difficulties. Mironova told me to go away and relax.

On 11 March Kiselev sent for me and told me to write out a statement to the effect that I was leaving the WHO at the end of May 1980, i.e. in two months' time. I would not agree, not only because I had no desire to leave Switzerland before my time was up, but also because I did not intend to be a scapegoat.

I decided to talk the matter over with Kondakov, as the representative of the Party of which I had been a member for thirty-four years. I was, after all, a man who, when Kondakov and Kiselev were small children, had been fighting Fascism, and who was one of the many to whom the Kiselevs and Kondakovs owed the fact that they were living happily in Switzerland. But Kondakov only talked a lot of nonsense about the importance of the 110th anniversary of Lenin's birth, and it was clear that I would get no sense or help out of him.

Later that day I learnt from my KGB friends that a ciphered message signed by Mironova, Kiselev and Kondakov had gone off to the Central Committee and Foreign Ministry in Moscow saying that I had, in a drunken state, run into another car, had run away from the place of the incident and had been arrested by the police. Such a charge was more than sufficient for a Soviet employee to be packed off immediately to the Soviet Union, if it were valid. A slightly more diplomatic and cunning way was found of handling my case.

On 20 March 1980, I was informed by Mironova's deputy Kolesnikov that, with Kiselev, I was to fly to Moscow on 22 March, supposedly to discuss my case in the Central Committee. I realized that I was simply being sent back to Moscow, and Kolesnikov knew it too, but, to give the lie the appearance of truth and to dispel my suspicions, a return visa was put in my passport allowing me to leave the Soviet

Union for Geneva within two weeks. My business in the CC would not take more than four days, Kolesnikov said, so that I would have time to see my relatives. I thanked him and left his office.

I did not believe that I was going to Moscow for discussions in the CC. But, clutching at a straw, I still retained a tiny shred of hope that perhaps, bearing in mind my long membership of the Party and my other services, I would get away with a reprimand and, after admitting my mistakes, would be allowed to continue working in the WHO and not have my record spoiled by a recall.

On Saturday, 22 March, Kiselev and I flew to Moscow, arriving in the evening. My wife and daughter remained in Geneva. Moscow greeted me with gloomy overcast weather which well suited my mood. The city looked to me even drearier than in the past. Dirty grey piles of snow lined the streets; there were queues in front of the cafés and restaurants; the people seemed all to be dressed in grey; the streets were hardly lit; and the food shops were empty, displaying in their windows only faded packets of macaroni, cornflakes, condensed milk, tinned fish, packets of salt, and so forth. My depression deepened.

I stayed in a flat belonging to a friend in the KGB. He had already heard something of what had happened to me and without further ado we set about alerting all my friends in the KGB, Foreign Ministry and Central Committee who could find out what the real situation was and even do something to help me. In fact they did everything possible, and although they did not achieve the result I wanted, they helped me to establish the truth.

On Monday, 24 March, I went to the Directorate for Foreign Relations in the Ministry of Health and wrote a detailed statement of everything that had happened, with a request to be allowed to return to Geneva and complete my period of service there until May 1981, as agreed with the WHO. I did this just in case a trick of fate might work for me. Podshekoldin, for example, who was in charge of the foreign cadres at the Central Committee, might possibly switch from being an *apparatchik* and behave like a human being. But this was pure fantasy. As I learnt later from the book by Arkadi Shevchenko, the former deputy to the Secretary General of the United Nations, even when Podshekoldin was working as secretary of the Party organization in the Soviet mission to the United Nations in New York, he was a pure *apparatchik*, lacking all normal human feelings. He is not alone; there are plenty like him, and they cheerfully take drastic decisions about other men's fates, treating people simply as the property, or personification, of the Soviet state.

It would be wrong, however, to give the impression that *all* those working in the *apparat* are soulless bureaucrats. There is a relatively small group of individuals who, although they carry out their bureaucratic duties faultlessly, do try to some extent to alleviate the rigidity of the Party *apparat* and to introduce some elements of democracy into Soviet life. I know those people, though I cannot name them. The so-called thaw that took place under Khrushchev was possible because of such individuals and had little to do with Khrushchev's admiration for democratic ways. These people understand perfectly well that the present dictatorship of the Party leaders and *apparat* not only causes irreversible harm to the country's economic development but also hinders the population's creative abilities, destroys initiative and gives rise to passivity and indifference.

They realize that fiery speeches and appeals on the part of the Party leaders, calling on the population to strengthen, increase, raise, develop and improve the situation in whatever field, will not produce any results without freedom of initiative and independence of creative activity, irrespective of whether the General Secretary is someone who has practically lost possession of his faculties, like Brezhnev, or a fully fit, educated person like Gorbachev. But there are only

a few individuals of this kind in the *apparat*, and there is no
reason yet to expect any substantial changes. There are
many people who think like them among the Soviet intelligentsia, but the artificially created wall which alienates and
isolates them is no less an obstacle than the security organs
that protect the interests of the Party leadership.

Consequently members of the Party, as well as those
who do not belong to the Party, prefer to say what they
really think about the situation in the country and its leaders
only within a narrow circle of friends, while at public meetings and gatherings they make speeches that follow the
official Party line and always vote in favour of proposals put
forward by the Party or government. In this way, following
the elimination at the end of the 1930s of all those who
opposed Stalin's leadership and in the mid-1950s of Khrushchev's opponents and then of the Brezhnev leadership, there
was created, with the active help of the *apparatchiks*, a unique
system to suit the needs of the Politburo and Secretariat of
the CPSU. Such a system has never before existed in history: I call it the 'system of mechanical agreement'.

The process began soon after the end of the Second World
War, when Stalin himself started all sorts of campaigns
against the obstacles 'preventing our advance'. What exactly
was hindering us nobody seemed to know, and so we waited
for a signal from above. Once we got it we dashed into the
struggle, now against jazz music, now against the linguistic
teachings of Marr. Stalin was cunning enough to realize that
by means of these campaigns, which never affected the top
Party leaders, he could give us the illusion that we had
freedom of expression and that the Soviet system was democratic as far as honest Bolsheviks and supporters of the Soviet
system were concerned. The majority of my generation
believed in the system. But after the reduction of the 'genius
and helmsman' to the level of a tyrant and murderer, performed by the 'true Leninist' Khrushchev, followed by the
reduction of the 'true Leninist' to the level of a political and

economic ignoramus, not only my generation but younger people too lost any faith they might have had and no longer believe in anything or anybody.

Today yet another campaign has been started up by the new General Secretary Gorbachev, against Brezhnev, Andropov and Chernenko, under the pretext of fighting against inaction, stagnation, corruption, drunkenness, underestimation of the progress of socialist society, exaggerated promises, etc. In other words, Gorbachev is fighting against everything that was typical of the post-Stalin period.

As in the past, promises and failure to keep them, a difficult economic situation and the continual propaganda conducted by the CC *apparat* under orders from the Politburo, have produced in the Soviet population a mood of total indifference to what is going on in the Party or outside it. To think one thing and to say another – that is the tragic situation in which Soviet people find themselves.

After coming finally to the conclusion that nobody at the Central Committee was going to talk to me, and was certainly not going to permit me to complete my span of service in Geneva, I wrote a request to be allowed to return to Geneva for two or three days to help my wife pack our possessions so that we could return together to Moscow. I asked for a speedy answer. I waited a day without receiving any reply and then phoned an official in the Ministry of Health who said that Kiselev would tell me what was happening to my case. I could scarcely believe my ears when I heard this, but that same evening Kiselev phoned me to say that he had indeed discussed my case at the Central Committee, that things looked bad for me, that he was flying to Geneva the next day, and did I want to send anything to my wife. Kiselev was obviously enjoying his victory. As far as he was concerned, I was finished, condemned to remain in Moscow with a black mark on my record.

I had, however, partly by chance and partly through my own foresight, one card left in my hand that would enable me to outwit Kiselev and all the officials who had neither the time nor the fellow-feeling to hear my side of the case: that was my diplomatic passport with its exit visa. With luck I might get back to Geneva in spite of everything. Then we would see what my next step would be.

On Tuesday, 25 March, with the aid of my diplomatic passport, I was able to buy an air ticket for Vienna. I could not fly to Geneva, because I might have found Kiselev on the same plane. And so it happened that, on the morning of 26 March, the victorious Kiselev took off from Moscow for Geneva to report that he had delivered Dzhirkvelov safely to Moscow, and twenty minutes later Dzhirkvelov himself took off from the same airport to fly to Vienna.

My next problem was how to get from Vienna to Geneva. I first thought of going by air, but then found I did not have enough money for the fare. In any case, it would have been very unwise to arrive at Geneva airport, where there were always a lot of Soviet officials. So I decided to take the train. My main concern was whether I could get to Geneva before the news of my disappearance in Moscow reached the mission. If it had, my wife and daughter would be taken into the mission, and I would have no choice but to go there too, because I had no intention of fleeing myself and leaving them behind.

A phone call to my wife established the fact that she was still at home and had not been disturbed. I told her not to talk to people and not to let any outsiders into our apartment. If anyone from the mission tried to force their way in she was to phone the Swiss police for help.

My train was not due to leave until eleven o'clock in the evening. So I went into the centre of Vienna and straight to a gun shop to buy a 9 mm gas pistol, which I intended to use if the KGB tried to seize me and my family after I reached Geneva.

I arrived in Geneva at the most inappropriate time – the middle of the day, when all the Soviet officials living in our building came home to lunch. But I was lucky and did not bump into anyone who knew me.

Having explained quickly to my wife what had happened in Moscow, I said that first of all I must have a rest, because I was exhausted after so many sleepless nights. I asked her to phone a friend in Moscow to find out if there was any news about my case. I had not yet taken a firm decision to go to the West, though I realized that all my bridges were burnt and there was no way to retreat.

While I was sleeping, my wife was visited by the wife of the deputy KGB *rezident*, a doctor neighbour and the wife of another employee of the WHO. My wife continued to watch the television as usual, and the curious visitors detected nothing suspicious, such as packed suitacases or anything suggesting a forthcoming departure. When my wife spoke to people in Moscow they told her that there was no news and asked whether I had yet returned from work. My wife said I had not. That meant that they realized that I had left Moscow and they hadn't given me away. Fine, I thought.

In the course of a long conversation with my wife I explained that I could not forgive the humiliation to which I had been subjected, nor the utter indifference and the inconsiderate manner in which my fate had been decided. I said I could no longer live among such people and under such a system, about which I had long since been disillusioned but which I had served honestly because I had believed that sooner or later things would change for the better. After what had happened to me I felt nothing but hatred, which I just could not suppress.

'What awaits us in the future I do not know,' I said. 'Since I have never worked for any other service there is nobody on whose help I can count. But to return and submit to even greater humiliation and undeserved insults – and from Party and other bureaucrats? That is quite out of the question. But where we are to go I do not know.'

To defect is always a tragedy and it is quite impossible to describe what it means on paper: you can only draw its rough outlines. I have never suffered from nostalgia, longing for the silver birches (of which there are plenty in Europe) or the wide open Moscow spaces, but it was difficult for me to imagine life without my relatives and the friends with whom I had spent my whole life. It was always people I became attached to, not to woods and forests or even herrings and black bread. I realized that my wife and I would be losing much more than we would ever acquire. To defect is a risk, and it is difficult and sometimes impossible to guess the outcome. But I have always been a fatalist, believing that if I am to be hanged I shall never drown, and I have always lived on the principle that he who risks nothing wins nothing.

My wife has always been my friend and adviser, and without too many words we reached agreement. She did not break into sighs or laments, but tears rolled down her cheeks. It hurt me to see her like that, but I realized that she could not leave me alone, just as I couldn't leave her and our daughter.

It took us very little time to pack. We took only the most indispensable things. I went down in the lift to the garage, holding a revolver ready in my pocket. There were voices down there, though it was only four o'clock in the morning. I listened for a few seconds and established that they were Swiss. Then I went to my car, checked that it would start and went back to the apartment. I made three or four trips down in the lift with a case in one hand and the gun in the other.

We woke our daughter, who immediately started to cry. We calmed her down, and then the three of us went down into the garage, got into the car and set off into the unknown, to the West, in the night of 27/28 March 1980.

INDEX